Education and Leadership

Role of Indian Universities and Colleges in Nurturing Future Leaders

Second Revised and Enlarged Edition

B.M. Naik

ATLANTIC

PUBLISHERS & DISTRIBUTORS (P) LTD

Published by
ATLANTIC
PUBLISHERS & DISTRIBUTORS (P) LTD
7/22, Ansari Road, Darya Ganj, New Delhi-110002
Phones : +91-11-40775252, 23273880, 23275880, 23280451
Fax : +91-11-23285873
Web : www.atlanticbooks.com
E-mail : orders@atlanticbooks.com

Branch Office
5, Nallathambi Street, Wallajah Road, Chennai-600002
Phones : +91-44-64611085, 32413319
E-mail : chennai@atlanticbooks.com

Printed in India at Nice Printing Press, A-33/3A, Site-IV, Industrial Area, Sahibabad, Ghaziabad, U.P.

Preface to Second Edition

Encouraged by the overwhelming response from readers of the first edition, the author is pleased to present the second edition with enlarged scope covering some more critical issues and challenges in global context facing the Indian higher and technical education. Universities and colleges in India, today do not stand high in the world list. Prime Minister of India is keen on making atleast some universities world class for which the Government has sanctioned more funds and more autonomy to twenty universities, ten from private and ten from government sectors. An article is included in this edition on why and how to make universities world class. If the universities become world class then only Indian human capital is likely to be enabled globally competent leading on the path to become a developed nation. Without world class universities students tend to go abroad, and India inspite of ample natural resources tends to remain a developing country.

Second important issue in India is unemployment of educated youths. Students have degrees in hands but many of them do not have jobs. There is a mismatch in education and needs of the employment market. Innovation, creativity and skill set possessed by graduates is wanting. This aspect is covered exclusively in another chapter. Funds for education are not adequately available. To augment funds and establish relevance of education to industry needs Government has made a law, namely "Corporate Social Responsibility". This aspect is covered in details in yet another chapter. A small country like Singapore with around 56 lakh population has three world class universities, and on account of them Singapore has become a developed country. Why India with 130 crore population cannot? This is explained in the present edition.

Faculty growth is the weakest point. Faculties are brilliant but they do not have opportunities to professionally grow. Service conditions are old, outdated. They need to be revised to global standards. Research facilities in labs need to be enlarged. It is well realised that faculty holds the key. A separate detailed chapter is devoted to this aspect. The readers will find this edition rich in practicable ideas. Indian universities are being transformed to world class level. The situation is optimistic. The book suggests bold policies and practices, makes valuable suggestions to transform universities and colleges to world class standard.

B.M. Naik

Preface to First Edition

"Where do we produce global leaders? Seeds are sown within the four walls of classrooms."

Does India Need World-Class Universities and Colleges?

Can India and its youth afford to do without them? Governments of various countries in the world have realised that in today's knowledge-driven society, no city, region or nation, even if endowed with abundant natural resources, can ever prosper fast and have sustained growth without having good institutions of higher and technical education. They are the main energy sources, and brain power factories needed to bring a developing nation at par with the developed world. Well educated competent citizenry is an essential condition for faster growth and prosperity. Having just higher educational institutes is good but not enough. They must be world-class and not mediocre. People's development is the key to national development. They need to be educated on priority and in the best possible manner, to the level they are capable of. It is the well educated men and women with imagination who generate ideas, capability and competency, required most in national development. Government of India is convinced that to run its affairs ably at national and international levels it requires globally competent leaders, engineers, industrialists, and various other professionals. Where are such professionals nurtured? It is well known that seeds are sown within the four walls of classrooms in universities and colleges. Mediocre institutes produce mediocre leaders. There should be a burning desire and passion to improve education by setting up standard institutes of learning. It is advisable to invest with priority on modernization of higher education to raise it to world-class level.

Why do the Students Go Abroad?

Every year, thousands of students go abroad to receive higher education, especially at PG/PhD level. They have been going since the Gandhi-Nehru period. How long will this continue? A major weakness of Indian education is that it is not able to provide standard higher education to the students. Many foreign universities are coming to India to meet the huge demand for high quality education. This underlines the need and importance of elevating the standard, especially of PG and PhD courses. Upgrading standard of PG courses will reduce the outflow of students. Intellectual capital must be preserved. Some institutes, if not all, urgently need to be upgraded to world-class level. The presence of world-class institutions is a necessary condition because it is reckoned as a differentiating factor between the developed and the developing nations. Nations develop faster only when world-class institutes are within the reach of common man. If India does not envision building world-class institutes with priority, then the country will only get increasingly more mediocre brains to run its national and international affairs. It is then destined to lag behind in the race for development. The book underlines the need and importance of creating world-class institutes.

How to Go About It

Indian Institutes of Technology (IITs) were conceived as world-class institutes. World's best professors from countries like Germany, UK, USA, Russia, among others were invited from the beginning to shape them. They were mentored by foreign collaborators constantly for 20-30 years. Programs like exchange of faculty, research partnership, global visions and missions, systems and procedures, gave them an international character, and so they could shine in the world. Establishment of universities even in developed countries is normally done like this under close supervision of world's best professors, some of them from within the country and some from abroad. They are appointed as mentors, as many as 15 to 20, at least one for each discipline. It is the mentors who accelerate the creation of world-class academic culture. Universities must groom the students to be fit for tomorrow's needs; they should teach that which will enable students to thrive in future. Presently, with a view to increasing gross enrolment ratio, many new universities and colleges are being set up in India. Should they not adopt such innovative approaches? They must, otherwise they are likely to be born handicapped, and removing the handicap afterwards is extremely difficult. Once the outdated systems and procedures, policies and practices set in, they tend to be perpetuated. The book explains in detail how to set up world-class institutes.

There is a thinking in some circles as to why involve foreign universities, when we have world-class IITs? Are IITs not good enough to guide? They are certainly good. But cross fertilization is better. Many new things have come up elsewhere in the world after IITs were set up. Good visions and missions, policies and practices from elsewhere in the world which are continuously coming up will have to be incorporated in Indian universities. It is good to involve existing IITs, but wiser to involve world's best universities and professors, Nobel laureates, award winning scientists, etc.

Envision Creating Imaginative Leaders

Can we afford to use old visions? Our children can't. We must depart from the old and adopt the new. The education scene in India must be transformed from mediocre to excellent. The importance of academic institutions in today's knowledge society is very high. It is they who are taking human civilization to greater heights. It is the academicians in them who provide new knowledge, new theories, new technology and competent manpower to business and industry. They are supposed to provide not only knowledgeable but also imaginative and ethical leaders to government, and to the world at large. In return, industry, society, and the government ought to provide adequate funds to the institutes to make them grow. India can be richer only by use of advanced knowledge. There is no other way. What kind of leaders the institutes produce will decide our future? If they produce mediocre professionals, the future of India will be mediocre. If they produce world-class professionals, India's future will be world-class. First we shape institutions, and then they shape us for generations. We need to ask: Are Indian institutes aiming at producing leaders of global standard? Do we have a mechanism for building leadership in educational institutes? Do the key people in government attach proper value to the upbringing of youths and provide adequate budget? Do they adopt world-class strategies and provide better governance to enable youth to harvest global job opportunities? The book attempts to answer these questions and provide guidelines for reformation.

Do We want to be Globally Competitive?

If we do, it essentially demands willingness to embrace change. The world under the forces of globalization is changing fast. Only those professors and institutes who change to innovate according to the changing time can educate the students on correct lines. Students now demand world-class education. They are ready to pay for it in terms of time, effort and money. But where do you find such institutes? IITs are very few. Thousands of students are forced by circumstances to go abroad to obtain quality education, and they have to spend huge sums of money. Universities and colleges in India now will have to be competitive with nothing less than world standard. Education has become a global subject. Some foreign universities have come and many more are coming in India. They are attracting the best of our talent and may soon dominate the Indian scene. Where do the Indian institutions stand in comparison? Let us humbly admit that Indian institutes are far too behind the world. None of our institutes stands in the list of world's 200 best. Have we made a gap analysis between Indian institutes and their counterparts abroad? Why are our universities woefully unsuited to the quality demands of globalization? Why are they far too behind their counterparts in developed world? Intellectually, Indian men and women are too good. They have contributed immensely in American universities and made them forerunners. In India, similar people fall too short because they are under poor governance, poor systems and procedures. We need to make an introspection, especially in the light of world's proven policies and practices. Do our institutions lack visions of new world? The present method of governance which is under the "grip of government" at one time served well, but today it falls too short of requirement. It needs to be reformed without any delay and made competitive in the global context. How can the institutions become autonomous? How can they become knowledge generators? How can they have effective governing boards? This is a challenge before Indian academicians. How to face these challenges effectively? You will find answers in this book.

The numbers of students and the institutions in India have increased tremendously. Yet the gross enrolment ratio is too low. In 2011, it was only 14 per cent, in comparison with UK, USA, Indonesia, Thailand, etc. where it is of the order of 30 to 50 per cent. The numbers of courses and the subjects are advanced and have become innovative in character. Transnational collaborations and networking with similar institutions in India and abroad, so also with industry, are becoming common. World-class education is eagerly being sought. But very few are able to offer it. Living up to the expectations of students and industry requires universities and colleges to have new organizational structures, new systems and procedures, flexibility, international perspectives, global visions and missions. The universities and colleges are now required to become innovative in character and give new technology to industry on a continuing basis. Students are expected to acquire skills for innovation and entrepreneurship, besides giving birth to start-ups in new technology. These are the critical areas which need immediate attention and exploration to generate new jobs and income. The book deals with them adequately.

India, in the recent past, has made a laudable progress in higher and technical education. It is producing today (2011) about 0.6 million engineers per year through IITs, NITs and other universities with thousands of government and private affiliated colleges. But the output of postgraduates and doctorates is too meagre. Scientific publications are far too few. Although Indian institutions have grown sufficiently well with respect to our own past, they are yet far too behind those of the developed world. They do not stand high in the world list. They have yet to go a long way to fulfil India's dream of being reckoned as a technological power. The government is aware of opportunities available in the globalised world and challenges to be faced. It had appointed National Knowledge Commission in the year 2005, and then appointed Yashpal Committee in 2008. The recommendations of the committee are being implemented vigorously. India has started Technical Education Quality Improvement Program (TEQIP), in association with World Bank, in which around 4000 crore rupees are being invested in about 300 colleges to bring them at par with world-class institutes. The government has set up a special organization, known as National Project Implementation Unit (NPIU) which has designed TEQIP with the objective of producing imaginative leaders in engineering and technology to manage its professional affairs at national and international levels. Where do you find strategies to deal with such situations? They are here in this book.

A study by NASSCOM reported (2010) that only 25 per cent engineering graduates are employable, the rest which are half-baked, have to make up the deficiency by attending finishing schools at extra cost and time. There is a huge energy in youths; they are brilliant, yet too few become technology pioneers, and technology leaders on a global plane, because that is not what present institutes are teaching students to become. The visions and missions mentioned on college brochures remain just slogans on paper. Commitment to implement them is lacking. Improving quality and relevance of education is the first and foremost challenge, addressed ably in the book.

Are Governing Boards Effective in Navigating Colleges and Universities?

In a time of transformation in higher and technical education, governing boards of universities and principals of colleges assume a vital role. Boards have to be adaptive and changing with time. They have to function like a navigator having long range perspectives with principal sitting in the driver's seat to tackle day-to-day obstacles. To build an exceptional academic institution of world-class standard requires, no doubt, adequate number of men, materials, and money. But it is not enough. It essentially requires proper policies and practices, visions and missions, systems and procedures. Only those institutions that use current and appropriate strategies are likely to win. Others may work hard, may have all the resources to draw on, but will lag behind without good academic culture. An institution with lesser resources but better strategies will undoubtedly do better than others with more resources but poor policies.

Nations are Prosperous where Institutes are Autonomous

An autonomous institution signifies its overall ability to act by its own choices in pursuit of its chosen missions. Autonomy is a dynamic participative model of governance based on continuous evaluation of performance. The evaluation needs to be done at regular intervals by internal as well as external agencies. Autonomy means freedom to think and freedom to act, but freedom also implies accountability and responsibility. Autonomy means self-determination, self-control and self-regulation with least interference from external sources. Autonomy implies going away from government, and closer to its own students, faculty and industry. Bureaucracy and politics are found the world over to destabilize education. For example, professors in government colleges are transferred more out of whims and fancies of ministers than due to a genuine reason. Long range policies change with the change in political party in the government. They should grant funds but not interfere as they are not qualified to steer the direction in academics. Capping imagination of institutions and students by the government should be strictly avoided. When asked, the Vice-Chancellor of Karlsruhe University, Germany replied that he did not remember if any minister had ever visited the university. Autonomy means internal debates and discussions. Autonomy enables to make best utilization of available resources and ideas to harvest opportunities. The Council of Europe Conference, 2003 said: "Institutes have to be autonomous at the heart, to be able to meet needs of world around it." Autonomous institutions think great, going beyond the government, in the global context. Those institutions which are going for autonomy should especially find this book useful.

Research is not a fancy affair. It is the corn seed for the harvest of benefit. Benefits from research far outweigh the costs. Research fuels education and makes it quality and cost-competitive. Research gives joy and sense of achievement. It provides economic security and confidence. It enhances the rate of return on investment and generates high-tech employment with high income. Education does not grow where research is absent. Presently, the syllabi are oriented to learning known knowledge and an established practice presuming that knowledge is finite. Truly, known knowledge is finite but imagination is not, and students essentially need to learn not only known knowledge but also learn to discover the unknown. Education without learning skills for research and innovation remains incomplete and irrelevant in the modern sense. So the Indian institutes do not rank high in the world list. The interaction between institutes and industry for research is too weak, adversely affecting competitiveness of both. Therefore, we should nurture an attitude for research.

Passion for research is the need of the hour. Lack of passion for research is the serious deficiency of our universities and colleges. How to motivate people for research? It must be the campus character. This is the way to win in world economy. If India does not create research-based universities and colleges, and industry does not involve colleges in this mission, mediocre graduates, far too low by international standard, shall come out and run India's national and international affairs.

Commercial exploitation of research fundings is needed. Teaching and learning in classrooms and doing research in labs are good, but not enough. It is essential for students to learn innovation skills for commercial exploitation of research done at doctoral, masters and bachelors levels. This is to increase the scholarship and transfer new knowledge, new technology from university to masses for their welfare. Experience of western schools in this respect is worth emulation. Majority of the western schools convert research into patents and IPR, and transfer them to industry through well-defined systems and procedures. Economic returns from investment in universities then increase, which brings more money for further research and makes it sustainable. Public service, carried out chiefly through teaching, was the motive for the creation of the earliest universities. Even today, teaching remains the core of the university's public service. But in today's competitive world, university's public service extends far beyond, to entrepreneurial activities like research park, technology innovation, patent and IPR. Intellectual capital of university which is so critical for national development is required to be converted into usable goods and services. For a country like India that aspires to be an economic powerhouse all the while, it is more important. Of what use are research, new knowledge, and new technology if these are not exploited commercially? Universities along with industry and alumni ought to think big in the global context and establish on campus a research park, like their counterparts in developed countries. Where do you get to know how to go about it? The information is here in this book.

Universities and colleges must integrate with community. Building bridges between institution and society is the need of the hour. To succeed and get support from local community they must establish organic links with the surroundings. Colleges and universities, large in number, have five star infrastructure, brilliant faculty and scholarly students, who do possess a lot of advanced scientific knowledge needed most by national and global economy. They continuously generate new knowledge through research at PhD, PG, and UG levels. Existing mechanism for transfer of knowledge from lab to field, in both the private and public universities and colleges, is however not yet perfect. It is insensitive to market needs. Feedback loop today is incomplete. As a result, continuous inputs to reform education are not provided, and productivity of various professions and vocations on this account remain low. In India, 25 per cent people live in poverty; the rate of return from investment in universities due mainly to lack of outreach is far too low. The book explains how to increase outreach and improve the rate of return on investment.

Experience of Western Schools: Many western schools are having well defined and perfected knowledge transfer systems and procedures. They are not only educating students to keep them competitive lifelong, but also teaching them marketing, new technology/new knowledge and transferring their full scientific capacities to the benefit of society in their vicinity and all over the world. The outreach of universities and feedback is far and wide, whereby they are enriching themselves and augmenting new ideas besides providing budget support for future growth. Universities, by virtue of knowledge in this period of knowledge society, have moved from the periphery to the centre. They have become the drivers of economic and social prosperity. The visions and missions of universities are required to be dynamic and adaptive, based on sharing experiences with people at large, and not just giving off-the-shelf, irrelevant and outdated prescriptions. Restructuring and repositioning of Indian universities and colleges with respect to society and the world is needed. The conventional wisdom of university system, with outdated visions and missions, systems and procedures, and policies and practices needs revision. Once it served well. But now in the free world, universities are expected to stand on their own merit and imagination. If innovation and creativity are to be given a boost, setting up of a research foundation for the purpose is must.

Thus far, it is the foreign collaborators who have gone nearer to Indian industry and propelled their growth. Indian universities remained away. Now is the time that our universities learn a lesson from their foreign counterparts and play a vital industry propeller's role.

Research parks, technological innovation centres, Patent and IPR centres being established in many universities for this purpose need marketing the products and services to Indian industry, so also abroad. Universities have to learn to give "technology push" matching with "market pull". This is the theme of the book.

Has Faculty Crunch Crippled our Institutes?

Is faculty crunch an outcome of poor national policies? It is the level of the faculty, their excellence in their fields of specialisation which decides the standing of an institution. No institution is taller than the professional height of professors. Five star infrastructures are not a substitute for good academic culture. Infrastructure does not teach. It provides an aid. The active resource is the faculty; they represent the real wealth of an institution. They ignite the imagination of young. Faculty status of an institution is the important measure of the quality of education. It is reported that there is acute shortage of well qualified faculty even in institutes of national importance like IITs and NITs. There is 30 per cent shortage. In rest of the colleges it is said that the situation is too bad; blind is teaching the blind. Lowly qualified faculty is teaching the bright students. Faculty shortage is an outcome of poor service conditions. India needs to make benchmarking in this respect with their counterparts in the developed world. I am optimistic that the solution to the problem is easy and possible. Professors need to be provided facilities to grow professionally like in foreign countries. Opportunities for growth are lacking; increased mobility in reputed counterpart institutes in the world is also lacking. Professors need to be viewed as research scientists, and provided grants for research. They also need to be given academic freedom to do consultancy like their counterparts elsewhere in world. Institutes will be able to keep pace with time only if the problem of faculty growth is addressed. How to create conditions favourable for faculty growth to attain international standard? Do the faculty members have to take an oath? If so, of what type? You will find answers in this book.

Institutes are expected to strike roots, grow tall and sturdy. Institutes are a place where creative minds converge, established notions of truth are challenged, and brainstorming takes place. Professors prefer hard truth to comfortable untrue stand, and self-respect to popular esteem. They normally do not yield to popular pressures but stand up with courage for truth. Public good is uppermost. For this they have to be autonomous in nature, with freedom to think and freedom to act. They ought to have organic links with the surroundings. Institutes function as a stepping stone to job market. They are the knowledge organizations meant for innovation and creativity. The book presents their status analysis vis-a-vis elsewhere in the world. It is urged that they grow soon to international standard. The book provides guidelines.

Have Students become Profit Centres?

Private institutions are seen dominating the scene, as 80 per cent of graduates are coming from self-finance institutions. Turmoil is however breeding everywhere because of high fees, not affordable to many. Strong signals that something is not quite right are being received. Frequent agitations have become common. Policymakers and educators must listen to their voice. It is feared that majority of the bottom half population are not able to send their children for higher education. The nation is losing their talent. Second grade but rich are becoming doctors, and engineers. Education has become a commodity on sale. Education institutes have gone into the hands of politicians who do not understand deeper purposes of education, and are exploiting the people. Court decisions are given a go by. The book explains these aspects and makes appropriate recommendations.

How Best to Bridge the Gap between Indian Institutes and their Counterparts Abroad?

India in the recent past has made progress in several fields. Yet there are many gaps. The book makes an introspection. The country lagged behind not so much because of lack of resources but more because of lack of visions. The same are presented in this book. It is pertinent to note the observations of the US Academy of Sciences given in the book, *Rising Above the Gathering Storm: Energizing and Employing America for a Brighter Economic Future* (2007). It says:

> Civilization is on the brink of new industrial order. The big winners in the fierce scramble for supremacy will

> not be those who simply make commodities faster and cheaper than the competition. They will be those who develop talent, technologies, techniques and tools so advanced that there is no competition.

These observations are addressed to US government to invest more in research and development and attract best brains from the world over. So as to rejuvenate the economy, Indian universities and colleges need more of intellectual inputs than financial.

The book is addressed primarily to thinkers in government; trustees and members of governing boards; principals and professors; and all those who seek reformation in education in India. It draws heavily on my experience as principal in the reputed Institute of Engineering and Technology at Nanded, and my visits abroad to study the function of universities in Germany, USA, UK, and China. It is hoped that the readers will find the book useful.

I hereby acknowledge with sincere thanks my academic colleagues, officers and managers in industry with whom I had fruitful discussions while preparing this book.

B.M. Naik

Contents

Chapter 1

Strategies to Make Technological Universities Globally Competitive

India is at risk, for want of research based, enterprising, world-class technological universities. If India does not make a head way in producing sunrise technology in universities, it will then remain a technology follower and less likely to become a technology leader.

ABSTRACT

Many technological universities have five star infrastructure, brilliant faculty and scholarly students, who do possess lot of advanced scientific knowledge needed most by national and global economy. They continuously generate new knowledge through research at PhD, PG, UG levels. Mechanism for transfer of knowledge from lab to land, in both the private and public universities in India, is however almost absent. Universities are insensitive to market demands. Government has perfected systems for import of technology, but it has not perfected systems for technology transfer from universities within the country to industry. Feedback loop today is incomplete. As a result continuous much needed feedback from students, alumni, and industry to reform education is not provided, as a result, productivity of various professions and vocations on this account remain low. Twenty-five per cent people live in poverty; the rate of return on investment in universities due mainly to lack of outreach is far too low. Technological universities are expected to be industry oriented. They are expected to be innovative providing ever emerging new technology to industry, to keep them globally competitive. But today their engagement with industry is far too low. What is the experience of Western schools?

Many Western schools, on the other hand, are having well defined and perfected knowledge transfer systems and procedures. They are not only educating students to keep them competitive lifelong but practically generating and marketing, new technology/new knowledge and transferring their full scientific capacities to the benefit of society in their vicinity and all over the world. The outreach of technology universities and feedback is far and wide. Thereby they are enriching themselves and augmenting new ideas besides providing budget support for future growth. Technological universities large in number exist in US, Germany, Japan. By virtue of knowledge, they have moved from periphery to the centre of development and taken the nations to greater heights. They have become the drivers of economic and social prosperity. The visions and missions of universities are dynamic, adaptive based on sharing experiences with people at large, and not only giving off the shelf irrelevant and outdated course prescriptions.

The paper presents from experience in the world new directions to the Indian technological universities so as to make them world-class. They should not remain mere examination bodies, as they are today, producing soldiers fit to do lower end jobs in the army of multinationals. Uniform standard of education all over the state, as is often talked, will not facilitate, rather is a hindrance in achieving excellence. Who wants uniformity? People want excellent education. They know creative and excellent things are never uniform. Students have to be educated in what they like. It is like, a fish should not be taught to fly, so also a bird should not be taught to swim. Freedom to learn as per liking is the need of the hour. India needs reformers, innovators, creators. India needs variety of engineers with capability of creating brand new ideas. Uniformity in education is not the solution; uniformity does not enable to achieve excellence. Uniform standard should find no place in technical education, for it generates mediocrity. The paper presents in brief, the need and importance of employing world proven current strategies to make technology universities competitive by world standards.

INTRODUCTION

Does India Need World-Class Technological Universities?

Can India do without them? A nation needs not only soldiers to win a war, it needs captains and generals. Producing graduate engineers [soldiers] is good, but not enough. Balanced output of MTechs, PhDs [generals] is needed. It is they who give strength to technological advancement. Governments in the world have realised that no city, region or nation, can ever prosper fast and have sustained growth without having world-class institutions of higher and technical education. They are the main energy/ idea sources, brain power factories needed to bring India at par with developed world. Well-educated citizenry in technology is an essential condition for faster growth and prosperity. People's development is national development. They need to be educated, on priority, to the level they are capable for, in a best possible manner. It is the well-educated men and women with imagination, capability and competency, who matter most for productive utilization of physical, financial and intellectual resources. Government is convinced that to run its affairs ably at national and international levels it requires leaders, leaders in engineering, industry, and all other walks of life having professional competency nothing less than world standard. Where are such professionals nurtured? Seeds are sown within the four walls of classrooms. Mediocre institutes produce mediocre leaders. They, in ultimate analysis are found to be more costly than the cost of their upgradation. So it is advisable to spend with priority on modernization. Presence of world-class institutions is reckoned to be a differentiating factor between developed and developing nations. Nations develop faster only when world-class institutes are within the reach of citizens. If India does not envision building world-class technological universities with priority, then India is destined to lose in world brain race. India will then trail behind.

World Experience in Technology Universities

Germany in 19th century with the help of its technical high schools is the first country to capitalize on technology. In German language, they were then known as "Technische Hoch Schule". Now they are upgraded to the level of "Technical Universities". Today, there are more than 84 technical universities, to name a few Berlin Technical University, Stuttgart Technical University, Karlsruhe Technical University, Aachen Technical University. The author, under a UGC scheme, has personally visited them and studied the organization, technology transfer and management style of them. The technological advancement of Germany is attributed greatly to the successful working of technical universities.

USA has more than 100 technical and research universities for example, Massachusetts Institute of Technology, California Institute of Technology, and Rochester Institute of Technology, etc. The model of technical universities is now adopted in almost all countries in the world. Japan, Canada, Korea, China has many technical universities. In the name of some universities the word technical may not be there, but essentially their character is technical.

On the campuses of these universities what we notice is that research companies are flocking round them. Technology incubators, research parks, innovation centres, patent and IPR bureaus are distinctly visible. Venture capital companies have opened offices in campuses in search of new technological ideas for commercialization. These universities are like magnets, which attract not only scholars but also industry, entrepreneurs, and VCF companies from across the world. Taiwan has set up a science town at Hsinchu with some 13000 researchers, in two universities, six national laboratories and around 150 companies specializing in electronics. Tsukuba Science City near Tokyo is another example of technical university—Science park collaboration. Another feature of Japan is that on the periphery of technical universities there are several specialised research institutes/companies to absorb persons coming out of universities with new qualifications. Students get access in these research labs and researchers get access in teaching, which make teaching, learning, research supportive to each other. Teaching, research and extension thus become more powerful by coupling with each other. This is achieved in Japan by locating research labs on the periphery of universities. Spin off of companies from universities is a common phenomenon, so also spin off of technologies. A foundation is set in MIT with facility of venture capital fund enabling professors and students to start new ventures based on technologies they develop during the MTech/PhD research effort. Every year as many as 20 to 30 new technology based firms [NTBF] are born in MIT. According to a study, around 3000 companies owe their origin to MIT. This is not unique with MIT. It is true of almost all universities in US, Canada, Australia and China. Universities have become maternity homes for safe birth of hi-tech companies. Indian technological universities will have to follow this route.

On the basis of successful working of technical universities abroad it is recommended that establishing technical universities is the only way for India to build its industry and economy globally competitive. We envision starting technical universities, not only to award ME and PhD degrees but also to become "light house" for industry. We have to have technical university model, with industry orientation, otherwise we will miss the bus or trail behind in Hi-Tech industrial development. Hon. Prime Minister Dr Manmohan Singh on January 3, 2012 in Indian Science Congress at Bhubaneswar has approved more budgets for S&T research and Development. Besides money he said this requires imaginative strategies. "How long India should play the catch up game in science & technology" is the major national concern. He appealed Indian scientific community to show creativity and build world-class universities and colleges.

How to Set Up?

IITs were conceived as world-class technological universities. From very beginning, world best professors in countries like Germany, UK, USA, Russia, were invited to shape them. They were mentored by foreign collaborators constantly for 20-30 years. Programs like exchange of faculty, research partnership, global visions and missions, systems and procedures, gave them international character and so they could shine in the world. Establishment of universities even in developed countries, today is normally done like this under close supervision, of world best professors, some of them from within the country and some from foreign. They are appointed as mentors, as many as 15 to 20, one for each discipline. It is the mentors who accelerate creation of world-class academic culture. Universities right at birth must be groomed to be fit for tomorrow. They should not be outdated or handicapped right at birth. Currently, with a view to increase gross enrolment ratio, many new universities and colleges are being set up in India. Should they not adopt such innovative proven approaches? They must, otherwise they are likely to be born handicapped, and removing handicap afterwards is so difficult.

The article explains in detail how to go about. There is a thinking in some circles why collaborate with foreign universities, when IITs within the country are available? Are IITs not good enough to guide? Many new things like patenting and outreach have come up elsewhere in the world after IIT were set up. Good policies and practices for industrial development from elsewhere in the world will have to be incorporated in newly coming technological universities. It is good to involve existing IITs, but wiser to involve world best professors in technical universities wherever they are and remain in global network.

Envision Creating Imaginative Technology Leaders

Importance of technological academic institutions in today's knowledge driven society is very high. It is they who are furthering human civilization to greater heights. It is the academicians who provide new knowledge, new theories, new technology and competent manpower to business and industry. They are supposed to provide not only knowledgeable but also ethical leaders to government, to the total economy and the world. Industry, society and government in return ought to provide adequate funds to academics to make it grow. India can be richer only by use of advanced technological knowledge. There is no other way. What kinds of graduates institutions produce decide the future? If institutes produce mediocre engineers, future of India will be mediocre. If they produce world-class leaders' future of India will be world-class. Are Indian institutes aiming at producing leaders of global standard? Do we have a mechanism for building leadership in academic institutions like principals, vice chancellors? The well-known saying goes, "First we shape institutions, and then they shape us for generations". Do the key people in government attach proper value for upbringing of youths and provide adequate budget? Do they adopt world-class strategies and provide better governance to enable youth to harvest global job opportunities?

Want to be Globally Competitive?

Then India ought to have many technological universities, of world-class standard. Students now demand world-class education. They are ready to pay for in terms of time, effort and money. But where do you find such institutions? IITs are very few. Thousands of students to obtain quality education are forced by circumstances to go abroad by spending huge sums of money. Some of them suffer bad treatment in foreign, like in England and Australia in the year 2011. Yet the number of students going abroad is increasing. Technological universities and colleges in India now will have to be competitive by nothing less than world standard. Education has become a global subject. Foreign universities have come and many more are coming. They are attracting best of our talent and may soon dominate the Indian scene. Where do the Indian institutions stand in comparison? Let us humbly admit that Indian institutes are far too behind the world. Have we made a gap analysis between Indian institutes and their counterparts abroad? Why are our universities woefully unsuited to the quality demands of globalization? Why they are far too behind their counterparts in developed world? Indian men and women intellectual potential is far too good. They have contributed immensely in American universities and made them forerunner. In India, similar people fail to perform because they are under poor governance, poor systems and procedures.

We need to make introspection, especially in the light of world proven policies and practices and improve governance of technological universities. Do our institutions lack new visions of new world? The present method of governance which is under the "grip of government" although at one time served well, yet today it falls too short of requirement. It needs to be reformed, made flexible enough without any delay and made competitive in global context. How can the technological universities become autonomous in true sense? How can they become knowledge generators? How can they have effective and imaginative governing boards? This is a challenge before Indian academicians. How to face these challenges effectively? You will find answers in this article. It essentially demands willingness to embrace change. The world under the forces of globalization is changing fast. Only those professors and institutions who change to innovate and again innovate can educate the students on correct lines.

Marketing is Essential

Marketing is a usual practice in profit-making companies. Companies earn money by selling their goods and services. In non-profit organizations like universities and colleges however, it is rare. Universities from developed countries have, of late, opened marketing departments and are adopting strategies to sell education and knowledge in international market. They have been organizing campaigns in India, so also in many other countries, to lure students. They, on campus, have been vigorously conducting scientific research, obtaining patents and IPR and selling technology brands to the whole world. Through technology transfer, they are contributing to human civilization. Thereby they are earning money which is ploughed back to support institutional budget, and contributing to make education affordable. Technology transfer from knowledge organizations to industry to improve productivity has become a major phenomenon. It is considered as the key to industrial development and competitiveness. Technology generation, dissemination, patenting and IPR, are some of the current important issues before the nations.

Technology Level of a Nation is the Key Determinant of its Economic and Social Well-being

Therefore, efficient organization and management of technology generation and its effective transfer to community in any nation more so in India, is the need of the hour. Will the present technological universities pay adequate attention to these aspects? They create the future of India. Will India remain a technology follower or become technology leader, matters for future of children and grandchildren.

Performance of institutions in isolation ought to be discouraged. Fresh initiatives to integrate the working of universities, CSIR labs, colleges, industrial estates, chamber of commerce need to be introduced forthwith. Gone are the days when universities enjoyed sellers market. Then they did not need marketing. Now transnational migration of students and high mobility in search of quality has become common. Indian technological universities now have to deserve rank on national and global planes on their own merit. They now face competition with domestic and international at their own door steps. Foreign universities are posing a threat to Indian higher education system. Indian universities will stand to gain from globalization only if they learn lessons from their counterparts, and quickly adapt to changing times. Otherwise they may trail behind.

Universities, world over, are getting less and fewer budgets from government, but are expected to produce more and more. Expectations of students are soaring high. They aspire to make career on global plane. Universities are expected to perform far better than in the past, for which they are pressurised to increase outreach for welfare of community and generate revenue to support their own activities. Self-finance universities and colleges are allowed by law. Universities and colleges are assuming key role in global economic systems, where new technological knowledge and highly skilled people are perceived as critical inputs for economic and social development.

Following observations are pertinent in this regard. They give a hint as to what our universities should be doing now and how they can stay fit and competitive in global market.

Participation in Exhibition

A few years back I happened to visit Hannover Industrial Exhibition in Germany. There was a pavilion meant for universities and colleges. It was most crowded by visitors. Students and professors were explaining the new researches, emerging technologies, like patents and IPR to visitors. Universities had come from all over the world to display and sell their research and innovation output to global industrial community. Visitors came to this pavilion to know which of the new technologies are on horizon and would dominate their business operations tomorrow. Japanese companies in particular were far too ahead, remaining in touch from research stage till completion with the universities not only in Japan but also those in USA, UK, and Europe. It is this strategy which has enabled Japan to become industrial leader. Good universities are aggressive in tapping the industrial clientele world over. Participation in exhibition presenting new knowledge, new technology, and new theories to create new society is demanded of a modern Indian technological university.

What is the Use of that Research Which in Spite of Potential is not Exploited Commercially?

Do our universities participate in industrial exhibitions? Do they have patents and IPR to sell like their counterparts abroad? Can we do this? We can, but we need to have a vision. In India, how many universities have so far obtained patents and marketed them. American universities obtain as many as 1000 patents each year, whereas Indian universities obtain less than 10, and they have no mechanism to market. Their use and application is left to chance. Students do research for PhD, masters and under graduation. In the absence of marketing mechanism, the theses remain in library on cupboards. Commercial exploitation is not done, and hence quality of research remains mediocre, less useful and irrelevant, and in turn the quality of education suffers. Full gains from research are not achieved. Many times papers are published in national and international journals, but patents on them are earned by foreigners. We need to make most of our capacities and outputs for which a well designed; well connected marketing and technology transfer department in a university is a must. Without that we are losing benefits and shall continue importing technology from foreign.

Technology Transfer from University to Industrial Estate

Can a university propel industrial development? A major reason for the success of the US computer industry has been the development of a host of small firms in Silicon Valley and in Boston. These firms grew directly out of research in neighbouring universities. Professors have acted as consultants to these firms, new grads have provided the workforce, and research projects funded by government have provided ideas. The companies benefitted, so also the nation with new products, new jobs and new market strength. Chinese universities are not behind, so also Australian. Can the Indian technological universities not do this? You need a swimming pool to learn swimming, so you need a technology transfer department to learn and practice entrepreneurship.

Marketing gives Feedback to Produce Technologies that can be Sold

A friend of mine 25 years back went from Pune to USA. He studied masters and PhD and then started a company in Silicon Valley. He returned to India after a gap of 25 years. We received him on Mumbai airport. He was curious to see the progress made by India. We were driving by car to Pune. He was happy to see the new express way, which is as good as in USA. When we came to Pune I was telling him we have entered Pune. He was not able to see any signs of his time on roads. He would not believe that this is Pune. He said how Pune can change beyond recognition. We came to Deccan Gymkhana. He did not see the shops and restaurants of his time, but saw a new flyover. He was not ready to believe that this is Pune. Then we brought him on Laxmi road. He did not see a single bicycle, which at his time used to be crowded. Then we came to railway station. He did not see a single horse cart. He refused to accept that this is Pune. Then we brought him to the university where he studied. Immediately, he exclaimed, now I cannot refuse. He said whole city has changed but the university has not. The same old buildings and roads, labs and classrooms, same old procedures and systems in university he could notice.

He said in USA, universities change faster than the cities. Universities change first, and then they show the way to cities and industry to change. In India unfortunately it is the other way round; universities have become bogies instead of engines. They do not drive but follow the change. It is mainly because they are not in touch with industrial and technological market. They have no knowledge/technology transfer and marketing departments. They have no eyes and ears to sense what the society wants and which way the world is moving. The situation can be changed if marketing departments, marketing studies and surveys are introduced. Marketing department will enable a university to be in driver's seat, and navigate university activities in needed direction.

Creativity, Discovery, Innovativeness Enable Nations to Win in Global Competition

I was reading an article written by an American author, in the magazine *Fortune*. The author, from US, was addressing the question, "Can India ever compete with US in software business?" To answer the question, he made an analysis of higher education in both countries and recorded that Indian system is rote learning that is to say it is mechanical, stereotype based on memorization and not creative thinking. Students are taught sunset knowledge, presuming that knowledge is finite. Institutes in India produce too less of sunrise knowledge, new theories. Students are not learning innovation, and hence they do not learn how to discover unknown. They are reflexion centres teaching that knowledge which comes to them from developed countries. It does not focus on creativity, discovery and innovation. He came to the conclusion that Indian institutions can produce at best followers in technology but not leaders. On the other hand, thrust of US universities is on producing leaders, discoverers, and creators who obtain patents and intellectual property. It is US which are pumping new technology most in the world market. Eighty-five per cent of world IPR is held by Americans. He said students of today are leaders of tomorrow. Their education is an enabler in competitiveness of software industry.

He came to conclusions that a nation creating followers can never compete with a nation creating leaders, unless in future it changes its strategies and improves. Universities in India need to incorporate creativity, discovery and innovativeness in syllabi and aim to produce leaders, which require market study to increase outreach on continuous basis. Technology generation, its marketing and technology transfer department is now a must, if India has to make a mark in world.

What is the New Agenda for Technological Universities? A university by definition is a place where knowledge is generated. They should be technology generators, obtaining patents and IPR, and transferring them to industry. To make this happen the technological universities should have to set up on campus research parks, incubation centres, patent and IPR centre, innovation centres, technology transfer centres, and marketing departments. This is what universities in foreign are doing. Why our technological universities cannot do?

Research Parks and Incubation Centres: It is the success of projects like Cornell's Centre for Advanced Technology that has led many universities all over the world to establish research parks and incubation centres on their campuses. In these parks, space is rented to small, developing companies—often headed by recent graduates—and the university provides facilities as well as scientific and business advice and support. The model is now adopted the world over. Research parks are providing spring boards for students to swim ahead of all in creative activity.

Success in the international marketplace in the coming years will depend chiefly on the successful and swift application of new S&T to manufacturing and processes and products. And that in turn will depend on close and effective partnership between university, government and industry. Are these models worth adaption for Indian universities?

It is the Apex Bodies like UGC/AICTE Which have to Show the Way

There is a story of two armies which were fighting a battle with each other. One army had a lion as its captain, but the soldiers were sheep. The second army had a sheep as its captain but the soldiers were lions. The lion captain employs bold strategies, while the sheep captain employs strategies like a coward sheep and looses battle, although the soldiers are lions, because the soldiers have to follow the strategies drawn by captain.

It is the strategies drawn by apex bodies like UGC/AICTE which can enable India to win. They have to make bold decisions like a lion captain. They have not yet drawn knowledge transfer and marketing strategies, nor conducted any studies and surveys. In India, it is only agriculture universities, which have research department with research staff with an extension department, and so productivity is increasing. Knowledge transfer from universities is solving India's food problem, although population has increased three times. Marketing will lead to improvement in quality of education; make it relevant and purposeful, besides cost competitive. Will UGC/AICTE benchmark with world best technological universities and adopt appropriate strategies?

Foreign Collaborators thus far have Propelled Indian Industrial Growth. Can Indian Universities not Go Nearer to Industry and Contribute?

Most of the companies have foreign collaborations. True that India is late starter in industry. Now enlightened industries are coming forward to join hands with universities to jointly conduct research and innovation. Department of Science and Industrial Research Government of India have started many schemes. It is good that they are recognizing their role and responsibility. They have to play a leading role in innovation and entrepreneurship. Foreign collaborators have so far been transferring technology to industry at high cost and with time lag, besides making us too dependent on them. Industry will be flocking round the technological universities if and only if they generate technologies.

Why India should Generate Technology?

Most of the time, it is the penultimate technology foreigners give and then they keep secret with them, and so we cannot be competitive in world market. Now organizational innovations like technology parks, innovation centres, patent and IPR centres, technology incubators are being established in many universities and colleges. This is a good sign, necessary to produce Indian brands of technology. This accentuates the need and importance of effective marketing departments. How can the products be sold in international market without marketing department?

National Knowledge Commission [2006] and Yashpal Committee Report [2009] have Prescribed Universities to be Enterprising

Both the reports have suggested reforms in governance and increasing outreach of universities. They said creation of new knowledge, discoveries and creative endeavours should be the integral components of higher and technical education. Technology innovation, patent and IPR, technology incubation, entrepreneurship, privatization, public private participation [PPP] are strongly advocated. They further said some institutes are planning to be in top 20 of world list. They certainly have the potential. But now it is not just a matter of putting more money or appointing more men on the job. It is more a matter of using current and appropriate strategies, including marketing and knowledge transfer. They should work with internal ideas but supplement them with the external ideas from industry and alumni. Winning institutes are those which are flexible, constantly changing with time. Indian universities must have to learn from case examples in foreign countries. How Japan with the help of universities has moved the nation forward? How Germany has maintained leadership by installing technological knowledge relay centres? How USA has created technopreneurs in Silicon Valley? All this demands universities to be not introvert but extrovert. National Knowledge Commission has recommended universities to be enterprising. How do they become enterprising? They have to resort to strategies like marketing, outreach, technology transfer through patenting, etc. US academy of sciences in its report, "Rising above the Gathering Storm" said:

> Civilization is on the brink of new industrial order. The big winners in the increasingly fierce scramble for supremacy will not be those who simply make commodities faster and cheaper than competition. They will be those who develop talent, technologies, techniques and tools so advanced that there is no competition.

These observations are useful to our universities also. Universities can be enterprising only if they have effective knowledge transfer and marketing department.

Characteristics of world-class technological universities. On the campuses of universities like Madison, Cambridge, Edinburgh, what we notice is that research companies are flocking round them. Venture capital companies have opened offices in campuses in search of new technological ideas for commercialization. Universities in developed countries have become like magnets which attract not only scholar students but also industry, VCF, and entrepreneurs, from across the world. They are globalizing their operations to meet the world needs in education and of technology. Students from many countries, so also industries from across the world are coming to their campuses and for which they are prideful. By virtue of strong research base, they have become a source of latest technological knowledge in education and a source of new ideas enabling companies to win. This has become possible because of strategies of marketing.

CONCLUSIONS

From discussions above following conclusions emerge:

1. **India desperately needs research-based, world-class technological universities.** They should not remain only as examination bodies. They are found to provide each new generation top leaders with creative, inclusive, inquiring, engaged and enabling mind. Brave new India of tomorrow is being created today in these temples of knowledge. Well-being of people critically depends on reforms in technological universities. Who will make millions of citizens fit for living in modern world? Who will create world-class leadership fit to run a big country, like India? It is the world-class professors in them who produce excellent able leadership. Therefore, they should be challenged, critically examined, and enabled to play an influential role in preserving traditional knowledge and rewriting the book of new knowledge.

2. **Technology universities should show lead in industrial development.** Technology clusters, innovation centres, research parks must be started in and around them. This will fire the imagination of young. IITs, NITs and state technology universities are good but their present impact by world standard is far too low. They should now emulate the models of Western schools. Technical Education Quality Improvement Program [TEQIP] Government of India through World Bank is aiming at this. Technological universities must make its fuller utilization. Universities must have to think out of box and enable industry to win.
3. **What should be the next big thing for universities to do?** Technological universities at this juncture of time must focus on generation and marketing of intellectual, technological capability in to saleable goods and services. Public service, carried out chiefly through teaching, was the motive for the creation of the earliest universities and colleges. Even today teaching remains the core of the university's public service. But now in globalized world, trend of public service extends far beyond, to entrepreneurial activities like technology transfer, research park, technology innovation, and patent and IPR, etc.
4. **Technological universities must be enabled to be responsive to world dynamics.** It is the technological universities in US, Germany, Japan which have enabled them to capitalize on technology. World experience tells us that but for effective knowledge generation and technology transfer with technology push matching with market pull; universities remain out of tune and isolated, as "Ivory Towers". They do not remain responsive to world dynamics and hence do not effectively influence people's life as much as expected.
5. **Restructuring and repositioning of Indian technological universities with respect to society and the world is needed.** The conventional wisdom of university system,

with outdated visions and missions, systems and procedures, policies and practices need revision. Once it served well. But now in free world universities are expected to stand on their own merit and imagination. If innovation and creativity are to be given a boost, creation of research foundations for the purpose is must. Industries should have to show a lead.

6. **Thus far, it is the foreign collaborators who have gone nearer to Indian industry and propelled their growth.** Indian universities remained away. Now is time that technical universities learn a lesson from foreign counterparts and play the role of "light House". They should present their research output, patents, etc. in industrial exhibitions.
7. **Technological universities can accelerate Brain Gain.** Thousands of students are going abroad every year. They have been going from Gandhi-Nehru period. This is happening mainly because our universities are highly deficient in knowledge generation and knowledge transfer to industry and society. Technological universities if enabled to upgrade they can stand high in world list bring back brains from abroad.

If India does not create research-based, world-class technological universities, if industry does not associate with them in this mission, the universities will be providing mediocre graduates far too low by international standard to run India's professional affairs nationally and internationally. India will then tend to lag behind.

REFERENCES

Fang, Zaho (2004). Academic Entrepreneurship, case study of Australian universities, published in *International Journal of Entrepreneurship and Innovation*, pp. 91-97. IP Publishing Ltd., Vol. 5, Number 2.

Frank, H.T. Rhodes (2001). "The Role of American University—The Creation of the Future", Cornell University Press.

Government of India, National Knowledge Commission Report, 2006.

Government of India, Yashpal Committee Report, 2009.

Green paper of European, "Union on Innovation and Technological", Transfer Enterprise Unit DG, EUFO, 2295-2920 Luxemburg.

James Duderstadt, A University of 21st Century, The University of Michigan Press, 2005.

Naik, B.M. and W.S. Kandlikar (2010). *Higher & Technical Education-Book of Knowledge*, Gyan Publications.

U.S. Academy of Sciences, "Rising above the Gathering Storm," report, 2007.

Chapter 2

India Needs International Standards in Accreditation Problems in Adoption and Implementation

ABSTRACT

The paper outlines in brief, need and importance of introducing global quality standards in accreditation, prescribed by the international agreement "Washington Accord". This agreement is initially provisional and after scrutiny, if found fit, it is upgraded to signatory status. It is this status which empowers students of engineering, to become internationally mobile to harness job opportunities in world market. It facilitates mutual recognition of professional qualifications and reduces barriers between nations for mobility of engineering personnel for employment, career advancement and pursuing higher education. However, there are problems in adoption and implementation. The problems are in respect of scope of the institutions which ought to include now more of research and development. Research needs to be increased with a view to enlarge student's innovation capacity and imagination to global level. The paper attempts to identify the problems and evolve possible solutions. India, to be able to fulfil its declared dream of becoming a developed nation by 2020, needs not simple professionals, but movers and shakers, technology pioneers and industry leaders of world-class standard, which can come only by becoming member of the international agreement.

The paper takes a note of the discussions and deliberations in World Summit on Accreditation (WOSA, 2012) held in

Delhi from March 25-28, 2012 and argue that now National Board of Accreditation (NBA) an autonomous body should not remain just doing inspection to measure and certify quality. But it should guide colleges to diagnose problems and give appropriate prescriptions to improve. NBA should assert and be objective enough without fear and favour, in public interest, to give signals to improve physical infrastructure and academic culture. It is understandable that to begin with only a few institutions will come up to global standards. But we must begin somewhere; the number will rise from year to year. Unaccredited institutions simultaneously may continue producing graduates, and they should be pursuing to attain international standards. International Accreditation Council of Quality Education and Research (IACQER) which is an organization in the world works along with the institutions to upgrade their education and research standards. Our institutions must have to associate to take guidance (Dinesh, 2012).

Although former HRD Minister Hon'ble Kapil Sibal in the conference speech expressed desire to make accreditation obligatory, at present juncture of time, due to inherent problems some of which are outlined below, it is difficult. In the initial stages till institutions are accredited they will have to remain unaccredited. They cannot be accredited right at birth. Younger generation is seeking increased mobility and wider access to opportunity in world market for employment, career advancement and pursuing higher studies. This necessitates adoption of international standards. Conclusions are drawn so as to enable India to join the band of developed nations.

INTRODUCTION

Need and Importance of Setting Global Quality Standards in Accreditation

The famous saying goes, "Low aim is a crime". Former President Dr. Abdul Kalam said India should dream big, think great and show commitment to implement dreams. It is time for India to aim high in quality and accreditation. Education without quality is no education. There can be no progress without quality.

It may take time to reach. But at the earliest India must sign Washington Accord, which originated in 1989, with the adoption of superior standards in accreditation. To qualify for signatory status of the same, most colleges may require redesigning their policies and practices, systems and procedures. The process should however begin somewhere. The colleges will have first to assimilate what the international standards are and then try to reach them. Initially, the number of colleges fulfilling standards prescribed by Washington Accord may be small but it in view of benefits from it will rise from year to year.

Lot of many opportunities due to emerging technology have and are coming up in globalised world. Indian youths need to be prepared to harvest them and go global (Paliwal, 2012). In this era of knowledge-driven society, development depends on people's intellectual and technological capacity to generate new knowledge, new theories and new technologies. Students, so as to harness them ought to have world-class competency, for which they are ready to work and pay in terms of time, effort and money. But not many universities and colleges in India today are able to offer. This is observed to be mainly because there is no performance evaluation of institutes by using international standards. The institutes have the potential, which can be unfolded only with the adoption of standards of Washington Accord. Thousands of talented students in the absence of quality education every year go abroad. They spend huge sums of money. They are going from Gandhi-Nehru period. How long should they have to go? Has India failed in creating a vibrant educational ecosystem that supports cutting edge research and in turn quality of education? Why foreign universities are coming? Is it not because the unmet demands are huge? Now Indian youth wants to go global and win. Signing Washington Accord to improve standard of education is therefore essential. Systems of accreditation should not let down youths any more.

India now is a rising economic power. It desires to reach to greater heights, for which graduates of colleges, universities and polytechnics have to have competency nothing less than world standards. Students aspire to harness opportunities arising out of globalization and rightly so India is intending to sign "Washington

Accord". To qualify for the same colleges require having superior standards in research, teaching, technology transfer and outreach. Reforming accreditation in isolation is good but not enough. Global standards cannot be reached without re-engineering of associated organizations, namely NBA, colleges, universities, government education administration and training in industry which are responsible for quality directly and indirectly. India, in 2007 is given provisional status in Washington Accord and not the signatory (WOSA). It means Indian degree is not yet recognised in world job market especially of member countries but will be recognised only after it gains signatory status. Till then Indian students are let down. So as to come out of this crisis, adoption of global standards in accreditation by NBA are urgently called for, implementation of which however pose many problems. Some countries which obtained provisional status in Washington Accord later than India have already obtained signatory status. This accentuates the need for India to move fast in resolving problems to adopt international standards. It is said, problems seen in proper perspective are half solved. With this intention the paper attempts to throw light on problems in adoption and implementation of international standards in accreditation.

Mediocre Institutes are More Costly than the Cost of their up Gradation (Naik, 2004)

Mediocre institutes appear to cost less but truly they are not. Out of pocket expenditure is less but it takes the toll of career of youth. They create mediocre graduates who cannot and do not ensure creation of the future at expected rate. Graduates remain dwarf, and unsatisfied. Nations remain underdeveloped and are left behind the world. The hidden loss is too big. To illustrate, let us assume there are two regions, say region A and region B. Region A has a world-class university but the infrastructure like roads, railways, etc. is poor. The region B has a mediocre university but the infrastructure is five stars. Which region between the two will progress faster and why? Which region students will receive better education and become more competent leaders to develop the region and ensure future of citizens? Knowledge is power, region A by virtue of superior knowledge in university will produce world-class leaders and so it tends to win. The other region in spite of five stars infrastructure because of mediocre university, people may lack in capacities to make full utilization of available infrastructure. The expenditure on creating infrastructure, in the absence of able leaders will not bring expected growth. This is to say that in the period of knowledge society, universities are now the main drivers of development. Upgradation of universities and colleges deserve much higher priority.

It is observed that the critical factor in national and regional development is the availability of world-class colleges and universities. NBA should move fast and in a firm manner to appraise government and AICTE of necessity to urgently build world-class institutes, which now are a differentiating factor between developed and developing nations. Demand for engineers now is from across the world, so also the supply. Indian graduates, in flat world, are now in competition with their counterparts in world market. Many of them are coming to India, so also many from India are going abroad. Indian engineers can fill up job positions especially in advanced countries where the population is aging. India would have to move ahead vigorously to avail the chances. This demands institutes to be competent by international standards. The question is how can they acquire world-class status and be recognized internationally? The only way to be recognised is the accreditation of courses and institutions with global quality standards, by following Washington Accord, which demands re-engineering of systems and sub-systems in that direction. Getting included in Washington Accord is not now an option but compulsion, without which India will not be able to reach to excellence to produce leaders and join the band of developed nations. It will otherwise trail behind.

Reaching to Global Standards is not a Matter of Only Pumping Money and Appointing More Men on the Job

It is more a matter of scientific planning and putting efforts in a systematic manner (Bush, 1945). There are many institutions in India, who spend money far in excess than necessary. But the expenditure is incurred in a haphazard manner. They are yet nowhere near global standards in quality. They need to follow quality assurance methods; they need systems. They need to have quality policy, quality manual and quality planning and monitoring cell. European University Association (2003) prescribed blending of internal quality assurance with external. NBA conducts external quality assurance (EQA), and is to be supported by internal quality assurance (IQA), through college-level monitoring cell. It has been opined by university associations in many countries like South-East Asian that both EQA and IQA are necessary to effectively ensure quality of education (Ganesh, 2006). Do the institutions have periodic review and feedback from students, alumni and industry? Now students demand quality in education. Education is now global and in buyers market. Competition is fierce. Will NBA give methods and improved systems to colleges? This will decide the success in reaching to global standard. Should NBA prepare documents of successful case studies in India and abroad, and provide to colleges so as to reach to global standards on sustainable basis? Should NBA give quality directions to AICTE and government? It is now an autonomous body of professionals and not subordinate of AICTE. In public interest, it should not hesitate. In AICTE and government, there are political considerations which, in spite of wish prevent professional development of colleges reaching to excellence. NBA without regard to politics should give valuable service in this respect. IACQER is reported to be giving matching grant-in-aid to institutions to raise R&D infrastructure, technical support and a wide platform of quality education and research. NBA should have to formulate schemes to associate.

Develop Awareness for Global Standards

Accreditation Board for Engineering and Technology (ABET) of US is the first body to have started accreditation 80 years before (Paliwal, 2012). All credible engineering programs in US today seek and obtain ABET accreditation. NBA started in the year 1994 has accredited so far very few existing engineering programs. Although India started late in accreditation, it is now moving fast. Government has made accreditation a precondition for obtaining financial support for modernization of research and education programs. Besides, employers are also giving preference to graduates coming from accredited institutions and courses. Students prefer courses for admission which are accredited. Foreign students now essentially prefer such institutions. The tempo in favour of accreditation is being built and soon will catch up. The route to accreditation goes through scientific approach in adopting global visions and missions, policies and practices, systems and procedures. Government will have urgently to mobilise opinion of colleges in favour of Washington Accord, create collective ambition, shared vision, and give technical advice for which several seminars country wide, are necessary. There is no short cut as well as no option to quality enhancement. If the institutions deserve global standards students and employers the world over stand to gain immensely. If not there is a threat to their survival from entry of foreign universities who are at our door steps. The external threat is forcing global standards in accreditation. Preparing ground adequately needs to be driven in the minds of those who manage and maintain institutions. Institutions ill-equipped will prefer not to be accredited. They will not apply till they fulfil the norms and standards and deserve accreditation. The colleges will have first to go through internal quality assurance tests. Good thing is that the momentum is picking up. Accreditation is giving impetus to quality enhancement. Washington Accord if adopted and implemented will internationalise Indian education programs.

REFORMS IN INDIA ARE HIGH ON AGENDA

TEQIP—Phase I is Complete and Phase II is in Progress

Government has undertaken reforms in technical education in association with World Bank through Technical Education Quality Improvement Program (TEQIP) from the year 2003 (NPIU, 2009). It has created National Project Implementation Unit (NPIU, 2009) for systematic implementation. The first phase covering 127 institutions is complete in 2009 and the second phase covering around 200 colleges is in progress. Government is pumping around ₹ 4000 crore, besides doing re-engineering of systems, which is crucial to quality improvement. TEQIP has made it obligatory to colleges to become autonomous, as well as have an effective board of governors, get courses accredited and recruit adequate qualified faculty and staff.

NBA is Evolving Improved Norms and Standards from Time to Time (Web-NBA)

It recognizes that with the increase in colleges in the country, accessibility has increased which is good but quality of education has decreased. A NASSCOM study indicates that only 25 per cent of Indian engineering graduates are employable. McKinsey Report observed that only 13 per cent are employable in multinationals. To re-educate the half-baked graduates "Finishing Schools" have been started. Currently, it is observed that infrastructure of colleges is far too weak. Qualified teachers are not available, competency of teachers is so low that it is said practically "blind is teaching blind". What is wanted is not taught and what is taught is not wanted. There is a serious mismatch. Technological research which is the basis of state-of-the-art education in most of the colleges is almost absent. Most of the self-finance colleges are behind time. They are producing soldiers to do lower-end jobs at best in multinationals. NBA is now activated to remove the ills. It must however move fast. Colleges, universities yet don't have the essential elements like research, innovation centres and so in a way they are handicapped like a human being with feet and hands.

Colleges have become "Black Boxes" consuming more inputs and giving less output.

Lack of Political Will is the Main Cause of Worry (Naik, 2010)

HRD is not yet given due importance in national and state planning. Only lip sympathy is offered. National budget allocation, although increasing, is far too low by international standards. Deeper purposes of education are not understood by the politicians who approve budgets for public education. Private coaching classes in India are booming. Privatization has set in, which is good, but most of the self-finance colleges are managed and maintained by politicians, who have no deeper insight in education. They have low value for academics. Today education barons have usurped the powers of academicians. Professors have no freedom to think and freedom to act. Fees collected in private colleges are siphoned for political purposes. Unethical trends like capitation fees, although banned, has become prevalent. Nobler aims of education are thrown to winds. They are found to be exploiting students and not offering quality education. Bottom 50 per cent of the population due to high fees is not able to send children even when they deserve and are willing. Lot of turmoil in disadvantaged class of people is breeding. There is a sense of betrayal amongst down and out people, that things are designed only for the rich. It is a hot topic of discussion in Parliament and most of the State Assemblies. Government is spending only around 3.5 per cent of GDP on education as a whole and out of which less than 1 per cent on higher and technical education. Government has announced several times from 1991 to raise budget to 6 per cent. But yet it is not practically done. It is felt that something somewhere is seriously wrong and the political will is lacking.

Introduction of global quality standards in accreditation to halt such things is a must, without which opportunities will slip out of people's hands. Engineers will be less mobile and stagnate; their career advancement will be less in globalised market (Paliwal). The future of younger generation will then be affected. The younger generation then will not pardon us for lapses. We must have to bring the world-proven systems and procedures, policies and practices to develop human resource and make them globally competent. This however demands re-engineering of the whole process of engineering education. Will the NBA and government show courage? Will the colleges make Gap Analysis between them and their counterparts abroad (Naik, 2010)? Creativity, discovery, innovativeness is the character of institutes abroad. Improvement in education has gone far beyond classrooms. Improvement in classroom teaching and learning is necessary but not enough. They have to be generating new knowledge, new theories and technologies and become maternity homes for safe birth of hi-tech firms. Institutes abroad are in driver's seat, Indian institutes are followers like bogies of a train. Why it is so in India? Indian people are rated to be brilliant but the quality of education and accreditation is lacking. An autonomous professional body like NBA, in the interests of future of youths, can play a crucial role in giving medicine to government and improving quality of education. Unless they do so more funds and higher priority is less likely to come.

Major Problems in Adoption and Implementation and Some Possible Solutions

An attempt is made in this article to identify the problems. They are presented with a view to evolve solutions. A well-known saying goes, "Problem seen in proper perspective, well in time is half solved." Ignoring problems is too costly. Future of youth and in turn of India is now at risk. India has to increase the competency of its workforce urgently. Do we realise this?

Lack of Organizational Capability, Systems Inefficiency and too Low Competency of Majority of Professors are Some of the Crucial Problems (NPIU)

No institution is higher than the knowledge level of professors. It is they who decide the level of an institution. It is they who fire the imagination of young. The real assets of an institution are the professors. But today it is our weak point. Developing capability of professors is the first and foremost need of the hour, which however is a long-drawn process. It will take years till professors become as qualified and competent as in foreign. The present systems for growth of professors are outdated. Indians in US perform far better because the systems under which they operate in USA are good. The professors in India however in less efficient systems remain dwarf. They lack international exposure. Only a small proportion of professors have opportunity to go abroad. This is their serious short-coming. Their service conditions are poor. Funds for research are not available. Research creates wealth; it is not a financial liability but an asset. This is less realised. Consequently, professor's growth in profession does not take place. They are almost disconnected from their counterparts elsewhere in the world. Hardly a few professors had chance to go abroad and see what policies and practices they follow. Their visions and missions, mindsets are not in tune with the dynamics of globalised world. Syllabi are outdated. They lack research infrastructure and research skills and consequently they teach yesterday's knowledge today. Our institutions today live in the past. They are behind time. They need to be oriented to teaching sunrise knowledge and skills needed in future. Time demands capacity building of professors and staff in colleges and universities. NBA will have to contribute on priority in this regard. It will have to suggest ways and means to strengthen capacities of colleges and professors in them. It should not only say that they are good or not good. Unless it overcomes the problem of systems improvement in accreditation, India may not be able to become signatory in Washington Accord.

Lack of Autonomy to Colleges is Another Problem

Many commissions from Radhakrishnan Commission have recommended autonomy to colleges. Kothari Commission of 1964-66 recommended, New Education Policy of 1986, so also National Knowledge Commission 2007 recommended. But the progress in this direction is too slow. Only a few handful colleges have become autonomous. There is a resistance to change from all stakeholders. Even the government and universities, although recommend autonomy, yet they do not hand over its powers to colleges. Permanent affiliation which is a precondition for autonomy is not given for selfish purposes. This is the root cause. Governments are recommending but with reluctance, there is no force in recommendation. World experience shows that nations are prosperous where colleges are autonomous (Rhodes, 2003). Government is not qualified in academics. It cannot steer the direction of higher education and so it should not interfere. But interference from government in academics is frequent. It grants autonomy with strings attached. So in real spirit colleges do not get freedom to steer their own direction. They have become like bogies of a train instead of becoming an engine. Unless government takes initiative in granting autonomy, its initiative in signing Washington Accord of accreditation may not bring desired results. Debates and discussions on autonomy, with case examples from India and abroad on how to implement it in real spirit are necessary, without which problems are likely to persist. Government, universities, colleges and professors and administrators have it seems doubts. They need to be thrashed out.

Colleges do not have Schemes and Means to Enable Professors to Grow to International Standard

Professors have become hirelings in colleges, both of government and private. They have no say whatsoever in reforming education. They are hired and fired at the sweet will of whimsical management in self-finance institutions. They just do not follow prescribed service conditions, which remain on paper. Professors have no academic freedom which truly is the backbone of reforms (Glen, 2002). They have become puppets in the hands of management. Research is given back seat in technical education. Many State Governments have approved contract appointments on too low salary to professors. Entry in this knowledge profession is being given to mediocre. This is a negative factor which is going against quality movement. Mediocre, lowly qualified professors are teaching meritorious students. They teach nothing other than how to be more mediocre. Majority of professors in colleges are of this type. They are appointed every year at the start of the year and terminated at the end. Regular faculty is less than half even in government supported colleges. This is a false economy. There is very little learning in colleges; careers of students are at stake, and so is India's future. Making accreditation obligatory to colleges as desired by the honourable minister is easy, but difficult to come up to expectations. It takes time, effort and money to upgrade standards. One of the basic principles of accreditation is that it should be optional and not compulsory. Secondly, there are different yardsticks for the measurement of accreditation. So, the first step is to make the concept popular.

Faculty Crunch has Crippled Education

Most of the students in private as well as in government colleges go to coaching classes, which are booming. Coaching classes teach and make more value addition. They teach parrot like. So creativity, imagination in students is not promoted. Besides, students have to pay fees in colleges as well as in classes. This is a national disgrace that colleges have become only registration bodies and not educating students to lead in creativity. AICTE has prescribed qualification as MTech and

PhD for higher posts. The existing teachers register the names in one of the colleges, where there is no learning worth the name, yet PG is allowed. Mostly, they get degree from universities by manipulations. Thesis for the MTech and PhD are available on sale in market. It is a very tragic situation. Under these circumstances how Washington Accord will make India a signatory? NBA will have to work hand in hand with AICTE and enlarge schemes for faculty upgradation. Increasing professional and organizational competency of professors is a gradual and slow process. It is relatively quick to build buildings, purchase equipment but to build faculty is time taking, requiring years. Do we realise this (Goheen, 1969).

Quality does not Grow where Research is Absent (Rhodes, 2003)

Professors have no research grants. Colleges have become teaching shops. Professors teach sunset knowledge. Students learn parrot like what is handed over to them. Unfortunately, teaching and research are segregated from each other and CSIR labs get most of the research budget. This leads to weakening of both. Unless professors are involved in research, there is no force in teaching, professors lack depth and relevance. They tend to teach irrelevant knowledge coming from abroad. They tend to produce technology followers and not leaders. They tend to teach stale knowledge. Washington Accord prescribes research as integral component of professor's duties and responsibilities. The principle is well understood. But very few colleges in India have research infrastructure and mind set in its favour. This is one major problem to be able to become signatory of international accord. It is a firm contention that without research base in colleges, quality of education is less likely to improve. India to be competitive globally must have to integrate research with education and industry. Education charged with spirit of discovery and innovation alone can move India forward. Colleges have major influence on improving innovation capacity of India. They are reckoned as mother of innovation. If colleges do not create centres of research and innovation, then there is no hope and other way for India to be a developed nation. It is more on account of lack of research that India does not stand high in world list. Research and innovation generate economic surplus and provide economic security. If India has to come at par with the world, it will have to take a drive for introducing research in colleges. IACQER can be a good guide to us in this respect.

Majority of research funding today is done in CSIR laboratories. The conventional system of funding may have to be altered and a big junk be created and diverted to universities and colleges. Our colleges will have to dream big, think great like their counterparts and teach research skills to students. Known knowledge is limited but imagination not. Students are expected to learn not only known knowledge but learn to discover unknown. Academicians and NBA will have to influence politicians to allocate research funding in colleges for the welfare of children and grandchildren. This will enable India to join international ranking. Research subsidises education and education subsidises research. Research funding does double duty in colleges. First, research skills are imbibed in youths and second technologies are generated at a much cheaper cost and least time. Most important, it makes learning joyful and effective. India should not lose sight of research. Research is not a fancy affair but it sows the seeds of wealth for future. Washington Accord norms and standards demand more of research output.

Commercial Exploitation of Research Findings is Our Weakness

Can we make it our strength? What is the use of research if although possible, is not exploited commercially? Our rank in accreditation will then go up if R&D is applied in professions and vocations and our graduates will then be in great demand. Our students will then create Indian brands of technology, products and sell them the world over. Research conducted in BTech, MTech, PhD often results in publication. This is good, but better it is if it is exploited commercially. Unfortunately, theses remain in library on shelf. No conscious effort is made to obtain economic value from them, mainly because vision and commitment in this direction is lacking. Today, students do not get opportunity to learn to convert inventions in to usable goods and services. Quality of research improves only when it results in commercial use. What use is of research if it is not converted in practical application? It is good that technical education in India is expanding. But acquisition of skills for commercial exploitation which is the demand of time is lacking. Research park, innovation centre, patent office constitute the infrastructure for research and innovation. It is found to create much needed enterprising culture in campus (Glen, 2002). Colleges then become like magnets to attract brains from anywhere and everywhere. Innovation in India is seriously lacking. This is a serious problem reducing our standing in accreditation. We need to consciously guard in this respect to get entry in Washington Accord.

Industry, in India is not Yet an Active Partner in Improving Technical Education

This is a vital problem in getting Washington Accord signed. It prescribes the two should work for each other. Institutes and industry have to have synergistic relationship between the two. They are interdependent. They cannot in isolation achieve peak performance. Industry should recognise their role and responsibility in long term and help institutes financially. It should sponsor technological projects and take active part in their implementation. It knows that it cannot do all the research it needs by itself, even if it has R&D centre. Industry cannot be globally competitive without research output from universities and colleges. They both cannot remain stand alone entities. It is too detrimental for their mutual good. Similarly institutes should contribute to corporate development. The character of the institution must have to be innovative contributing value to industrial development (Glen, 2002). This is what Washington Accord requires.

Research Parks, Innovation Centres, Patent and IPR Centres are Some of the Projects to be Undertaken in Collaboration (Fang, 2004)

Theory says that if there is no significant industrial research in college then there is no significant education. Industrial research and education are like two ends of a bow. The arrow does not move fast unless the two ends are tightly tied together by a string. Neither end has a force without the support of other. An institute binds the two, namely industrial research and education together to provide quality education. Education then becomes a creative learning. Today, most of the industries have foreign collaborations. Their development plans are propelled by foreigners. They do not go nearer to institutes and institutes do not go nearer to industry. The situation will have to be changed, which is possible, only when colleges are engaged in research, and the professors have knowledge to give to industry. Will NBA play a role in attaining synergy?

Colleges do not have Transparent Accounting Systems

Intensions of many self-finance colleges are not fair. They do not have professional effective, imaginative Board of governors. Corruption in AICTE, state offices, universities are of high order. This has a negative impact down below. Under these and many more difficult circumstances NBA has to find its way to global standards in accreditation. They must have a conviction to win. Where there is a will there is a way.

Government's Poor Vision and Too Low Value Attached to Education is a Serious Problem in Government Supported Institutions

Government attaches too low value to it in national budget. It is mainly on account of this that India ranks too low in the world list. Nobel Laureate Dr. Amartya Sen when asked by the then Finance Minister Yashwant Sinha what priority should he give to education in national budget. Amartya Sen replied India should give first priority to education. Then he asked what should be the second priority? He again said education. When asked what should be the third priority? He repeated education. He said education-education-education should be the priority in national budget. He said that there is no project more feasible at this juncture of time for India than education. The rate of return from investment in colleges and universities are reported of the order of 50 to 100 per cent, which very few projects yield. The present budget allocated is around only 3 per cent of GDP, whereas many countries in the world are allocating up to 10 per cent, USA 12 per cent and so they are winning in brain race. India has brainy people, but their brains are starved. They need better nursing. Government has been announcing again and again from 1991 that it will allocate 6 per cent of GDP to education. It however gave only lip sympathy.

If government does not increase public budget on education, international standard is less likely to come and signing Washington Accord on accreditation will be difficult. Government needs to be provoked for quality education. How to provoke is a problem? Who can provoke? Policymakers in India are not galvanised with new ideas. Strategies employed are behind the world. National Knowledge Commission 2007 and Yashpal Committee Report 2009, gave valuable recommendations, which however are too slow in implementation. Those who should show lead like UGC/AICTE themselves are found to be opposing. Academicians like Prof. Yashpal have so far failed to pursue government. Although budget for education is increasing from year to year yet it is too low by international standard. Unless public budget is increased reaching international standards is difficult, especially in aided colleges.

Most of the Universities and Colleges are Like a Physically Handicapped Person

A person without a hand, leg or eye, etc. is considered to be handicapped. He cannot perform the operations like a normal man/woman. A college or university without research centre, patent and IPR, technology transfer department, innovation centre, etc. is also a handicapped institution. Nowadays, institutions should enlarge their scope to cover above-stated organs besides teaching and learning in classrooms. The activities are interactive, supportive to each other, strengthening learning. Teaching and learning without these organs remain incomplete, irrelevant, non-viable and out-of-date. The multifaceted activities are reinforcing the teaching and learning. Without them learning of students learning remains incomplete, and deficient. Do we realise this? Institutions in India by and large are really deficient in respect of research and professional requirements. They cannot run in global race with handicaps and hope to win. They cannot rank high in world list and become innovative, creative and world-class. The framework and scope of the institutions first must have to be made comprehensive covering the elements needed. The conception of the institutions will have to be inclusive of multifaceted activities. Shall we not envision the modern institutions? The old type of institutions based on only classroom teachings have gone out of date. NBA will have to assert to change mind set of key people in colleges to enlarge scope of colleges.

CONCLUSION

The paper has presented major obstacles for attaining global standards. The problems are huge. But they are solvable. Accreditation cannot be seen in isolation without re-engineering of key stake holders, namely industry, government, and colleges. Indian institutions have the potential but for awareness and high aim the potential remains unexplored. Conferences to develop awareness are necessary.

An international accreditation standard in Indian colleges and universities to ensure recognition and mobility of students, their career advancement, and availing growing opportunities in business world and to enrich human civilization is the need of the hour.

Rapid upgradation of quality of education through accreditation in the light of experiences in the world should urgently be taken up. There is nothing more urgent for India at this juncture of time than reviving technical education to make youth more mobile. We should not close our eyes and ears to good ideas from abroad. We should not miss to benefit from them. It is too costly not to interact with the counterparts elsewhere in the world. Accreditation by standards of Washington Accord is the need of the hour.

Accreditation for institutions, the world over, is optional and not obligatory. In India too it should not be made compulsory. The benefits from accreditation nationally and internationally to an institution should be an attraction to the colleges and universities. Incentives may be given, so that more and more seek accreditation. Besides, unaccredited institutions have also a place in society. If unaccredited institutions do not survive, it will give a setback to much desired increased access to education to masses.

NBA should not become just an inspection and certifying body, but it should offer technical advice to colleges to improve. It will have to work hand in hand with AICTE and state governments to reform. Industry should not remain a silent spectator but become an active partner. The problems are possible to be solved. Alumni and industry must have to support.

Restructuring and repositioning of NBA with respect to society, government and the world is needed. The conventional wisdom of NBA, with primitive visions and missions, systems and procedures, policies and practices need revision. Once as a part of AICTE they served well. But now as an autonomous body in free world NBA is expected to stand on its own merit and imagination. It should take least support of government, rather it should give support. If innovation and creativity are to be given a boost, NBA should have to show a lead and imagination in getting Washington Accord signed.

NBA now should have to do its home work efficiently, avoid delay and win the confidence especially of self-finance colleges, which turn out 80 per cent of graduates. It will have to be objective in purpose giving warning signals if necessary to AICTE and governments to increase budgets for quality infrastructure, equipment, research and education.

India, without international standards in accreditation, is at risk, industrial productivity is at much greater risk. NBA should play a key role in resolving problems in adoption and implementation in achieving international standards.

REFERENCES

Academy of Sciences, USA book *Rising Above the Gathering Storm*, 2007.

Bush (1945). Commissions Report, 1945, US Academy of Sciences.

Economic Times, Editorial, 2.1.2005.

Fang, Zaho (2004). "Academic Entrepreneurship, Case Study of Australian Universities", published in *International Journal of Entrepreneurship and Innovation*, pp. 1-97. IP Publishing Ltd., Vol. 5, Number 2.

Gautam, Dinesh Kumar (2012). "Accreditation of Engineers for Effective Implementation of Washington Accord", Souvenir, WOSA-2012, New Delhi.

Hegde, Ganesh (2006). "Blending of Internal Quality Assurance with External for Quality Enhancement". *University News*, Vol. 49, No. 44, November.

Jones, Glen A., Patricia L. McCartney and Michael L. Skolinik. "Creating Knowledge-Strengthening Nations." University of Toronto Press, 2002.

Naik, B.M. (2004). "Needed Innovation & Entrepreneurship in Higher Education Institutes", published in *Journal of Technical Education*, January-March 2004, Vol. 27, No. 1, pp. 27-32.

———. (2010). *Higher & Technical Education—Book of Knowledge*. 2010, Gyan Publication, New Delhi.

NPIU (2009). Government of India, Technical Education Quality Improvement Program [TEQIP] Phase-II Project Implementation Plan [PIP].

Paliwal, D.K. WOSA-12, Excellence in Education, Students Mobility and Opportunities for Accreditation Agencies. [Background paper].

Rhodes, H.T. (2003). *Role of American University—The Creation of the Future*, Cornell University Press.

Robert, Goheen. Princeton University Press, 1969, *The Human Nature of a University*.

Website of NBA.

Website of Washington Accord.

WOSA-12, World Summit on Accreditation-2012, New Delhi, March 25-28, 2012, Souvenir.

Chapter 3

Autonomy Policy for Higher Education in a Changing World

If we grant autonomy to colleges, our efforts and investment are likely to be fruitful. If we don't grant, and even provide abundant financial and other resources, all that is not going to be much useful.

STATEMENT OF PROBLEM

Absence of autonomy is found to have created almost a complete lack of competitive environment in institutions and loss of spirit of academic leadership. In the absence of autonomy, colleges have become like bogies, having no authority to steer the direction by themselves. They have become too much dependent on universities. They do not have authority to self-monitor and self-control and hence do not move with the times. There is a time lag between the action initiated by university and action taken at college level. This slip is a cause of worry. It is this slip which is avoided in autonomous structure. When institutions become autonomous, they become self-actuating, self-driven, shaping future on their own, and not depending on university.

In India, autonomy is talked more but little practiced. Government, universities, colleges and policymakers in public interest need urgently to act together with dedication and not merely provide lip service. They ought to consciously chart the road map for installation of autonomous structure.

Educating and training the concerned persons for effective use of autonomy, and changing their mind set, is the need of time. Learning to use autonomy is relatively easy, but unlearning the old style of working in affiliating system is difficult. Hence, brain washing is necessary. It is therefore advisable to make colleges autonomous right at birth.

Autonomy is effective in increasing the response ability of an institution to the changing situations. It requires consistent efforts over a period of ten to fifteen years to learn successfully to use autonomy. Mere declaration of autonomous status to institutions does not bring autonomy. People have a tendency to cling to old systems. The leaders of the institutes must have to change their mind sets, and consistently practice democratic functioning as is demanded, in autonomous structure.

They should have to abandon bossism or bureaucratic culture, and refrain from autocracy. So as to enable youths to make most in globalize world India needs urgently to initiate steps to adopt and implement the policy of autonomy.

Introduction of autonomy is not like a magic wand. Its successful use is a long-drawn process, which requires patience and consistent efforts. Once perfected it lasts longer.

CONCEPT OF AUTONOMY

An autonomous institution signifies its overall ability to act by its own choices in pursuit of its chosen mission. Autonomy is a dynamic participative model of governance based on continuous evaluation of performance. The evaluation need be done at regular intervals by internal as well as external agencies. Every stakeholder's viewpoint is valuable and this needs to be respected and cared for. Autonomy means freedom to think and freedom to act but freedom implies accountability and responsibility. Greater autonomy means greater accountability and greater flexibility, relating to budgets, admission of students, degrees awarded, quality of teaching and research. Autonomy means self-determination, self-control, and self-regulation, with least interference from external sources. It means greater economic freedom, to raise the resources. Autonomy implies going away from government closer to its own students and faculty, who are the main stakeholders in an institution. Autonomy means internal debates, discussions, continuous improvement for the public cause of education. Autonomous institutions are found to be innovative and innovating non-stop. Autonomy enables to make best utilization of available resources, available ideas to harvest opportunities.

Stimulant of Excellence: Institutions by practicing autonomy over a period of years are found to become innovative and rich in terms of knowledge. Knowledge and decision-making are distributed throughout the organization. An autonomous institution is characterized as a knowledge organization. Creativity and innovation; trust and confidence, are the main pillars on which institutions rest. They attract brains from anywhere and everywhere. Scholars dream to study in them. They tend to become creative by keeping role models of internationally known institutions before eyes. The professors in these institutions not only teach and research but think great in global context and provide guidance to government, corporations, and other public bodies in respect of public policies. Autonomy provides freedom to professors to enable them to be equal to world-class professors. An academic institution is not only a teaching institution but a knowledge source for the society; a think-tank, it ought to be so in public interest. However, government which is least qualified in academics is found occasionally to interfere in these institutions even in academic matters. This kind of over stepping by government is required to be stopped forthwith. This is in public interest.

An Autonomous Institute has an In-built Mechanism for Continuous Reformation

It should be allowed to function; even if it fails for failure teaches important lessons. In any case freedom which is the main strength of an institution ought not to be curbed. Government has a tendency to interfere unnecessarily, and to kill its self-improvement ability. Institutions ought to have immunity from arbitrary exercise of disturbance from external authority. It should be allowed to enjoy self-ruling and ought to have exemption from external control. It is like learning how to ride a bicycle. It takes some time and requires self-effort to learn. But once learned one keeps on refining it. Autonomy signifies the state of being free or at liberty rather than in confinement. It has the power to determine action without restraint. Pursuits of truth, innovation, discovery, creativity which are the main functions of an institution require minimum interference, demanding more autonomy. This is for larger good. Government and its other agencies should consciously avoid interfering. But autonomy does not mean monarchy. Institutions must have to follow the law of the land.

Leadership Distributed: The concept of autonomy is intertwined with decentralization and privatization. Powers are not centralized at one level but distributed at various levels with various persons. Financial resources and newer ideas available in private sector besides in government need to flow in education. Hence, private sector leadership with continuous experimentation, in autonomous structure is the accepted way of working.

An academic institution is a knowledge organization, consisting of innovative people. The academic leadership in the institution is scattered throughout. Leaders create leaders. This is their distinguishing feature from other organizations. The people are worthy and autonomous structure enables them to become further more worthy.

These autonomous institutions by virtue of self-control are a security for the economic future of people and the nation, so said Mr. Jefferson former President of US. The autonomous institutions, public and private both, tend to make full utilization of the knowledge available in the society. Education needs of the people cannot fully be visualized by people only in government. It needs to be assessed at every institution level, both in public and private sectors. Knowledge available out side government must be allowed to flow in the system.

HISTORY

The first autonomous college in India "Hindu College of Calcutta" came in existence in the year 1817. This was followed by Agra College in 1827, Poona College in 1833, and Elephantine College, Mumbai in 1834. Eight autonomous colleges came in existence before the universities like Bombay, Madras were set up.

Education Commission under the chairmanship of Dr. D.S. Kothari in the year 1966 recommended grant of autonomy to colleges. National Education Policy of 1986 recommended granting autonomy to colleges. World over, colleges and universities by law are autonomous. In India today there are more than 18000 colleges, but they are not autonomous, mostly affiliated to universities, offering stereotype, irrelevant and standard courses. Only about 200 colleges are autonomous. Affiliating system has resulted in a huge waste of intellectual and physical resources, besides misdirection to younger generation.

Government of India, with a view to make education responsive to people's needs, recently had appointed the committee under the chairmanship of Kanti Biswas, which submitted "Report of the Central Advisory Board of Education on Autonomy of Higher Education Institutes, in 2005".

The terms of reference were:

(a) To suggest measures for enhancing the autonomy of higher education institutes, especially those with potential for excellence.

(b) To institutionalize regulatory provisions for promoting autonomy and accountability of higher education institutes.

The committee has strongly advocated the implementation of the policy of autonomy to make education flexible keeping in tune with worldwide latest developments.

Some of the important recommendations are:

(a) Freeing higher education from unnecessary controls and regulations and withdrawing avoidable state interventions.

(b) Institutes need to be insulated from internal and external pressures, of political, bureaucratic and other groups.

(c) UGC/AICTE and government should evolve strategies to achieve this end.

(d) There is a need to grant autonomy for designing curriculum.

(e) To bring innovative approaches in teaching and research.

(f) To make more funds available for education.

(g) To start self-finance courses.

(h) To set up internal quality assurance cell.

(i) To improve PG courses and research.

(j) To fix number of posts of professors, assistant professors, etc.

(k) To train academic administrators.

(l) To provide block grants.

The report observed with surprise that the associations of professors, like MFUCTO are objecting for the implementation of autonomy. Autonomy empowers professors. Then why do they not want autonomy? The government administrators and universities are perhaps not serious about releasing authorities to professors. For small little things, they have to take approval from government. Today, professors have many responsibilities and no authority. Who will take responsibility without authority?

National Knowledge Commission, Government of India in its report of 2006 has analyzed the problems in higher education, and said, "most obvious solution is to provide autonomy to colleges either as individual colleges or as clusters of colleges."

WORLD EXPERIENCE

International Association of University Presidents (IAUP) in its meeting December 8-9, 2006 in Thailand discussed the issue, "the anatomy of autonomy".

Views were expressed on institutional autonomy in this meeting by experts from various countries. They differ considerably from country to country. Perceptions of autonomy change over time as well. Governments in almost all countries have been interfering not only by the power of purse; but they have been interfering in respect of rules of admission, recruitment of staff and faculty, courses and deciding how an institution should be governed. Interference from Government of India in IIM Ahmedabad is a well-known recent case. The ideal situation IAUP recommended is that, "Government should put trust in institutes to carry out their designated public roles without government intervention."

They should be permitted to fight out for themselves and evolve solutions. But unfortunately this does not happen. Institutions are given freedom with strings attached. This should be avoided by government.

AMERICAN COUNCIL ON EDUCATION

According to the report, "Shifting Ground-Autonomy-Accountability and Privatization in Public Higher Education" of 2004, it is observed that demand for higher education in US is increasing. The report recognizes that "Good health of higher education is a necessary condition for good economic health of USA".

The relationship between higher education institutes and their states is undergoing a profound restructuring. States are funding less and less, leading to increase in tuition fees. Financial grants are being converted in to loans. Some feel public purpose of education is at stake. Autonomy and privatization are not mutually exclusive concepts. Privatization in all sectors is found to yield higher productivity; in higher education also it should be so. Debates are going on how autonomy is useful or how it is hurting the ability of higher education institutes to serve public interest. Some look at autonomy especially in financial respect and privatization as a threat to academic success. Some fear that the changes will lead to negative social consequences. Autonomy however is in practice in varying proportions in various states. In sum total, significant trend is observed in favor of autonomy and privatization.

It is realized that it is the autonomous status of universities and colleges which has elevated the scholarship, and economic performance of US ahead of European counterparts. Greater autonomy is being perceived as the strategy to cater to increasing number of students in higher education. Freedom from state regulation is often exchanged for increased accountability, demonstrating how the institute will meet state needs in a fiscally responsibly manner. Rigid regulation is being replaced by a focus on performance and learning outcomes, with smaller share in funding from states. The report applies to both public and private institutions.

University of Massachusetts in its report of the year 2000 says autonomy means ability of institutes and particularly of faculty to carry out the primary mission of higher education in a manner with shared visions. That mission is to educate (not just train, as politicians and others urge), the general population for intelligent participation in the public realm and to contribute to the understanding (not just of knowledge, as urged by those who think education as marketing of ideas), of how physical, aesthetic, political and social worlds work.

If some one comes along proposing a change in an institute, public policy or ways of doing education business, the institute does not compromise on academic freedom. The central question to be answered is, whether the change will preserve or enhance the autonomy of the academy? Whether the professors are involved more in academic or administrative matters? If the answer is not yes, the institute says people should resist the change, and fight tooth and nail.

Council of Europe Conference in the year 2003 prepared and adopted a report, "Institutional Autonomy and Higher Education Governance".

It said that institutions have to be autonomous at the heart, to be able to meet the needs of world around it. Its research and teaching must be morally and intellectually independent of all political authorities, and economic power. Academic freedom to students and faculty it said is the integral part. It advocated student's participation in governance of the institutions. Freedom was related to academic matters, and not organizational and economic. It recommended self-governance with invited external participation. It advised the academic community. "To elect its own offices like vice chancellor, director, dean, professors, etc. with little or no external interference".

Hidden interference of political persons is discouraged. Autonomous institutions are expected to open up new sources of income, as the state is not able to meet the demands fully. It is expected to co-operate with business and international agencies. Increase in efficiency with the association of business is expected.

It further said, law must delegate the necessary decision powers to the institution, for changes in curricula, teaching and research, interaction with their counterparts nationally and internally and for economic transactions. Transparency in transactions is prescribed. Quality assurance system should be independent of political system. Autonomy is desired to set the institution in motion. We must see continuous improvement, not uniformity, but variety. It further said realization of fruits of autonomy will depend on co-ordination between government and institutions for change, and willingness in national interests.

With the emergence of globalization, fantastic opportunities have opened up, requiring higher knowledge, and hi-tech skills to perform the jobs. A knowledge-based economy in the whole world is being pursued. Higher education institutes are obviously at the centre and going to play a key role in meeting the challenges of globalization. Consequently, every one in every country is for changing the higher education.

A report from Germany, entitled "Financial Autonomy of Higher Education Institutes, the Necessity and Design of Institutional Framework" recommended autonomy for only academic purposes. It suggested giving flexibility in budgets and lump-sum grants to institutions is necessary. It recommended authority to institutions to raise resources from several other sources. Absolute financial autonomy it said is not desirable. Government, ultimately, should bear the financial burden, yet grant liberty to the institutions in operations. Total autonomy may do more harm than good. Decentralized decisions are better characterized by better knowledge of problems and needs greater flexibility. Hence, it recommends autonomy.

Bulgaria in 1993 has made an act of academic autonomy for higher education establishments. According to which the state has granted autonomy to higher education and research establishments. The act delineates the relations between the institution and the government, other establishments, in the country and outside. The act empowers the institutes to define independently operative rules and regulations. It prescribes methodology for upgradation of faculty and staff. It empowers them to create their own funds. Rights of IPR, patents are granted. It empowers fundamental rights to students and faculty. Mobility of professors and students is encouraged. An opportunity for training and retraining for faculty and staff is prescribed by law.

A report from Japan says autonomy has played an important role in promoting lifelong education. The corporate education in Japan is rising, mainly because the institutions have been granted autonomy. Education only once in initial stages is good but not enough. People change jobs three to seven times in service career, for which they need retraining, which the institutions are providing. But for autonomy this would not have become possible.

Vietnam has recently accepted the need for a comprehensive transformation of its higher education system. In 2005, the Ministry of Education and Training developed a Higher Education Reform Agenda (HERA), a blueprint for reform of the system by 2020. The Government of Vietnam recently approved the main elements of the Agenda, including a proposal to give universities and colleges the right of autonomy. Measures supportive of institutional autonomy in higher education now need to be addressed. In particular, there is a need for legislative and regulatory reform, the establishment of appropriate accountability relationships, the development of leadership and managerial expertise at the institutional level, and the building of confidence and trust in the processes of institutional self-governance.

UK recognizes autonomy as an essential tool for success. The strength of UK higher education is founded on its autonomy and funding structures that support universities and institutes ability to respond flexibly and according to institutes priorities. There is a shared responsibility of funds. All those who benefit from higher education contribute to its cost, including individuals, employers, and the public purse. Universities and government have a shared responsibility to protect the reputation of UK higher education at home and abroad. Higher education continues to expand in response to changing student demand and also to respond to the needs of diversity of markets in which it operates. Public funding in UK fell by 37% in the year 2002. But the total budget of each higher education institute has increased. Institutes are earning money from multiple sources. Block grant scheme is in practice. There is a commitment from government to funding through block grants. Institutions have mobilized funds from various other sources with almost no control from government.

China. In the recent past, a tremendous change is noticed in higher education in China. This is solely on account of decentralization and autonomy and granted to them. Institutes lacked autonomy and flexibility in the past. Now administration has been decentralized, and local private participation has gone up. Provincial governments have been given more decision powers. Institutions have now more rights for decision-making.

"Incentives have been designed for the institutions which use autonomy to the advantage of students and the economy".

Internal management of the institutions has substantially improved. More number of courses with flexible curriculum has been introduced. Moral of professors and students has gone up. Management of education and research is according to the market demands, and needs of society. The institutions are giving a much different look than in the past.

Autonomy and decentralization have put more enthusiasm in the education domain. Consequently, the number of students studying has gone up. Post-graduation and doctoral courses have been increased. State funding has gone up. The number of publications, patents earned companies spin-off from universities has shot up. Undoubtedly, one is conspicuously struck by the impact of autonomy and decentralization.

POLICY IMPLICATIONS FOR INDIA

Do we want the education to be relevant and purposeful? Do we want education to be innovative, creative and flexible enough suiting to the current global needs? Do we want it to be qualitative and cost competitive? Do we want institutes to produce pioneers in technology and world-class leaders in industry? Should the institutes be producing new technologies, patents, and first mover entrepreneurs? This will not happen unless the institutions are autonomous.

"Government should put trust in institutes and empower them to carry out their designated public roles without government intervention".

Solution to improve higher education does not lie in providing more funds, but in making effective utilization of provided funds, which essentially requires autonomy. But for autonomy, public and private investments in higher education are used less productively. Autonomy, at the moment, is the single most solution to many ills in higher education.

Autonomy is a world proven model of governance. There are however problems in its adoption and implementation. Teething troubles like everywhere are here in initial stages. They need to be identified and solved with determination by concerned through teaching, debates and discussions.

Once used to affiliating system, an institution finds it difficult to abandon it and switch on to new. It is easier to introduce autonomy at start of college. New institutions should therefore be permitted only with autonomous status. IITs were born autonomous and hence they could shine in world.

Autonomy is a world trend. Debates and discussions for refinement are however going on; they are not limited to India. Academicians in India ought to hold many conferences and seminars to discuss pros and cons. Key persons in government, universities, and colleges need to take initiative.

US economy is reported to have advanced mainly because of its world best higher education system, which owes credit to its autonomous institutes. Students all over the world dream to study in US. Why? It is mainly because the professors in institutions are teaching the latest. This attracts best and brightest brains from everywhere and anywhere in the world. Many of them settle there adding to intellectual capital.

World-class institutions are using autonomy with higher degree of success. They are managed and maintained by local trusts, on which scholars, scientists, industrialists, educationists, noble laureates are represented. They have much less of bureaucracy and much more decentralization, and autonomy.

Today, in India, higher education is over administered. Decisions which matter most are in the hands of bureaucrats in UGC and AICTE. The engine of development of academics must move out from distantly located administrative bodies to professors close to students.

Government by legislation should grant autonomy and permit the institutions to use autonomy in right spirit. It should not stifle the autonomy. Government is neither designed nor capable to steer higher education, it should therefore not interfere. It should leave it to academicians and the governing board. Interference is found to kill the internal curative strength.

Presently, in India, there is an over regulation from government in higher education. Institutions and universities have become mere tools in the hands of bureaucracy. Institutions badly need liberation from government clutches. Too many controls from unqualified have spoiled education.

Interference in academics by government is however observed in almost all the countries, more so in developing. It is being resented by academicians. Frequent interference by government is observed to be damaging public good.

World over, a gap exists in perceptions on autonomy between the law makers on one hand and the academicians on the other.

It is up to the leaders in education to explain to legislators and convince that lack of autonomy threatens the economic security of the nation. This must be realized by both. Initiative must come from academicians.

IITs and IIMs have become world-class because they are autonomous right from birth. More money and more autonomy is the right kind of solution to problems of higher education in India. Government should only give adequate funds and yet not interfere in their administration. Simply because it gives public funds, it does not get authority to interfere. It should appoint a professional body, neither political nor bureaucratic to monitor. This is in public interest.

Autonomy means ability of institutions especially of faculty to carry out the primary mission of higher education. A professor is a hero. Autonomy should enable him to be so. He should be permitted and enabled to have freedom to be innovative and creative. Then and then only autonomy is meaningful and it delivers expected results.

Institutions are now at the core of knowledge-based economy; hence they have assumed the position of drivers of development. To be a winner in global competition, India has no way other than making its universities and institutions autonomous.

Indian institutions and economy have a high potential to leap frog their counterparts in developed countries, which is hindered by lack of autonomy.

Autonomy is the only way to achieve excellence in higher education, which unfortunately today in affiliating system is blocked. The blockage needs to be removed urgently. Grant of autonomy will enhance the chances of India becoming a world leader.

"If we don't step up the challenge of creating autonomous institutions, we undermine every thing else we are trying to reform higher education".

Traditional regulations by universities and government in today's stormy weather of globalization do not suffice. Higher and technical education must remove constraints, and introduce flexibility, and autonomy. Virtual and for-profit universities from across the world are on the horizon, and posing a serious threat.

REFERENCES

American Council on Education, "Shifting Ground-Autonomy-Accountability and Privatization in Public Higher Education", 2004.

Bulgaria, Academic Autonomy for Higher Education Establishments, 1993.

Financial Autonomy of Professional Higher Education Institutes, Comparison between Finland and Some European Countries, by Voukko Kohtamki, Finland, 2003.

Higher Education in Australia, Structure, Policy, and Debate by Jim Breen Monash University.

Naik, B.M. *New Vistas in Technical Education*, Vivek Publication, Aurangabad, 1999.

Report from International Institute of Education Planning, 7-9 Rue Engne, 75116 Paris.

Report of Council of Europe Conference, Strasburg, "Institutional Autonomy and Higher Education Governance". December 2-3, 2003, Bologna Secretariat, Dr Per Nyorg.

Report of National Knowledge Commission, Government of India, 2006.

Report of the Central Advisory Board of Education [CABE] Committee on autonomy of Higher Education, Government of India 2005, under the chairmanship of Kanti Biswas.

Chapter 4

Colleges Need Research Parks to Make Education Globally Competitive

ABSTRACT

Research park is a joint effort between an academic institution and industry. It provides a common platform to both industry and academic personnel for innovation, creativity, technology generation, and product/process development. It binds together the two, namely industry and institutes for mutual growth and prosperity. It is a place where innovative minds of students and professors on one hand are matched with innovative minds in industry on the other.[1] Establishment of research parks in universities and autonomous colleges is recommended by Anil Kakodkar Committee in its report to government. It is a means to convert intellectual capital of both the university and industry in to usable goods and services. It is a Profit Centre. It generates wealth and employment. It is a mechanism to build synergy between industry and institutes. It enables university to upgrade quality of UG, PG, and PhD programs. It converts research output in to patents and IPR, and makes their commercial exploitation. It generates surplus after meeting all the expenses and plough it back on continuing basis to further research. It enables university to be the "Light House" for industry. It facilitates students to earn and learn hi-tech in knowledge environment and become globally fit for future. Innovative students, professors and industry personnel are the key players and drivers of park. It believes in,

"Look ahead to stay ahead". Research park enables a university to keep progressing in research and its commercial exploitation, from generation to generation. It increases the rate of return from investment in universities and industry both.

Institutes and industry are interdependent. One without the support of other cannot stand high. Research park is a project to be established in partnership preferably with the alumni and industry. All the partners, namely colleges, alumni and the industry could share development and its management besides the costs and benefits. Research, innovation and testing of materials labs which are costly could be established as common facility centre. The capital cost could be borne by all the partners. Grant from DST Government of India and Rajiv Gandhi Commission for S&T of about 4 crore is available. More than 15 parks in various institutes have obtained grants from them. Thousands of parks all over the world are successfully contributing from the last more than 50 years. They are improving quality of education and simultaneously giving fresh technology inputs to industry to improve competitiveness.

Good teaching in classrooms and labs is necessary but not enough. It has to be supplemented with learning innovation and research skills for which a research park is necessary. The paper explains how to go about.

It is a Meeting Place for Innovative Minds

Research park is a common platform, where innovative minds from industry and from academics meet. Professors of university and colleges along with scholar students meet industry personnel to exchange each other's progressive ideas and stretch imagination to bring them to reality. It is a place meant for cross fertilization of ideas in addition to giving feedback for making education more relevant and purposeful. Research park is meant more for giving birth to new technology-based firms.[2] Research park is a mechanism to commercially exploit the research output of PhD, masters, and bachelors thesis in to usable goods and services, and simultaneously give feedback to improve their quality. It converts intellectual capability and technological strengths in to new products and processes. It is a

university to masses for their welfare. Experience of Western schools in this respect is worth emulation. Majority of the Western schools convert research in to patents and IPR and transfer them to industry through well-defined systems and procedures. Economic returns from investment in universities then increase, which brings more money for further research and makes it sustainable. Public service, carried out chiefly through teaching, was the motive for the creation of the earliest universities. Even today teaching remains the core of the university's public service. But now in competitive world university's public service extends far beyond, to entrepreneurial activities like research park, technology innovation, patent and IPR. Intellectual capital of university which is so critical for national development is required to be converted into usable goods and services. For a country like India that aspires to be an economic powerhouse all the while it is more important. What use is of research, new knowledge, new technology if not exploited commercially? Universities along with industry and alumni ought to think big jointly in global context and establish on campus a research park, like their counterparts in developed countries.

All World-class Universities have Research Parks on Campus[9]

Quality and relevance of education in universities has become superior because of park. Studies indicate that enterprises born on park are observed to be more successful than those born off park. A university can become centre of excellence only if it ventures in innovative efforts as this. So as to obtain innovative character it is essential that the Indian universities adopt this new strategic direction.

National Knowledge Commission 2006 and Yashpal Committee Report of 2009 both have recommended innovative projects like research park, so as to create new knowledge, new technology, discoveries and creative endeavours to be the integral components of the university. FICCI Higher Education Summit in its report of 2008 has recommended their creation and urged the colleges to show a lead.[10] It suggests PPP mode for implementation. In a nutshell,

- Research park is a cradle for entrepreneurs.
- Its output is in terms of new technology-based firms, patents and IPR.
- It makes commercial exploitation of research done in various departments in university and colleges like in PhD, MTech, MSc, BTech, etc.
- Research park converts intellectual and technological capability into usable goods and services.
- It inculcates research and innovation skills amongst students.
- Research park produces Indian brands of technology.
- It increases financial rate of return from investment in university.
- It creates entrepreneurial culture in campus.
- Facilitates synergy of university and industry.
- Research park generates employment in hi-tech of high income.
- It produces world-class leaders in industry, leaders in technology and first movers in industry.

The Indian universities ought to dream big, think great to create new capacity to succeed in competitive world. Research park attracts great people from across the society with the possibility of great success.

Research Park Increases Universities Out Reach Far and Wide[11]

Universities world over with research park are observed to be enriching them and augmenting new ideas besides budget support for future growth. They are getting well integrated with society and industry. Universities by virtue of research park and knowledge in it have moved to the centre of development, they have become drivers of economic and social prosperity. The visions and missions of the universities then become dynamic, adaptive based on sharing experiences with people at large, and not only giving off the self-irrelevant prescriptions. UGC/AICTE in various projects in the past have invested good amount of money on research. How much is the return obtained from them? In the absence of research park, returns on investment are too little. Replenishment of funds for research slows down. Research park is designed to generate economic benefits for people in the region, by bringing intellectual discoveries of scientists, professors and students to the world. It accelerates the speed of research and makes it more focused and effective. It brings risk taking entrepreneurs, investors, expert advisors, youthful scientific minds together in the same place at the same time. Can Indian universities afford to neglect?

Programs and events in the park are consciously designed to encourage networking among innovators, entrepreneurs, and investors. Thought provocation speakers from around the world are invited to inspire and inform new ways of working. Entrepreneurship programs aim at inventor-entrepreneurs and leadership teams of emerging companies, to help bridge knowledge gap. Creative people with brand new ideas are a great resource. Can university/college become a light house for industry without it? How can globally successful companies come here in search of new ideas and technologies? Establishment of research park is the answer.

Prof. Terman of Stanford University gave the following philosophy,

> An industry to be globally competitive needs an access to first-class research in universities. So also universities and professors/scholar students need an access to industry to commercialize findings of their research.[12]

Industry and institute, by being stand alone cannot achieve peak performance even if they deserve. They need to synergies their efforts for which research park is essential.

Research parks are found to have given stimulus to increase the scholarship of the university and colleges, made the education at UG, PG and doctoral levels more relevant and purposeful. Universities have thereby become innovative in character. Research park is a place to sharpen ideas and to connect with business advisors to explore market potential of these ideas. It is a launching pad for spin off companies to world market. More and more application of knowledge leads to more discoveries. Universities can acquire much desired innovative character by installing research park on campus. They get a feel which way the industrial world is moving and orient them to enable youths to harvest opportunities.

Harness the competitive Advantage: Universities are offering UG, PG and PhD programs in science, engineering, arts and commerce, etc. Students and faculty are brilliant. The university continuously generates new knowledge, new theories through research at PhD, masters and bachelors level. The theses most of time remain on cupboards in library. No worthwhile use is made of the research findings, except a few publications. If research park is established the research done can be most effective to obtain patents and IPR, spin-off companies in hi-tech, taking technology to masses for their welfare. Full capacity of intellectuals in the university and surrounding area can be utilized only when platform of such a park is available.[13] Similarly, there are innovative people in industry, for want of infrastructure and synchronization their capacities remain unfolded. Can the universities aim to be equal to world-class? Should we not expand our visions and missions? Low aim is a crime.

PURPOSE

To provide an organizational base.

To Transfer Technology through start-ups in hi-tech.

To attract and create new companies to use intellectual capacities.

To accelerate and stimulate research, innovation, patent and IPR and centres of excellence in close collaboration with industrial world.

More commercial exploitation of research is an incentive to researchers. It stimulates young minds to be more innovative and creative.

To develop entrepreneurship culture, research and innovation culture.

To generate innovation and research skill set amongst scholars. Students tend to become creative and not remain parrot like mugging up.

To generate employment of hi-tech, hi-pay and bring about economic development with higher productivity.

Returns on investment in university/college increases, which attracts in turn more investment.

To enable students to reach out to industry at global level.

To reduce time gap between invention and its application.

To conduct strategic research in conjunction with industry.

To make both the university and industry more enterprising.

To develop bond between institute and industry.

To apply findings of research done in industry.

To create knowledge-based society that is to say technological society.

To enable university graduates to start companies.

VISIONS

An institution/university of 21st century to be successful must adopt new visions of new world. It should not function like yesterday. It should along with all neighbouring colleges synergies its efforts of development with industry. No university, in spite of potential, can become excellent all alone by its own internal efforts and ideas. It must take the support from industry, give birth to knowledge and research industry. Alumni should put their full strength in terms of ideas and money behind academics for long-range gains to themselves industry and student's community. The university/institute essentially should have to show lead. An institution has knowledge strength. It should attract like a magnet knowledge industry around.

Do we want to initiate a project to create Indian brands of technology? Or follow the brands like in the past from foreign? Do we aspire to make most of our abilities and become a technology leader to sow the seeds of development and not remain copy cat? Research park is then the answer.

How can we create world-class institutes/universities? World-class universities produce not only graduates but produce new technologies and new technology based firms.[14] They create a new industrial society, fit for future. Universities elsewhere in the world are doing this. Many companies are in continuous contact with MIT Boston. They derive technological strength, like blood supply to our body. We can if we envision. Low aim is a crime. We should dream big and think great.

China, one time behind India, is now way ahead, producing two times more PhDs and MTechs. They have adopted a vision to produce 100 hi-tech firms each year. Does it pose a challenge to Indian universities and colleges?

Present status: Around 15 Indian universities, like Poona University, IIT Chennai, Cochin University have set up research parks under DST program called as Science and Technology Entrepreneurs Park (STEP) and are also spinning off hi-tech companies. As you need a swimming pool to learn swimming, so you need a research park to learn innovation skills. A university without research park in modern world is incomplete, irrelevant, non-viable, and outdated.[15] The conventional wisdom of university which once served well is not fit for today and tomorrow. They must transfer new knowledge to society, for which research park is a means. India needs many more of them to be globally competitive.

MISSIONS

To contribute to technology development, patent and IPR in the region:

(a) To facilitate new knowledge transfer to society.

(b) To make commercial exploitation of research, of MSc, MA, MTech, PhD thesis and enhance their quality and relevance.

(c) To convert intellectual capability into usable goods and services.

(d) To spin off hi-tech firms.

(e) To inculcate innovation and discovery skills amongst students.

(f) To increase scholarship of courses.

(g) To enable grads to start enterprises.

(h) To provide a platform to industry and alumni to contribute.

All world-class universities have innovative and creative character. Can we envision?

Incubating Talent for Global Competitiveness

Why thousands of students every year go abroad? They have been going from Gandhi-Nehru period. How long they will have to go? Can all students go? What do they learn, which is not available in Indian university? Have we failed so far as a society to provide adequate opportunities to our youth to be educated in world-class manner? Have we failed in creating a vibrant educational eco-system that supports cutting edge research? How are counterpart institutions in developed countries different? We have too much of rote learning. They have more of innovation, creativity. Students abroad are challenged to create, to discover and innovate.[16]

Universities abroad essentially have research parks, science parks, incubators, patent and IPR centres, entrepreneurship centres, which yet majority of universities in India do not have. In the absence of which, innovation talent remains idle, and underdeveloped. Returns from investment in university and colleges are less. We are importing technology and foreigners are exporting. Bright students are migrating to greener pastures. Knowledge IPR has become more important than resources. Indian universities may like now to be more innovative in character and become enterprising. It should enable the talent to grow to the level it is capable for. Do we lack visions or resources?

Research park is like a magnet to attract and retain talent. It has the potential to arrest brain drain and bring back previously gone, to convert it in brain gain.

Organization for Research Park

Public-private participation model consisting of some or all of the following is recommended

Local Industry Association

State Industrial Corporation

Leading banks

Leading industrialists

Leading persons from IIT incubator, STEP IIT KGP, UICT as advisors

Organizational head and professors

Municipal Corporation

The university may have to plan, install and monitor the progress.

Steps Involved

Develop awareness among industry and academic personnel

Prepare a project proposal

Discuss and make critical analysis of the proposal

Obtain approval from government, obtain grant

Appoint head

Collaborate nationally and internationally

Appoint expert advisors

Appoint a separate governing board

Depute people to attend international conferences of Association of science/research parks.

To recapitulate,

World experience tells us that institutions/regions/cities develop faster which have established research parks in universities and colleges.

Research parks brings long-range thinking, long-range planning and advanced research so badly needed in a university and in Indian industry. University and industry to remain globally competitive ought to carry out jointly functions of research and innovation to keep them fit for future.[17]

Today success in the global marketplace means creating and applying new knowledge—which is to say new technology—faster than one's competitors. World winners will be those who develop talent, technologies, techniques and tools so advanced that there is no competition.

Innovation potential of youths in the absence of research park today is wasted. It enables it be unfolded and put to fuller use.

How to produce more entrepreneurs and how to encourage more firms to grow are the main visions and missions of this project.

A university to create and maintain its leadership position needs forthwith to establish the park.

The park works as magnet to attract best and brightest from anywhere and everywhere in the world.

One of the essential ingredients to generate hi-tech jobs, well-paying jobs, industrial cluster is the creation of research park.

Research park if established will make a big difference for industry, economy and university.

Without a research park, the university, industry and institutes, so also cities and regions howsoever hard people may work will remain behind in international competition.

A university with park will turn out leaders in industry and leaders in technology with knowledge qualitative by international standard. It will create technology pioneers. The quality and relevance of education would become fit for future. Why students will then migrate elsewhere?

The university without park will remain incomplete, ineffective and outdated in modern sense. When shall we realize this?

The region can win in global competition by establishing research park and not without it.

"Success in international competition depends now on turning intellectual strength in to marketable commodities".

Let us dream big, think great to make college in long-term a world-class institute.

College of Engineering Aurangabad may like to install research park, patent centre, innovation centre, in campus in partnership with alumni association, to make education globally competitive.

COEP is in the process of installing, IIT Chennai and many others have already done, Anil Kakodkar Committee has recommended to Maharashtra Government, Institutes in foreign are having from many years, DST Government of India and Rajiv Gandhi Commission on S&T provides funds.

NOTES

1. "The Role of Science Parks in the Promotion of Innovation and Transfer of Technology", Proceedings of the Science Parks Association, Annual Conference, 6-7 April 1989.
2. *Ibid.*
3. *Creating Knowledge-Strengthening Nations, the Changing Role of Education*, Edited by Glen A. Jones, Patricia L. McCartney and Michael L. Skolinik, University of University Press, 2002.
4. Wisconsin Alumni Research Foundation, Research Park, website.
5. Green paper of European Union on Innovation and Technological Transfer Enterprize Unit DG, EUFO, 2295-2920, Luxumberg.
6. H.T. Rhodes, *Role of American University—The Creation of the Future*, Cornell University Press, 2003.
7. *Ibid.*
8. Fang Zaho (2004), "Academic Entrepreneurship, Case Study of Australian Universities", *International Journal of Entrepreneurship and Innovation*, pp. 91-97. IP Publishing Ltd., Vol. 5, No. 2.
9. James Duderstadt, a university of 21st century, the University of Michigen Press.
10. FICCI, website.
11. B.M. Naik, "Strategies to Make Universities Globally Competitive", *University News*, Vol. 49, No. 26, July 03, 2011.
12. H.T. Rhodes, *op. cit.*
13. B.M. Naik, "Needed Innovation & Entrepreneurship in Higher Education Institutes", *Journal of Technical Education*, January-March 2004, Vol. 27, No. 1, pp. 27-32.

14. B.M. Naik and W.S. Kandlikar (2010), *Higher & Technical Education—Book of Knowledge*, Gyan Publications, Delhi.

15. Government of India, National Knowledge Commission 2006-07.

16. B.M. Naik, "Gap Analysis, Between Indian Institutes and their Counterparts Abroad", *University News*.

17. U.S. Academy of Sciences, "Rising above the Gathering Storm", report, 2007.

Chapter 5

Envisioning Higher and Technical Education to Meet World of Work Needs

> Institutes will be successful which give birth to new knowledge, new theories, new technologies, patents and hi-tech startups.

NEED AND IMPORTANCE

It is a proven theory that where there is vision people flourish, and where there is no vision people perish. In the knowledge driven economy of today 'vision' has achieved significantly high importance. Vision ignites minds for creative action. Indian economy, in spite of abundant resources, it is said has lagged behind because of a lack of vision. About 25 per cent of the people are still living below the poverty line. Per capita income is only around 1000 dollars, whereas that of Japan is 30,000. How do we explain this big difference? Do they work 30 times more? Certainly they do not. It is mainly their higher and technical education system which has moved the economy forward. A country like Japan from the last 50 years has gross enrolment ratio of the order of 50 per cent, where as India even today has only 14 per cent. They adopted vision to build knowledge society long before.

The Govt. of India has recently announced the national goal to become a developed nation by the year 2020. Prime Minister Hon. Atal Bihari Vajpayee in his address to the nation on 15th of August 2002 has proclaimed to have conceived this goal and expressed commitment to build India into a technology oriented nation. India aspires to be free from poverty, and to sit in line with G-8 nations. Our past President, Hon. Dr. Abdul Kalam wrote,

> A developed India by 2020 or even earlier, is not a dream. It need not even be a mere vision in the mind of many Indians. It is a mission we can all take up.

In order to achieve this goal, the Technology Information and Forecasting Council (TIFAC) of the Department of Science and Technology, Govt. of India, has been preaching that technology has to be the driving force for development. The council in its reports of 1998, has underlined the need and the importance of creating knowledge society, for which reorientation of technical education is an essential prerequisite. TIFAC has recommended to AICTE to revamp technical education system so as to realize the dream of a developed India by 2020.

The Vision to Build World-Class Institutes

The important questions that must be addressed are how long should students go abroad for higher education? And can all go abroad? Thousands of students from India have been going abroad every year for higher education. The trend is increasing year after year. In the year 2012 as many as 1,30,000 students left the Indian shores. This figure is higher by 12 per cent than previous year. Indian brains are in search of quality education within the country, but the supply is inadequate. The trend to go abroad is continuing from pre-independence period. How many more years should this continue? Foreign universities from countries like England, America, and Australia are also coming here to attract the students. What do these trends mean to our institutes? Should they be welcomed or opposed? What is in the interest of our students and of this nation? We have no alternative than to face competition. We have to acquire better polices and practices, systems and procedures from our counterparts in developed countries. It is now not an option but compulsion. Education institutes, except IITs are far too behind their counterparts. Can we not build our universities like IIT

MIT, Oxford and Cambridge? We have not been able to do so, thus far.

This was largely not on account of the lack of resources but more due to a lack of vision and lack of commitment to implement.

The key to accomplish this vision does not lie in collaboration, and waiting for foreign aid. Some times the aid is counter-productive. The key lies in creating motivated education entrepreneurs, professors, principles and vice chancellors. Previously, colleges and universities were designed at best to become technology followers. Now we have to redesign them to become technology leaders. India now holds a vision to become a developed nation by 2020, free from poverty, and on par with G-8 countries. Technical education has a key role in achieving the same.

Vision to Re-engineer Universities, Colleges, and Polytechnics to Lead a Change

Can India hope to become competitive with the existing old model of higher and technical education? Should we throw out the dysfunctional model of affiliated colleges and adopt a new model where educational institutions are more autonomous in nature? How can the institutes become enterprising, setting up innovative activities like patent centre, research park, etc. and integrating them with education and research? How can we go about using new technologies, virtual classrooms, and sharing development efforts with private agencies? We need to set up more technical universities, and if so how many?

It is the agriculture universities which have solved the food problem of India. We need to emulate this model to solve the problem of industrial competitiveness. Starting many engineering colleges is good, but not enough. Without setting up technical universities, such a move will not bear the expected fruits. This is the opinion of 98 per cent of respondents in a study conducted recently. Innovation is the origin of progress. Policies, practices, and also an overall climate favourable for innovation are the essential prerequisites for growth and prosperity. Institutes legitimately are the crucibles of reformation and advancement.

They are the centres from where economic and industrial reforms should originate. They should earn the status of initiators of change, and function like spark plugs to release the energy for reformation. This has to be borne in mind by the education planners, administrators and professors. Accordingly these institutes need to be energized to enable them to lead the change. More importantly, the institutes themselves have to deserve to become the drivers of change.

It is relatively easy to bring about road development, housing development, etc. in shorter periods. But it is quite difficult to bring about development of universities and colleges worth the name. Pandit Nehru on the occasion of laying the foundation stone of IIT, Mumbai in 1959 said, "It is easy to install and run a big factory but it is more difficult to establish and run a small higher education institute competitive by world standards."

Future of people undoubtedly depends on what vision we adopt today. Implementation of vision needs resources. There is a well-known saying, "Where there is a will, there is a way." There are resources available now, and many more will follow, running of mediocre institutes' turns out to be more costly than the cost of their upgradation.

Where do Our Universities and Colleges Stand in World List?

According to a worldwide survey, only IITs, and IISc, Bangalore stands in world list. However, the students in many other colleges like Mumbai University Delhi and Pune University are world best, students get into them after stiff competition. Many institutions are very good in dissemination, but they are functioning like Departmental Stores. They are borrowing knowledge generated else where, which is acceptable only up to a certain point. We need to contribute to increase the pool of knowledge, and teach from our own first-hand research.

The areas, in which we lag, are low level of faculty research and low visibility. Generation of new theories, new knowledge is almost absent. Best minds can be attracted and nursed well only through active involvement in research. Recognition to institutes comes from the quality of its alumni. The infrastructure of most of the institutes is good. What is lacking the proper direction to their working. We have to be world-class in research. Then, and then only our institutes can become world-class in education. Teachers should not fall behind in their research commitments. Good teaching skills go hand in hand with good research capabilities. Teaching without research involvement results in mere dissemination of obsolete and irrelevant material.

It is the research output of an institute that creates its reputation. Management and government should invest more in research. This makes education cheaper and better. If the institutes acquire research capabilities, there is no reason why they cannot become world-class.

What we notice in foreign universities is that research companies are flocking round the universities in search on new technologies. The institutes on their periphery have units like Patent and Intellectual Property Rights (IPR) Centre, Technology Incubator, Innovation Centre, Industrial Services Centre, etc. Venture capital companies open offices nearby for early commercialization of brand new technologies. Spin-off start-up companies are born one after the other. The Institutes attract both scholars, and companies from the world over. Thus the technical educational institutes have become a source of new ideas enabling them to win. All these multifaceted activities have a positive effect on education. Students get access to these centres of research and technology transfer. They feel happy to take active part in the research activities and thereby elevate their capabilities. It is such schemes that have turned the universities into wellsprings of new knowledge. It is mainly innovative activities such as these that are attracting scholars and industries from the world over to US.

Adopting an Inquiry-based Learning Model

This is a model that is currently being followed in some of the world's best universities like Oxford, Cambridge and MIT. This model was recommended by the Boyer Commission in USA in 1998. In this model, students are introduced to research right from the first year. They learn both through discovery, and transmission. The important characteristic of this model is that all persons, namely professors, senior and junior students, lab assistants, etc. are learners, researchers, and discovers. They all have a shared vision to achieve a common goal of inventing new knowledge, which bind them together. What matters most is the skill of the professor to synergizing the efforts of individuals to create a community of learners. The first year is the most vital of the formative years and hence senior professors choose to address them.

The model is recommended for innovative institutions which aspire to excel. The institutes which possess a commitment for creating new knowledge and new technologies are fit for the purpose. They ought to appoint professors who have research capability and who can create an environment favorable for innovation, such institutions prefer international market orientation and invite scholars from the world over, junior students work with their seniors under the guidance of professors to generate new technologies. The institutes integrate the education of their undergraduates with research projects. Such institutes do not function like departmental stores. It is this approach which is found to result in continuous supply of eminent scientists and professors to the economy.

Reverse Brain Drain: Time is Ripe Now

Shall we not realize and implement the schemes like research parks, which are well proven elsewhere in the world over a period of about 30 years? When shall we realize our strengths? MIT is earning about 100 patents every year. Twenty per cent of the institute's budget is met out of technology sale. Here research is observed to subsidize education, and education to subsidize research. Research and teaching are like the two ends of bow. Neither gets force without the other. Shall our institutes not adopt this logic and become a Lighthouse for industry? This is the trend worldwide which India ought to emulate. When institutes elsewhere in the world could do this, why can we not do so in India? Should this not be the vision for the next 20 years? Who will provide this vision? The institutes would have to adopt modern vision to bring fruits of globalization to its people. China has been successful in attracting its brain back with huge FDI.

How to Abolish Limit to Growth?

The question is: Have we put uppcr limits on ourselves by worthless systems and procedures? Private universities, although new to India, have existed in the USA for over hundred years. Almost half of the universities there are private. They arc managed and maintained by the church, industry, or philanthropic organization. The standard of education in them and the quality of research vis-à-vis to that in state controlled universities is frequently found to be superior. The best institutes like MIT are private. USA has progressed well and due credit must go to private institutes. Many important inventions and innovations have taken place in them. Today a large proportion of patients and IPR are earned by private universities. The human civilization would not have progressed so well, if there were no private universities in the world. On the other hand, all universities in India are state funded and hence state controlled. Their performance due to inherent weakness of the model is however far below expectation. They are over centralized, bureaucratic, and monopolistic, thwarting and impeding ideas of students and professors. The appointment of vice chancellor is politically motivated. Does the answer lie in setting up of private universities? The state universities need to be supplemented by private universities to pose competitions. The systems of accreditation and ISO have now been introduced world over, which assure recognition nationally and internationally.

Are there risks in starting private universities? Are there greater risks in not starting private universities? Do the private universities deserve fair considerations? US universities have overtaken European universities because of privatization. Private universities do not need not to toe the government line of thinking. They do not become routine, like government departments. On the other hand, they become innovative and generate new knowledge and provide the same to government to improve administration. They are in search of truth, working for high ideals and enrichment of minds and lives of students. They have to have academic freedom to think, and the freedom to act. Then only can they do justice to their existence. For, independent and free thinking privatization helps. Hence, we have to learn to believe in privatization and strive to make its success. The private institutions will not fail to tap the talent regardless of whether they have money or not. The institutes will install scholarships. New vision and insights are necessary in privatization.

LIFELONG EDUCATION

"They know enough, who know how to learn." Learning only once in the initial stages is good, but not enough. One has to learn again and again nonstop. Continuing Education for increasing the competency of in-service personnel has assumed high degree of importance. There exists a gap in knowledge level between the Indian engineers and their counterparts in foreign companies, which has made survival difficult for the Indian corporate sector. Indian companies are being merged, amalgamated and purchased by foreign companies. Many persons in mid-career are being thrown out of jobs. They have to learn new technologies and acquire new skills to get re-employed. A learning organization with learning individuals alone can win in the world economy. Many people are re-learning at their own time and cost.

Have companies in India given sufficient thought about training of employees? Employing persons, giving them high salaries is good, but not enough. It is essential to provide them an opportunity for lifelong learning, to increase competency to the level they are capable for. It is reported by International. Association on Continuing Education that it yields more than 100 per cent return on investment. It brings back sick units to good health. Motorola observed that when it invests one dollar in training it generates 30 dollars in three years. Sixty per cent productivity gains it has realized through training of employees. Only 5 per cent of employees in India get a chance to receive training, where as in Finland 90 per cent do. Countries like France, Finland and China have made legislation and made training obligatory for both the companies and individuals. Continuing Education activity in India is insignificantly small. A wave in this is perhaps needed. Will the institutes, government, and the industry not come together? Who will show them the vision? Higher Education Institutes will.

ARRIVAL OF THE DIGITAL LIGHT

Education today is in the wonder-world of Internet economy. With the advances in communication technology, World Wide Web and personal computers, the traditional methods of learning and teaching have been threatened. Virtual classrooms and virtual universities are coming into existence. IIT Mumbai, MIT Boston, and several other universities are launching programs which can be attended at home and at leisure. The academic community is having a fear that the emerging technologies will undermine what many deem best about traditional instructional practices and academic experiences—that is the personal contact between learner and teacher and among students. Many others feel that the arrival of new technology will bring instruction to them at cheaper cost. What lies ahead for universities and other sectors of education? What consequences will technology have on the institutional mission and mandate of universities? An extreme view has been offered by management sage Peter Drucker that traditional universities would not survive. Higher education is in deep crisis. Already we are beginning to deliver more lectures and off campus classes via satellite or two way video at a fraction of the cost of traditional courses. The colleges' campus would not survive as a residential institution. Today college buildings are hopelessly unsuited and totally not needed. The university colleges however should have to evaluate how fast this can happen? Should the institutes welcome new technologies? Undoubtedly, yes, and accelerate their arrival. India should exploit new technology to the benefit of masses.

Finance for Innovation

The government has created many schemes for financing industrial development IDBI, ICICI, IDCs, etc. have been providing finance and support: this is good, but not enough. It is the scientific and technological innovation which need a boost. The government would have to create "Innovation finance" in universities and colleges.

The industry, bankers and institutes would have to come together in this common cause. Innovation finance has modernized both the institutes and the industries in foreign countries. When they could do this, why can we not do so in India? Such financing has become essential a prerequisite to cope with demands in competitive and dynamic economy. Does the connection exist properly in India, between the industry and institutes? Without such interaction, the education and the economy of India will be crippled. The key person's, viz. policy makers, administrators, and professors would have to expand their thinking, and open up to new possibilities and global opportunities arising out of ever emerging technologies. They need to adopt a new agenda for the thought and action that would enable them to become more capable leaders. Not all the inputs given in this article are applicable to every college. They can choose what suits them. Who will show the way to create innovation finance? The learned professors will. At least 2 per cent of industry budget should be diverted to innovation to make fruitful investment in industry.

Preserving the Global Culture and Heritage

Ability to communicate well is essential in the present era of globalization. In this interdependent world, familiarity with foreign languages and foreign cultures, tolerance towards other faiths, an awareness of the benefits and differences in civilizations assumes importance. One of the objectives of education is that it helps to preserve the sanctity of human civilization. Education is directly concerned with moral power. In the past, institutes have neglected this aspect. It is only through moral education that we can work through, and find solutions to the problems of unemployment, poverty and terrorism. Most of the time, religions have been educating the people in improving morality. That is necessary, but not enough.

Corruption has grown beyond limits. Disparities between the rich and the poor are increasing. Educated people hold the key to progress. It is they who spend most of the budget. Unfortunately, they in general, do not have a good image in society. Introspection needs to be done. How the educated people look at the situation would decide the future of the world. Should education institutes not take a note and apply corrective measures? Imparting technical skills and knowledge are essential, but making them good human beings should not be forgotten. Deliberate and well thought out effort needs to be made in every institute to hold human civilization together.

Creating World-Class Technology

The questions are: can academics in India propel industrial development? Industrial goods from China and several east-west countries are flooding the Indian market. Many domestic industries are finding it difficult to survive the global competition. India ranks 43rd in world list of competitiveness. Some of the industries are becoming sick; some are being amalgamated, and purchased by foreign firms. Unemployment is rising. Can the Indian industry compete in a globalised market without modernizing the higher education? There has to be a close bond between the two. Gone are the days when Indian industry development plans used to be propelled by foreign collaborators. In those days, it was believed that technology can be generated only in foreign countries and after testing, it could be imported at high cost. Now it is proved beyond doubt that technology can be generated in India on par with that abroad and that too at half the price. It is no more necessary to knock at the doors of foreign countries for technology India should hold the vision to propel the industrial growth indigenously.

GOVERNMENT FUNDING OF EDUCATION

There is a school of thought that, if the state spends more on education, there will be a faster rate of growth. That if it is does not, growth will be slower.

Education is a wealth generating mechanism. Even in the hours of financial crisis, increase in budget to education is advocated. This is because it increases competency of people to utilize physical and financial resources. Nobel laureate Dr. Amartya Sen advised government to increase budget allocation to 6 per cent. When asked by Mr. Yashwant Sinha, the then Finance Minister. What should be the first priority in budget? He replied ‘Education.’ What should be the second priority? He replied ‘Education.’ What should be the third? He replied ‘Education.’ Indian has failed to grow faster so far, in spite of enormous promise only because of its weakness in education in general particularly, technical education. Many countries like Indonesia and Philippines are more advanced because of education.

Education alone can move a nation forward. The future belongs to those who understand this. We need a cultural and attitudinal revolution in favour of education.

There is, at present a wide gap between urban and rural areas in both social and economical development. Poverty anywhere is a threat everywhere. The people in rural areas do not have access to education. It is the scientific and technological capability of the people which enables them to strive and reach to higher income.

Adopting Internationally Proven Policies

The education should not depend on short-sighted whims and fancies of politicians. It should go on and on, uninterrupted, non-stop, regardless of the ruling political party. Academicians should be allowed to think and act freely. Higher education is more important and should go ahead even in times of war and peace. The earlier it is liberated from the vested interests of politicians and bureaucracy the better will it be for the state. Arrival of professionalism in education is hindered so far by politics and bureaucracy. Bringing policies and practices, systems and procedures from developed countries and adapting them to local situations is the crying need of the hour. People's minds need to be prepared for autonomy. The universities which are supposed to lead a change in favour of autonomy are found to be actually obstructing the process solely based on narrow selfish interests. In the wider national interest they should in fact dedicate their efforts to the cause of reformation in education.

The author suggests that the chancellors of universities in the face of rising challenges and increasing complexities in higher education essentially should have an independent office. The chancellor should be an academician working full-time, the present system in which the Governor of the state is the ex-officio chancellor, needs reconsiderations. The bottleneck today is at the top. The problems are being ignored and not attended to. The chancellor who is a Governor of the state remains too busy in his other legitimate duties and responsibilities. Any person, howsoever efficient may he be, cannot do justice to both. The origins of ills in higher education today, lie at the top. The situation demands urgent correction.

Universities as Maternity-homes for Safe Birth of New Enterprises

It is necessary for the universities to establish Patent and IPR Centres, Innovation Relay Centres, Research Parks, Incubators, Industrial Services Centres, Entrepreneurship Centres, Venture Capital Fund, Technology Transfer Office, etc. The above-mentioned centres are commonly seen in all universities abroad. Companies like HP, Apple, etc. were born in university incubators. It is these centres which have taken their countries ahead of others. But they are conspicuous by their absence in our institutes. If the state of Maharashtra takes this vision to set up such centres and succeeds, brain drain will be converted into brain-gain. Poverty will be wiped out, and employment generation for vast masses will take place. The schemes are known for income and employment generation.

Scientists from labs will have to be offered chairs in academic institutes and professors be offered chairs in laboratories. The practice of exchange of academic leaders prevails in Germany and many other countries. Networking of innovators on the one hand and the technology users on the other hand, to obtain push-pull effect will have to be done.

A committee must be appointed to prepare project reports and monitor implementation of establishment of such centres. The committee must be comprised of representatives from industry, laboratories and institute. Bhatnagar award winning scientists, Nobel laureates, NRI professors be specially invited to work on these committees. Innovation culture will not come automatically in the academic institutes and the state. It will have to be deliberately planted. Hence is this recommendation. 93.03 per cent respondents in a study, recommend the establishment of such a committee.

TOTAL QUALITY MANAGEMENT TECHNIQUES

According to a study conducted recently, 91 per cent respondents recommend use of TQM in education institutes. Eighty-eight per cent say investment with out TQM does not improve quality. Ninety-seven per cent respondents say TQM should be made compulsory where public funds are utilized. Ninety-six per cent say use of TQM will lead to improvement in quality and productivity. Ninety-one per cent say that there should be a state council for quality assurance. This will ensure higher efficiency in the state level systems. Due to the lack of TQM approach, our resources are wasted and are not available where they are needed.

Accreditation has been introduced at the national and state levels. This is a good scheme. But it has to be implemented in a right way. It has to be realized that accreditation is the last step of Quality Assurance. The preceding steps of Quality Assurance are not cared for. Benchmarking, identification of systems, inputs and outputs, use of statistical methods, making a survey on how satisfied the students, the faculty, the employers, and other stakeholders are, must precede and become a part of accreditation. Doing accreditation has unfortunately become a cosmetic exercise. The spirit is forgotten. The norms and standards prescribed by accreditation board are backward by world standards. Mediocre are being declared excellent. It has become like conducting of examination without the prior conduct of lectures and practical. This is precisely contrary to the principles of Quality Assurance. There is a plentiful of scope for improvement. In universities in UK that receive grants-in-aid, quality assurance is compulsory.

ISO head quarter at Geneva first arranged education programs and created a cadre of LEAD ASSESSORS, then gave them authority to educate persons in industry, to install Quality plans, Quality manuals. The exercise of training personnel in an enterprise continues for a year or two, and after they are prepared, they make application for ISO certification. Some such preparation of the institutions will essentially have to precede accreditation. Shall the NAAC/NBA devise mechanism to install quality assurance?

Industry-Institute Interaction

American industry has helped institutes to transform them into Power Houses of economy. Can Indian industry not do this? Industry and institutes can achieve peak performance only if they go hand in hand.

According to the study 93 per cent say that there should be a committee at state level to plan and implement industry-institute interaction. It is a well proven theory that industries in isolation from institutes cannot progress and become competitive, so also the institutes. In order that they are productive they must marry with each other. The proven theory says new technologies must be born in institutes and they should be transferred and used by industry in production of goods and services. The efforts of both needs to be synergized. There is a University Industry Science Partnership Program (UNISPAR) of UNESCO. Funds and guidance are available Maharashtra state has appointed a Director for Industry-Institute Partnership. This shows vision on the part of Govt. of Maharashtra. What remains is to activate the Directorate, to forge links between the industry and institutes? Who will show the way to activate it? The academicians will.

CONCLUSION

What then is our vision for the year 2020? The vision is to make India a destination of world-class technical education. The vision of India is to become a world-class fountain head of S&T, a wellspring generating and disseminating new technology to small, medium and large scale enterprises, both in India and abroad.

Can India hope to become a developed nation with the old outdated model of technical education?

Certainly not! We need to throw out the dysfunctional college-affiliation model and grant autonomous or deemed university status to them. This has not happened so far. The bottleneck lies at the top. There is a need of full-time chancellor.

Government in associations with ISTE would have to carry out restructuring of existing education and research organizations. This will make the institutions more productive, putting idle resources to effective work. However, there remains a need to increase the Govt. budget up to international norms, i.e. 6 per cent of GDP.

We shall have to bring world best policies and practices like in MIT, Oxford and Cambridge to our Institutes. Institutes will have to acquire a vision to become world leaders in technology. However, moral education must no be forgotten.

We envision starting technical universities, not only to award ME and Ph.D. degrees but also to become lighthouses for industry. The models of private university, virtual university need be given a fair chance. The youth must be given full access to research in public and private labs.

Education must be made research-based. Installation of Research Parks, Incubators, Patent Centres, Venture Capital Foundations, and other centres of excellence deserves high priority. Education has to be made innovative. Creating a culture in colleges and polytechnics that favours creativity and new ideas is the patent need of the hour.

Appointing state level and national level committees to achieve technological innovation, industry-institute interaction, etc. in a proper way must be done.

Upgrading the skill sets of vast masses so that they may perform jobs in modern industry to earn higher pay will have to be given priority. Centres for continuing education to fit people to job requirement will have to be established. Many jobs in India and in the world market are lying unfilled due to non-availability of proper people.

All aspects of this vision are not for all institutions. What will colleges and polytechnic look like in the year 2020? If the vision stated above is implemented in letter and in spirit, they will be much different. The Indian economy will then quickly grow stronger.

It is hoped that the leaders in industry, academia, religious, social and political systems will come together, work together, use collective wisdom and give a proper shape to build India into a developed nation by the year 2020.

An academician to a society is like a navigator of a ship. He does not take wheel in hands, but gives directions to the captain, either to evade or meet the waves.

Chapter 6

Risk Factors in Privatization

We find today a time bomb ticking under India's social and economic foundations. At a time when the level of education needed for productive employment is increasing, opportunity to go to college for economically bottom half population is decreasing. The academic values in institutions are eroding. Sweeping changes to halt sharp increases in tuition fees and increase of public and other sources of revenue for higher education is the urgent need, lest India will miss the valuable best possible contribution from brains of bottom half population.

INTRODUCTION

In an age of knowledge economy in which educated people and their ideas have become the wealth of nations, the universities, higher and technical education institutes have become of critical importance. The education opportunities offered by institutions the knowledge they create and the services they provide are the key to economic competitiveness and well-being of people. The impending revolution in the structure and function of higher education stems from the worldwide shift to knowledge-based society, that is to say more brain means more gain. The principal challenge now is how to discover new ways and means to respond vigorously to rapidly evolving world, and creating opportunities of quality education at affordable cost for vast masses. Privatization of higher education provides a means to achieve this. Private institutions must have to preserve the cherished aspects of the core values like academic freedom, autonomy so essential to ensure better future. Opportunities in private are always accompanied by risks. Which need to be assessed and guarded?

STATEMENT OF THE PROBLEM

Privatization is presently a flash point of crisis, in whole of India and elsewhere in the world. This is the central issue of debate and discussion in Parliament and assembly of various states. Turmoil is breeding every where, because of rising fees in self-finance colleges. Pretty strong signals, that something is not quite right, are being received in India. Frequent agitations from poor and disadvantaged families for whom it is difficult to bear rising cost have become common. The policymakers and educators need to listen to their voice. It is feared that if majority of the bottom half population are not able to send their children to college, long-term damage is likely to be caused to the fabric of Indian culture. The poor and disadvantaged people feel that the nation in its attempt of development will lose the talents of majority of population, and undoubtedly will miss the cherished goal of development. Poor and middle-class people feel that programs in government are perceived and planned only for the rich, adversely affecting them. They have a feeling of betrayal causing resentment which may lead to discontent, instability, even riots, which may be very costly.

Private self-finance institutes, in India, are mostly managed and maintained by political leaders, rather than those who understand it. They have little understanding of deeper purposes of education. In most of the cases, they are self-centred going to the extent of causing damage to the core function of academics and jeopardizing education. They put the students and public to disadvantage. Short-term gains dominate the long-term objectives, like raising people's intellectual capabilities. Concern for students, faculty and staff is likely to be lost, in favour of management whims and fancies.

Government, in the recent past, has reduced investment in higher education and as a result privatization has spurred.

Private institutions have become practically tools in the hands of politicians and businessmen who do not appreciate academics. Consequently, the deeper purposes of education are lost. Loyalty to the cause of education is reduced. Admissions are practically being made in spite of Supreme Court decision on capacity to pay for, rather than merit. Brainy students who are a national asset, from half the population are excluded from education.

Academics is getting back seat and money making has become prime. Professors have become employees having almost no say in governance. Professors are required to bend before politicians and industrialists. Respect for them in the eyes of students and management has gone down, adversely affecting creativity. Short-term private gains are getting priority and long-term nobler public interests are sacrificed. Professionalism is adversely affected. Governing boards, it is said, have polluted the academic atmosphere.

These risks in privatization need to be understood, analyzed and accounted for. US Government has appointed recently a commission to examine how privatization is undermining core academic values and its long-term impact on national economy. Many people in India, also have fears that uncontrolled privatization, in the long run will shadow Indian intelligentsia.

Higher education leads to both public good and private good. With the increase in education, economy grows, so also the tax collection. An educated man benefits the whole society. This is the public good. The individuals also earn more, which is termed as private good. Both the beneficiaries should share the costs. This is the pattern accepted world over. Can we in India not accept it? Government today is gaining additional tax without paying for costs, cent per cent cost is borne by students, which is unethical. Government should have to pay its share. When other countries are spending up to 10 per cent of GDP on education why India cannot? Spending on education is wealth generating. Those who understand this will win.

The paper identifies the risk factors and delineates what universities, government, and academics at this juncture of time should do to limit damage and yet make most of privatization.

POSITIVE ASPECTS OF PRIVATIZATION

Wisdom to establish and run an institute of higher education is not the monopoly of government. It is available also in private. India cannot forego imaginative ideas, funds available, organization and management capability so abundantly available in private, so as to win in global competition. From 1981, a wave of self-finance private institutions has been initiated, and now proposal of private universities is being moved.

Private institutions being relatively thin and lean are quick to respond to opportunities in changing times. They enable people to learn that which is relevant and encash income and employment chances in global market. Private institutions can afford to take more risks and thereby avail more opportunities. Their rules are flexible, and this is their strength. Privatization of higher education is found to accelerate industrial development, generate employment and income. Governing boards of private institutions are mostly consisting of professionals like lawyers, industrialists, doctors. They can better regulate higher education institutions than legislators in government, who hardly have any orientation, and priority so is the observation world over. Private institutes are nearer the free market, which facilitates them to adapt quickly to changing situations, which leads to effective governance. It is obviously wiser, to use money, energy, talent, etc. of private for the public cause of higher education.

It is not a matter of only providing financial resources for higher education. More it is a matter of organization and management capability. If the same amount, for example, as invested by private institutions, was invested by government, for establishment of new institutions, they would certainly not have come up as fast and better as they have. The limiting factor for success, it is realized, is not funds alone but the expertise. India at this juncture of time needs to depend not only on government institutions but to exploit the dormant capacity available in private and without which its economic and social development plans will undoubtedly lag behind. Hence, opening of private institutions and universities should whole heartedly be welcomed.

This does not mean that all is well with them. Only private institutes do not suffice. Education should not be the monopoly of private. Equally important and essential for competition is the opening of new government institutions. A national policy favorable to both is the need of time.

The one time leading universities of Europe today are falling behind, mainly because they have not adopted privatization. American universities are leading. Nine out of ten world best are from USA. US were the first to adopt privatization, and hence are ahead.

INVESTMENT IS REWARDING

Governing boards of private institutes are found to be active and more successful in raising funds from alumni and others. They also collect innovative ideas, to orient institutions to scientific management practices. They provide increased access to more number of students of all ages. They successfully raise intellectual capacity of the nation. They are found to give more and better leaders to government, industry and to various walks of life. They have in the past given many inventions and innovations, which have enriched the human civilization. They would now shake up not only the higher education sector but also the national economy. India, so as to fulfill its dream of becoming a global power needs to harvest capacities in private institutions most. The rate of return on investment in higher education is reported to be very high, of the order of 70 to 100 per cent, which very few commercial projects can achieve. More investments India makes in education, more financial returns it can obtain. It is a case fit even for borrowing from international market.

Privatization of higher education in India, since 1981, has delivered good results. Private, self-financed institutes have contributed remarkably well to economic and employment growth. For example, in IT sector it is observed to have made a mark on international plane. It has raised the image of India in the world market. In USA almost half the institutions are private.

RISK FACTORS TO BE GUARDED

Privatization is good provided it is planned and regulated well. But when uncontrolled it may harm the society. There are limits [Laxman Resha in Marathi language] within which if they remain privatization succeeds. If they go beyond they enter danger zone. The limits need to be borne in mind by all concerned and especially the governing boards, government and academic leaders. They have to guard against the risks at their respective institutions. This is so essential for their survival, and to make most of privatization.

Future of Higher Education at Stake—The Long-term Risk

The Supreme Court of India in its various rulings time and again, have stated that admissions be made on merit and not on the capacity to pay for. All merit students however may not have money enough to take admission in private institutions. True that education loans have now become available. Yet they are not that easily available. Today in the year 2010 as many as sixteen lakh students have taken loans. This figure is increasing from year to year. They need guarantors, land, buildings, etc. for mortgage, and capacity to repay. Such merit students may be deprived of making a better career they are capable for, and ultimately the institutions will be without brains from poor people, and hence the nation stands to lose to that extent. These colleges in turn may become institutes only for the rich, mostly mediocre. Instead of bridging the gap between the rich and poor they are perpetuating to widen. They themselves and the nation at large may in long term become socially unstable. The limits of privatization need to be understood and followed in spirit. Scholarships need be provided to poor meritorious students.

Fees in the self-finance colleges in medical and engineering courses have sky rocketed. Institutions are found to admit students on the capacity to pay for, rather than merit. The standard of education in private colleges has been diluted. Private colleges have taken a hold on most of the universities, and have been bending rules to preserve their interests, resulting in dilution of standards. The board sometimes appoints only such professors who would be co-operative. The institutions have turned mediocre. Imagine the plight when students from such institutions get degrees and join professions, and thereby license to practice profession. Would you take your patient to a doctor passed from such an institution? They do not follow the ethics but exploit situations. Institutions would have to guard against this tendency.

NOBLER AIMS THROWN TO WINDS

The motives that inspire professors may be nobler, going far beyond those that animate political and business leaders. Commerce is irrelevant to learning, discovery and acquisition of knowledge. Nothing from politics or corporate sector can measure the value of research output or determine reliably how valuable is the knowledge. Academic institutions should therefore be meticulous in following the norms and standards of faculty, staff, and infrastructure, laid down by academic authorities like UGC/AICTE. Professionalism should be maintained at all costs.

Management of college has a tendency to appoint experts from corporate sector to economize expenditure and yet improve performance. These experts who do not understand the pulse of academics may try to apply corporate methods. They may identify redundant positions in science departments but this may diminish quality of education and research. So as to really encourage innovation and creativity, you need to have a good deal of slack time. Ways of corporate sector are however neither consistently useful nor wholly irrelevant. This makes problem handling in academics more difficult. Educators must have to use their own judgments to decide how to pursue improvement, and economize. Simple cost benefit analysis will fail. Would you like to admit your son or daughter in an institution where there is no professionalism?

There is a growing influence of business on academics. Interaction between the two for exchange of ideas and experience is essential. Some observed that working of academics for business is beneficial and not at all harmful. While this is true, academics must remain academics and business must remain business.

Separate identity of the two is essential. Companies provide funds for research and wish that for competitive reasons the result should not be published. This secrecy is not desirable for a public institution, although desirable for company. Institutions should have to prepare the rules, legal framework, and professional ethics without which they will yield to pressures from companies. Academics should not be required to bow down to business. This in long range is too damaging. Corporate money, it is said would try to subordinate the public aims of research and education to private ends. Governing boards ought to hold academic values even at the cost of lucrative opportunities to earn money, win public trust, and retain the interest of faculty and students. They should create an atmosphere favorable for truth to prevail. Academic institutes by virtue of research and innovation should show the way to industry. They should be like light house for industry. It should not be the other way round. Academics and institutes should remain in driver's seat, and not be driven.

ACADEMIC FREEDOM USURPED

Government is asking institutions to speed up innovation, inventions, job creation, and income growth by co-operating more closely with industry. There is a growing demand from society to benefit from academic works and draw rewards from marketplace. Academics should certainly put academic work to practical use by selling patents, scientific discoveries and earn money. While this is true the ties between the two should be open and follow sunshine laws. They should not be suspicious. Academic institutions private or public both work for the public cause. Academic sanctity should be maintained. Academicians should essentially have academic freedom to publish the findings of their research, so also conduct research they like. These limits should be observed by both the academics and business. Business should not impose a constraint on them.

Academics are expected to play their legitimate role of critic for both the government and industry. They essentially should remain autonomous, for maintaining a healthy national economy. Would good professors like to join as faculty in such on institution where there is no academic freedom?

The sanctity of professorate in private institutions is also likely to be adversely affected. The respect of professors in the eyes of governing board and students is going down. They are treated as simple employees available on payment and not as gurus. Their emotional involvement in education is not tapped. They are not permitted to possess academic freedom. This in ultimate analysis may damage the creativity so badly needed, for a nation to prosper.

It is further observed that government has reduced investment in education and hence students are forced to go to private self-finance colleges. Some feel this is a plot of politicians who on one side sit in government, and on the other as chairman of private self-finance colleges. Loyalty to education of governing boards in the eyes of public has become doubtful. This is the finding of a study conducted in the year 2003. Ninety-five per cent of the respondents from college professors said they have no confidence in the political leaders for the cause of education.

Institutions as Business Concerns Lead to Catastrophe

Governing boards should primarily be guardians of academic values. They should see to it that academic values are not compromised. Many are afraid that private universities if started will shadow in long run the intellectual and academic culture. Irreplaceable values may get permanently lost in relentless growth of privatization. These are the negative side effects which need to be guarded.

Linking academic research to business, only in a limited manner is good. Opening offices by institutions for commercial sale of patents and technology is good, but within limits. The limits need to be defined and identified in rules of the institutes. Nothing should be at the cost of education. It should only supplement. This however is not an easy job.

Institutions should not become tools in the hands of those who do not realize the value of academics. Academics should not be viewed as business but service to society. It is now time proper, in the face of globalization to revamp higher education. We must accept the challenge, in spite of difficulties and tap opportunities in world market. Academic professors and directors of the institutions should be appointed who bring scholarship to the institutions. Often professors and principals are appointed who are good in raising funds. This is the side effect to be guarded. Business effects are for short term while academic effects are for long term.

Privatization affects the behaviour of professors, and officials. The element of social service is being driven out. This may change their character for worse. Self-finance institutions are tending to become business concerns instead of moral and intellectual. Privatization leads to surge in money making activity in campus. It stems from the attitude of top management. Education values are likely to be sacrificed. A wrong message is likely to go to younger generation. Are teachers granted role in governance of the institutions?

The institutions in private sector also are accountable to public interest. University or an institution is a means to prepare a brave new India. It is a national asset of very high value. Therefore private colleges should be regulated well. Education has assumed a central role in national development. Are institutions accountable to public interest?

Status of Professor, the Key Player, In Danger

Business executives are being appointed on boards of institutions. They are appointed even as chairman. This is welcome with reservations. Many professors in all their humbleness do not appreciate the move. They feel institutions should not be run like General Motors. Principal purpose of institution is academic. They should be run by academicians who are specialized in them and not by administrators, politicians or businessmen. Success is measured in terms of research output and education quality. Cost saving in teaching and researching by those who do not understand the pulse of academics is hazardous, which can do more harm than good. Long-term damage to institution may take place. They may make a business of institutions and academics may be given back seat.

The time and energy of students may be diverted to commercialization and not education. Long-term damage for generations is therefore possible and guarding against this happening is of vital importance. Non-academic things like campus maintenance, food service, etc. may however be better managed by persons from non-academic fields. Governing boards may be oriented to changing academic needs in global environment. People at the time of elections have their votes in their hands. They should cast them in favour of those who attach high priority to education, and fund adequately, equal to if not more than defense. What is the value of that governing board which does not win confidence of faculty, staff and students?

Students from bottom half of the population is observed to be late developers, having greater enthusiasm and having a greater drive for higher education. Many of such persons after graduation have grown faster into successful professionals, and leaders in social and community activities. They are observed to become more productive and ease tensions in the society. It is these common students who often do uncommon. The governing boards ought to give consideration to these aspects, give poor and middle class students wider access to private institutions.

SUMMING UP

Risk factors involved in privatization of higher education demand a wide scale debate and discussion. This is essential so as to understand the gravity, and keep in check the negative side effects arising out of privatization. The paper has attempted to identify some of them.

Higher education institutions essentially should not go too close either to business or government. It has to have academic freedom to be able to play its legitimate role as critic. It should essentially therefore be autonomous.

The honor and respect of professor, which is the highest post in academics, should be by law, maintained at all cost. The authorities and responsibilities of professor should be written down in university act. This is essential in public interest. It is they and the students who make on institution. Others even chairman, governing board, etc. although important, are ancillary.

We need to appreciate that higher education is public good, besides private.

The two namely public and private beneficiaries must have to share costs in a proper mix. In USA, fees paid by students is 31% of the cost of education. Central and State Government contribution is 48% as public good; rest is contribution from donations and earnings from technology sale.

We have entered a period of significant change. We must ask two questions to ourselves, whom do we serve? How can we serve better? Certainly, the need for higher education will be of increasing importance for masses in knowledge driven future. The current paradigms of teaching, research, and service to society, and of obtaining finances all must change. During change, interests of lower and middle-class people should not be forgotten. Without increased access in higher education to down and out people undoubtedly India will remain poorer.

If institutions keep on increasing tuition fees and state does not support financially, as an obligation of public good, one day India will be socially unstable. Instead of becoming a power in the world, it will then remain one of the poor most countries. If we stay on our present course, and do not change we are more likely to encounter disaster, in the years ahead.

New paradigms for providing and financing higher education are required for longer term. Shifting the financial burden from previous generation to nest allowing the generation proper to bear the burden is one possible solution. Students should take loans today and pay back from their future income. It is like present system of housing loan or car loan. The debt on student will be too big. Assimilation of this will take time. Have the previous generations paid for establishment of institutions for generation of today? They have paid when the country was poorer. Why now prosperous India cannot?

The tuition should not be too low, to mean that tax payers are paying for the rich. We must re-establish our priority, to provide educational opportunity to all, who have the desire and ability to learn. We must sustain these institutions to serve our children and grandchildren, by abandoning the erosion of government support. Human competency increases with education, and the government will only be richer if it does so. When other countries are spending 6% to 10% of GDP on education why India cannot? Roots of poverty lie in low level national funding for education.

While most of our institutions are already trying to change and adapt to a changing world, they are yet far too behind the target. Actually, due to privatization the standard is falling down, when the need of knowledge and skills in competitive environment is rising. They must, regardless whether they are private or public, maintain fundamental scholarly commitment and values required for a worthy democratic society. The key persons should keep in mind the deeper purposes. Those institutions which show visions, wisdom and courage will lead in years to come. Poor and middle class people are looking with hope to them.

It is hoped that the governing boards and academics that control the institutional performance, will show wisdom to recognize their obligation to community, region and even the world. They should take their duties and responsibilities as a moral vocation, show scholarship in public trust they govern, and provide public service in an exemplary way. They can certainly cover all the risks arising out of privatization, and make it a success.

"The solution of virtually all problems with which government is concerned like housing, poverty, health, education, environment, energy, urban development, international relationships, space, economic competitiveness, defense and national security, all depend on creating new knowledge, producing competent manpower, and hence upon the health of academic institutions."

REFERENCES

Bok, Derek, *Universities in the Market Place, the Commercialization of Higher Education*, Princeton University Press, Princeton, New Jersey.

Bombardieri, Marcella, Elite Colleges Increase Aid to Woo Poorest Top Recruits, Boston Globe of July 16, 2005.

Bowen, William G. and Derek Bok, *The Shape of the River, Long-term Consequences of Considering Race in College and University Admissions*, Princeton University Press, Princeton, New Jersey.

Commission appointed on 19.9.2005 by Secretary Spellings, on Higher Education for America to remain a global economic leader. Serious implications of the ability of millions of Americans to pay for college are to be examined. College affordability is the issue.

Duderstadt, James J. *A University for THE 21st Centuries*, The University of Michigan Press.

Naik, B.M. *New Vistas in Technical Education*, Vivek Publication, 2001.

THE GUARDIANS: *Boards of Trustees of American Colleges and Universities, What they do and How Well They Do It*, by Clark Kerr and Marion L. Gade, Association of College Boards of Universities and Colleges of America.

Vaishnav, Anand, *Out of State Schools on the Move*, Boston Globe of August 28, 2005.

Chapter 7

India Desperately Needs Research Based, Innovative World-Class Universities and Colleges to Nurture Leaders for Tomorrow How to Go About?

India is at risk, for want of innovative, research based, world-class universities and colleges.

ABSTRACT

The paper presents in brief, need and importance of research-based innovative world-class universities and colleges, so as to keep India globally competitive. India needs professionals and leaders in all the walks of life of world-class standard, with higher imagination who can take it to greater heights on international plane. Students need nurturing to become pacesetters, technology pioneers, political and industry leaders. Institutes have to be ahead of time, to do this. They have to have research and innovative character of global standard. Conventional institutes in the absence of high-end research base are unfit for the purpose. They produce, by and large, mediocre, only soldiers at best fit for multinationals. There is huge energy in Indian youths, yet too few become leaders in industry and technology on global plane, because that is not what present universities are teaching students to become. The number of world-class institutes is now a differentiating factor between developed and developing countries.

If India does not envision and show commitment for building research-based world-class institutes, it will lose in brain race; India will continue to trail behind the developed world. More and more foreign universities will come and displace Indian universities. World experience says that the cost of upgradation of universities is far too less than the cost of mediocrity.

The paper identifies strategies which when adopted institutions become world-class. The strategies are grouped as governance, academic, administrative, financial, etc. They are however tough to deliver and essentially call for a political will.

INTRODUCTION

Students demand world-class education. They are ready to pay for. But not many universities and colleges are able to offer. Thousands of students every year go abroad. Foreign universities are coming. Institutes which are innovative in character only are likely to earn the status of world-class. They are always ahead of time. They generate jobs, entrepreneurs and high income. In knowledge-driven economy of today, they assume high significance. Society looks at these institutes as “Light House”. They are an idea source. They energize national and international environment. Spending necessary amount to make institutes world-class is justifiable. Mediocre institutes are more costly than the cost of their upgradation. Can India hope to be a developed nation with present poor quality higher and technical education? At least some better performing institutions should forthwith be enabled to reach to world-class status. Can we create world-class centres of excellence? They are the places to create and nurture leaders of each new generation. The output of such institutes is not only learning, but the bold new society of tomorrow. Tomorrow’s society is being created today in colleges. It will decide the character of India, and increasingly the character of many of the leaders in India and possibly foreigners who come for education to India.

Envisioning bright future for young generation demands high dreams, thinking great and commitment to implement reformation plans. Will the people who matter most show reformative spirit? Will they abandon bureaucracy, become more imaginative?

Where does India Stand in World Ranking?

World ranking of universities for the year 2010[1] indicate that first eight out of ten universities are from USA. Merit students in all the countries in the world dream to study in US universities. Many of them after studies settle in US adding to its intellectual capital. World-class institutes in any nation are like a magnet to attract brains. Seeds of leadership are sown in the minds of students while they are studying within the four walls of classrooms. Chinese universities in world list went up from 16 to 34 in one year. Whereas only two of our institutes, namely IIT Kharagpur and IISC Banglore figure in first 500. With so small a number of world-class institutes can India ever win? So India Government is installing afresh many new IITs, IIMs and universities.

You lead only when you create world-class institutions. Where do you produce imaginative leaders? They are produced within the four walls of classrooms. Leaders for tomorrow, who would be the movers and shakers around the world are strolling today in quadrangles of institutes. USA could become world power mainly because it tops in the list of universities. US produces leaders for itself and also for other countries. Many world leaders have received education in US including India. Thomas Jefferson the founder President of USA then emphasized in US to improve higher education to world-class standard so as to enable US to become world power.[2] He said unless until US establishes lead in higher education, it cannot show lead in economy and industry. US Science Foundation and research-based universities came out of his initiative. The strategy worked well. It will work well also in India, and so Government of India has initiated Technical Education Quality Improvement Program [TEQIP]. Around ₹ 4000 crore are being invested in 300 well-performing colleges with the assistance of World Bank.[3] We need to implement TEQIP effectively, and enlarge its scope to cover all colleges. National budget on education should be raised from 3 per cent to 6 per cent of GDP; higher education budget needs to be increased from 0.65 per cent to 2 per cent.

"Where once nations measured their strength by the size of the army and arsenals, in the world of future knowledge will matter most. Now strength is measured by the number of world-class institutions that germinate, innovate and incubate new knowledge and new technology," India needs them most for it is aspiring to be a developed nation by 2020.

World-class institutes provide imaginative leaders with global visions. They are driving force to run a nation.

Reformation in universities and colleges in India presently is high on agenda. According to the recommendations of National Knowledge Commission (2006) and Yashpal Committee Report (2009), attempts are being made to enlarge Gross Enrolment Ratio, achieve excellence, and make education inclusive. India's economic and political standing in the world is dependent on its winning in "Brain Race" that is to say on higher education in global comparison. With this in view government is allocating huge budgets, opening more institutions and appointing more professors, which is necessary, but not sufficient. Critically important is adoption and implementation of world-proven visions and missions, policies and practices, systems and procedures. Learning from world experience, it is necessary to re-frame the visions and missions and link them up with internal institutional programs and activities. Questions are being asked whether the institutions will adapt to include, knowledge/technology generation, technology transfer, innovation, creativity, patent and IPR, spinoff of new technology-based firms, corporate development, lifelong education in their visions and missions.[4] They have a deeper impact on improving quality, without which, in spite of having all the resources they turn out to be mediocre. Mediocre institutions teach nothing other than how to become more mediocre. Most of the institutions in India produce graduates today who can at best become efficient technology/knowledge followers and not leaders.

In the absence of research base professors do not bring cutting edge technology to classrooms. They teach yesterday's knowledge today and are not able to produce technology leaders and technology pioneers.

Without world-class institutions India's dream to become a developed nation certainly cannot be fulfilled. This is writing on the wall. The knowledge, technology content in the society then remains low, keeping people's income and standard of living at low level. The paper gives a suggestive list of strategies which when followed will enable an institute to make most of its existing intellectual resources to become forerunner.

The higher and technical education institution, in the coming time, although will undergo substantial changes, driven by new learning technology, harsh financial constraints, changing public demand, globalization and growing intellectual opportunity, it must keep learning and especially student learning at the heart of its mission. Creativity, innovation, discovery, patent and IPR, spin off new technology-based firms should have to become the new targets. Only teaching and learning in classrooms although essential, is not enough to turnout world-class graduates. Campus of today indicates larger society of tomorrow. With this in view institutes need shaping.

Institutes are known as powerhouses to produce knowledgeable leaders to lead India at national and international levels. They produce intellectual and technological power to run a nation. Today, the vector direction of higher education in India is undoubtedly misplaced. There is almost a complete lack of good leadership and proper governance, which makes the problem huge. Government is simply providing lip service, and hence India remained a lowly educated country, with 25 per cent people riddled in poverty. That is why on one hand we have unemployment of educated and on the other shortage of well educated. What is wanted is not taught and what is taught is not wanted. It needs immediate correction. It needs more than 6 per cent of GDP budget for education. This requires political will, without which the people below poverty line, nexalism and suicides of farmers will keep on increasing.

Arjuna was asked by guru Dronacharya while hitting the eye of parrot "what do you see". When he said "I see only the eye of parrot". Then guru asked him to shoot. The direction of the arrow was right. It was not necessarily with high speed, or high force. The strategies of institutions would have to be right to win in world competition. How would the winning institution in coming time look like?

An institute which has characteristics as under is more likely to win; others may work hard, may have all the resources to draw on but will lag behind.

An attempt should therefore be made to change mindset of key people to upgrade existing institutions to acquire following characteristics.

Many institutions in India are planning to jump up to higher orbit. They are pumping huge amount of money, appointing more professors. This is all necessary but not enough. To enable an institution to become world-class essentially requires change in policies and practices and change in style of governance. How to go about is attempted in this article.

Strategies Enabling an Institute to Become World-Class

The following strategies and their combinations in various proportions enable an institution to achieve excellence. Systems of operation internal and external, in an institution may have to be redesigned to align them to fit in globalized world.

GOVERNANCE STRATEGY

Institutional Autonomy with effective board of governors well engaged with college is essential. It is only an effective, imaginative, and committed BOG which can enable an institution to become world-class. The successful higher and Technical Education institution in coming time will be that which will maintain institutional autonomy, lively faculty, independence, and vigorous academic freedom, but will enjoy strong, impartial, public governance and committed institutional leadership. All good institutions, world over, are essentially autonomous. Professors and students ought to have freedom to be innovative and creative. Politicians and bureaucracy should not put a cap on their imagination, although they provide funds. Government is not qualified to steer the direction and hence it should not interfere. Institutes themselves ought to steer the direction of academic pursuits. There should be almost no interference in academics from outside. This has to be so in public interest. More governments believe that institutions serve their nations better if the institutions are managed and maintained by governing boards consisting of professionals. The trust should not supervise the college directly. It should appoint a body of experts as governing board to supervise. AICTE has shown wisdom in making it a precondition for new institutes starting from this year (2011-12). This will undoubtedly lead to enhance the quality of education. Autonomous status is a prerequisite to succeed. This should be accorded in letter and spirit. Faculty and staff should be allowed developing taste of autonomy for which mixing with their counterparts, in world best institution is necessary. It is observed that government grants autonomy to institutes but with strings attached. This is not in larger interest. Bureaucracy needs to be curbed. When will the government realize this?

All developed nations have only autonomous institutions. One and all are born autonomous. Those which are not born autonomous they believe they are like children born handicapped.

Compatibility to opportunities and challenges in globalize world. The winning institute in coming time will be that which runs programs compatible to the opportunities arising in globalization. Indian institutes are yet not aligned and tuned to world dynamics. They have in the recent past progressed well quantitatively but are yet poorly equipped and woefully unsuited to the quality demands of globalization. Transformation to world-class status demands more of intellectual inputs, systems inputs. There is a mismatch in education. What is wanted is not taught, and what is taught is not wanted. Conduct of courses is diverse from opportunities for employment and income generation. They run behind the time. That is why there is unemployment in educated youths.

Privatization ought to be publicly accountable and socially committed. The preferred institution will be increasingly privately supported but publicly accountable and socially committed. Privatization of technical education is certainly good. But there are some risks, which need to be guarded so as to make most. Private institutions in India are mostly managed and maintained by political persons. They should keep in mind the deeper purposes of education. Students should not be exploited but helped. It is hoped that governing authorities would show statesmanship and use the institutes as means to build a national unity they seek, and to develop the human resources needed by economy.

Educate local people in hi-tech. The successful institution will be technologically sophisticated but local community dependent. Quality of education does not depend only on instructions in classroom and laboratories. It depends more on building synergy in institutes and local society/industry. Indian institutes need to learn commercialization of new knowledge/technologies. It needs multifaceted activities like entrepreneurship, technology incubators, patents and IPR, lifelong education centre, research parks, enterprise development centres which bring about a marriage between industry and academics. They are new in India and should be set up as early as possible. Only classroom teaching although essential is not enough to improve quality, and relevance. Only pumping more money and appointing more men in institutes is not enough. National Knowledge Commission[5] has recommended establishment of above centres of excellence, as integral components of the institutions. They have a deeper impact on quality of education. Solution lies in sensitizing institutions as well as industry in the potential synergy between the two.

Institute has to be Competitive internationally. Each successful institution in coming time will have to be competitive, not only by national standards but by international. The visions and missions of the institutions, policies and practices, systems and procedures should be made responsive to the changing world. Indian universities, colleges and polytechnics till recently were ahead of their counterparts in China.[6] But now they are far too behind. Do we realize this? Only those who realize, and do benchmarking with others will improve.

Addressing local problems with an eye on international. The successful institution will be campus rooted but internationally oriented. The professors in the past did not have adequate opportunities to go abroad and see what and how their counterparts are teaching. They were practically disconnected from rest of the world, and not familiar with the global developments. In order that they become equal to world-class professors they need to be granted increased international mobility. Sachin Tendulkar could not have become world-class cricketer if he was not allowed to play international cricket. Cost of providing international exposure to professors is high but far too less than the hidden cost of not providing, which ultimately reflects on competency of the society. Ignorance is far more costly than the cost of education.

Create academic partnership with many institutes. The successful institution will be academically independent but constructively having partnership with many others. If the institution is to meet the increasing range of social needs, it will require new alliances within the academic community and new partnerships outside it, with communities, local, state and national agencies, corporations, libraries, museums, publishers, professional associations, scholarly societies, and other institutions. It will establish closer cooperation with other "providers" and "users" of knowledge including commercial vendors of educational hardware and software. Institutions will be successful who nurse public private partnership (PPP).[7] Success of an institution will depend on how many partners national and international it is able to carry with.

Institutions will be successful only if the mechanism of governance at all levels, i.e. governmental, university and college levels is modernized by using scientific approaches. It should be made flexible, participative, and responsive to the aspirations of youths. Government is devising policies and practices so as to make it inclusive. Universities and colleges should bring them in practice. Professors are yet poorly paid with stringent work conditions, which constrain them from achieving international standard. Sabbatical leave which adds to quality is not yet provided. These are the critical inputs to academics to make it grow. When shall we realize this?

What is then the vision of India for the year 2020? A developed nation? Then we need to throw out old dysfunctional college affiliation model and resort to autonomy. So as to achieve this dream, institutions must have to become fountain heads of S&T, a well-spring generating and disseminating new technology to small and medium enterprises. The orientation of institutions is still towards training in known knowledge and practice, rather than creation of new. It is presumed in system that knowledge is finite, already discovered and written up, so that a young scholar is needed to study only the established facts. Research, discovery of unknown is not yet an integral part of curriculum. This new vision must prevail.

Academic Strategies

The successful institution will be knowledge based but student centred, research driven but learning focused. There is an acute need of establishing technical universities. It is this strategy which enables to achieve excellence.[8] It is they who can focus better on technological research, and to become "lighthouse" for industry. Universities should go beyond puppet-like teaching. Students should not become teacher puppets. They should aim to become pace setters and path finders in changing world. They should create an atmosphere of competition and avoid monopoly. The present universities are fat and flabby like an elephant. They are running like in the past. They are doing what their forefathers did, but not able to adopt new directions with changing times. Universities should be lean and thin like a deer, and possess agility. For want of technical universities opportunities are dying and being taken away by foreigners. World experience tells us that technical university and other specialized universities is a more effective model than multi-faculty model. It consumes fewer resources and gives more and relevant output. We need to realize this. Present multi-faculty universities consume more resources and give less output.

The successful institution will be that which will produce new technologies in its laboratories. By importing and following the technologies from abroad, India cannot hope to be a technology leader. Institutions should aim at producing new knowledge, new technologies, and leaders in industry. How can Indian youth become technology pioneers? They should aim to learn from student age to produce Indian brands in technology and industry. Entrepreneurship is almost absent in syllabi of all disciplines. CAFETERIA approach needs to be adopted and rice plate approach abandoned.

Successful institutions will be that which acquire new vision of the new world. The industries need continuous input of new knowledge and new technology, so as to remain competitive in global market. Institutes and universities should acquire this new vision of the new world. Visions should include corporate development and enable industry to win. Institutions will be successful who provide new technologies to industry. Institutes and industry in isolation cannot achieve peak performance.

Indian institutes will be successful which produce balanced output of UG, PG and PhD. Present output of PhDs is 0.5 per million populations. The corresponding figure of USA and Japan are 30 and 28 per million population. With this abysmally low figure of PhDs can India hope to win in the world brain race? TEQIP-II Government of India, 2009.[9] In its document has estimated that India needs 30,000 PhDs and 24,000 MTech.

The successful institution will be quality obsessed but procedurally efficient. Many institutions in India are spending money far in excess but due to lack of Total Quality Management (TQM) approach they do not excel. Implementation of TQM does not require additional money, it results in saving. The Governing boards, UGC/AICTE should prescribe, make it obligatory and facilitate use of TQM. In United Kingdom Government does not grant financial support to an organization which does not use TQM.[10]

Institutions will be successful which give birth to new technologies, patents, hi-tech startups. Do we want to use only imported brands of technologies or generate Indian brands? Then industry and institutes should look to each other's support for growth. They cannot produce in isolation from each other. Youthful talent in institutes is a great force. Synergy between institutes and industry is the only way to achieve peak performance by both of them. Industry should change their mindset and learn to support technological research in institutes. They should jointly undertake activities like research parks, innovation centres, technology incubators, etc. One is less effective without the support of other. They should do so on sustained basis over a long period.

ADMINISTRATIVE

The institution will be successful, where the chancellor of universities is competent academically.[11] Governor of a state is presently the ex-officio chancellor of universities. This system coming by tradition does not suit today. Now when education has become so vast and complex, stakes involved are so high, the chancellor of universities cannot be a decorative figure. He needs to be an academician with wide open experience in the world of academics. Today the problems in higher education remain improperly diagnosed, inadequately analyzed. Hence, solutions are not forthcoming. A separate office of chancellor with qualified staff is the need of the hour. If this is not done foreign institutes will find it easy run over and capture the vast Indian education market. Who pays the price? Innocent people!

Industry should take a long-range view of the interaction with institutes. Industry cannot do all the research technological, social and financial all alone by itself needed for becoming globally competitive. It must think differently and align with institutes for research. With this approach it is much cheaper, quicker and better to develop indigenous technology and/or absorb technology coming from abroad.

The skill set of the vast population of India is far too low by international standard India, today is a lowly educated country by world standard. The Gross Enrolment Ratio is only 14 per cent as against world average of 30 per cent. It needs upgradation forthwith. Both young and adults in urban as well as rural areas should be uplifted in knowledge and skills. Not only machines become obsolete but men also. They need to be enabled to become globally competent and remain so lifelong. This demands lifelong education, continuing education programs. Learning only once is not enough. Lack of access to learning skills leads to unemployment, increases in poverty, naxalite tendency, crime rate and in turn forced for investment in security measures, etc. Shall we then not choose to invest in favour of building world-class institutions rather than being forced to build prisons?

Higher and technical education in India will be successful only if the recommendations of National Knowledge Commission

(2006), and Yashpal Committee (2009) in respect of grant of autonomy to institutions should be urgently discussed debated and implemented. Innovative and creative budding minds demand reforms. Nations where institutions are keeping pace with time progress faster. They must change with changing world. The challenge is to enlarge capacity of colleges.

Institutions will be successful which identify internal weaknesses, revise structures, systems and procedures. A world proven theory says that some of the authorities in chair and politicians in particular may obstruct even sabotage and slow down the process of transformation. Resistance to change, inertia of the system is natural.[12] This is usually done to keep alive their personal vested interests putting public interest in danger. This is human tendency. Therefore, transformation of higher and technical education should not be left totally in the hands of authorities in chair. An independent body to plan and monitor reforms must be constituted. Implementation of recommendations of NKC and Yashpal Committee 2009 should not be left to existing authorities of universities and colleges like in the past. A separate independent task force of dedicated educationists, industrialists, and social reformers is necessary to be constituted at state and national levels for the purpose. Recommendations of earlier education commissions, like Kothari Commission, New Education Policy 1986, Radhakrishnan Commission (1959) have not been seriously implemented because of lack of independent task force.

The institutions will be successful which replace traditional bureaucratic approach in governance and management of academic institutes. Bureaucracy in institutions is no more relevant today, it should be abandoned forthwith. Indoctrination of ideas, rigid framework, and inflexibility has no place in academics. They throttle emergence of spontaneous, breakthrough ideas. Higher and technical education will be successful if it gives go bye to the present degraded policies and practices and pulls them up from the ruts and takes up to higher orbits.

If the reforms are delayed, foreign institutions are likely to establish education hubs in India and exploit the vast education

market. Indian academics will then go in service of foreign masters. Consequence will be that Indians will be branded inefficient, incompetent and less knowledgeable to govern institutes in global context by themselves. They will become subservient to foreigners. Education may slip out of our hands in favour of foreign, which is too detrimental. Foreign universities once they come in India they will not remain limited to education but interfere in industrial, social and political affairs of the country. India will tend to become like Afghanistan and Pakistan. Foreign universities will not come if we become equal to them, hence is the importance of world-class standard.

Institutions will win which view professors as researchers, discoverers, innovators and creators.[13] They should be enabled to grow to the level they are capable for. They are a great force in pulling the nation forward. They are an insurance against obsolescence. They should be encouraged and enabled to discover new S and T, write books, research papers, obtain patents, etc. How many of our professors have travelled abroad? How many have written books? How many have published articles in journals? How many have obtained PhD, patents and IPR? Then how shall we inspire younger generation to be innovative, creative? A saying goes "if there is no water in the well from where it will come in bucket"? A change in mind set of people who govern is the need of the hour. An investment in professors to upgrade their knowledge and skill is the first and foremost need. Capacity of colleges to produce more output will increase if the professors grow to the level of their counterparts.

Institutions will succeed which empower professors with necessary freedom to think and freedom to act. This is essential in the interest of public at large. It is they who design and shape the future of the younger generation. They create tomorrow's leaders today. This is a very important job. This should be borne in mind by professors, planners and administrators. Institutions must have to be manned by high quality devoted people. They should be viewed beyond doubt. Professors need encouragement, inspiration and support. They don't need control.

echnical education will take the nation forward are differentiated from government servants. nks. They are like race horses not like horses carts. Institutions will be preferred by students which value not only acquisition of knowledge and storing it in brains but learning innovation skills, creativity and discovery skills and learning to discover unknown are given higher priority. *Students should learn to capitalize on technology, and knowledge.* Institutions will win which make a paradigm shift in the teaching methods in the institutions making use of modern technologies like computer, telecommunications distance education, etc. This is found to bring down the cost yet improve effectiveness. Should we not permit more experimentation?

FINANCIAL STRATEGIES

India needs to increase education budget from present 3 per cent of GDP to 6 per cent, which has been announced by government way back in 1991 and several times, but not yet done. It should be realized that spending on education is far more rewarding. Not spending is a false economy, and certainly planning for failure. Not investing in education is more costly. Mediocre institutes are more costly than the cost of modernization. Do we realize this? It is the education which has failed India. But for education India has lagged behind. India in world eyes is a less educated country. If you do not upgrade the higher and technical education, the economy will weaken, and outside elements may exploit. Let us remember that the institutes are best levelers in development and who create the future. Bright future could be created only if institutes are made world-class. Institutions in Malaysia, Thailand, and Indonesia are investing 10 per cent of their GDP, in education. Why India cannot?

Institutes will be successful which establish technology transfer offices. The know-how possessed by these colleges is very much needed by SSIs and SMEs. The institutions should not run after only big industries that have their own centres. Technical education institutions, students and professors must adopt global perspectives, global mindset. They should attract talent and ideas, like magnet from everywhere and anywhere in the world. They must remain constantly in touch with the market. The world experience tells us that high tech industries are flocking around the institutions which are able to generate new ideas and new technologies. Scientific institutions are a pre-requisite to industrial development. This model is being replicated in China, Japan, Philippines, and all over the world. Institutes will win which open marketing departments and increase their outreach.

Institutions will win which harness strength of their alumni. Alumni associations play a critical role in modernizing the institutes. No world-class institute exists without active alumni association. They bring fresh ideas to institutes to remain in tune with world. So much is demanded from college that all alone an institute cannot give. It must be backed by ideas from alumni who are their ambassadors, so competent and scattered the world over. Regions/nations/cities will develop faster and better where the institutions are excellent. Regions without them even if endowed with plentiful natural resources do not develop well. Regions/nations do not develop where scientific and technological capability of institutions and people is limited. Putting more money and putting more men on the job is good but not enough. What is essential is using current and appropriate strategies, adopting flexible rules and regulations.

Nations will succeed more where innovation fund for students studying in colleges is provided. A national level as well as state level committee needs to be constituted in education to give boost to innovation. Potential of innovation in youths in colleges is high but unexplored. If they develop innovation skills in young age they use them lifelong. If not, it is less likely that they become innovative in service career. Education charged with spirit of discovery and innovation alone can move India forward. Future belongs to those who realize this. Government of India has recently appointed, 2011, a commission on Innovation under the chairmanship of Dr Sam Pitroda. States are advised to constitute similar commissions.

Nations will be progressive which establish new universities and colleges by following principles of scientific project

management. This ensures optimum utilization of resources, in achieving the institutional objectives. The age-old method of sanctioning resources, in government in a piecemeal manner is wasteful, besides missing institutional targets. The old outdated practice should be abandoned forthwith.

In establishing world-class institutions, it is necessary to appoint subject wise "Mentors" from different universities across the world. It is they who by cross fertilization of ideas would create sound academic culture demanded by world around. Best of the professors' subject wise could be chosen and appointed as mentors on long-term basis, for five years or so.

Higher and technical education institutes will be in top demand where teaching and research are treated as inseparable.[14] Every teacher will be a researcher and every researcher a teacher. Nations will be winning in global competition where government makes it a national agenda to educate "every one—lifelong—nonstop" and earmark budget for the same. Keeping skill set of people up to date is of paramount importance.

Nations will be successful where exclusive well-focused technical universities exist. They are spear headed organizations capitalizing on technology. It is these universities which can take the nation forward at a faster pace. Earlier they are established better it is. Nations will win which recognize that education the world over is getting deregulated. It is more due to distance education, open course ware on Internet, reducing monopoly of universities, for profit institutions, etc., Multiple approaches in private and public sectors will grow. Last but not least; nations will be successful which nurture today the young minds for entrepreneurship, so as to ensure that they become global players.

Modern technology can solve many problems in teaching and learning.[15] Do we teach the same old way we learned? It is high time to deviate by blending distance education methods, computer-aided instruction, video films, etc. with classroom teaching. The new methods are cheap and more effective. Institutions will be successful which employ new technology for learning.

CONCLUSION

Foreign institutes are waiting at our doorsteps to enter. Some have already entered. If we delay reformation and delay adoption of above-stated strategies foreign universities may displace Indian institutes, and we may in spite of all brilliant people lose in national and international market. Transformation of an institute to world-class status is a long journey, requiring not only resources but good visions and missions, policies and practices, above all patience.

The task in which world-class institutions are engaged is "The pursuit of learning is not the passive conveyance of information; it is the passing of torch, the sharing of the flame. It is igniting the spirit of leadership, entrepreneurship and innovation". It is not just learning known established facts but learning to discover unknown. Knowledge is infinite.

If the institutions trivialize that responsibility, if they reduce it to distributing the stale food of disarticulated information or limit it to sharing lifeless elements of technical competence, they will fail those who have entrusted them with responsibility, who have upheld their freedom, who have provided them resources, and who have supposed they were meant about doing a greater task. It is recommended that the concerned authorities, in all seriousness shoulder their moral responsibility and prove worthy. Children of India look at them with high hopes.

Higher education drives and is driven by globalization. It has become a vibrant business. Strategies outlined in this paper should therefore be given serious consideration.

How is world-class institution created? What is the world experience? Appointment of meritorious professors' subject wise as mentors, to upgrade academic culture and create scientific research ambience in institutions should be done forthwith. They may be part-time visiting, available on e-mail. Internationalization of education is insurance from obsolescence.

India desperately needs world-class institutions which will provide new generations' top leaders with creative, inclusive, inquiring, engaged and enabling mind. Brave new India of tomorrow is being created today in these temples of knowledge. Well-being of people critically depends on reforms in higher and technical education. Who will make millions of citizens fit to live in modern world? Who will create world- class leadership fit to run a big country, India?

It is the world-class professors working in them who produce able leadership. Therefore, they must be challenged, critically examined and enabled to play an increasingly influential role in preserving traditional knowledge, and rewriting the book of new knowledge. Technology innovation clusters must be started in and around the institutes.

To fire imagination of young, innovation fund must be provided to colleges and polytechnics. Every professor should be given adequate fund for research, right from his appointment, which he should have to multiply further from funding agencies. It will increase innovation capacity of India. Full scope of innovation needs to be explored.

India's future, the future of children and grandchildren depends on the creation of the world-class institutions. Large numbers of institutions in India today are mediocre who can produce only mediocrity, at best produce followers, soldiers fit for recruitment to do lower end jobs in the army of multinationals. At least a few better performing institutions must therefore be enabled forthwith and upgraded to world-class status. This is the only way for India to prosper, which TEQIP is aiming at. All other institutes must aim at that or else they stand a risk of falling behind. Nation is at risk for want of reformation to world-class status. It is therefore recommended that TEQIP is implemented forcefully and expanded to cover many more institutions.

Education is the public obligation of the government. How it fulfills the same decides the future.

If India does not create research-based world-class universities and colleges, and if industry/society does not join them in this mission, the universities and colleges will be providing mediocre leaders, far too low by international standard, to run its national and international affairs.

NOTES

1. Editorial, *Economic Times* of August 21, 2010 entitled "Just two institutions in the world's top 500".
2. H.T. Rhodes, *Role of American University—The Creation of the Future*, Cornell University Press, 2003.
3. Government of India, 2009, Technical Education Quality Improvement Program [TEQIP] Phase-II Project Implementation Plan [PIP].
4. *Ibid.*
5. Government of India, "National Knowledge Commission Report 2006".
6. *Op. cit.*, 1.
7. Government of India, Public Private Partnership—FICCI document on internet 2008.
8. B.M. Naik and W.S. Kandlikar, *Higher and Technical Education*, Gyan Publishing House, 2010.
9. *Op. cit.*, 3.
10. *Op. cit.*, 5.
11. *Op. cit.*, 8.
12. World Bank Working Paper No. 190, "Governance of technical education in India, Key issues, Principles, and Case studies edited by Andreas Blom and Jannette Cheong, 2009".
13. Bush Commissions Report, "Science the Endless Frontier" US academy of sciences, 1945.
14. *Op. cit.*, 4.
15. US Academy of Sciences, "Rising Above the Gathering Storm, 2007".

Chapter 8

Indian Universities and Colleges Need Professionalism in Governance for the Creation of the Future

Universities and colleges need less of inspections, less of audits and control. They need more of inspiration, encouragement, empowerment and freedom to think and freedom to experiment. Future belongs to those who understand this.

ABSTRACT

The paper presents, in brief, need and importance of introducing professionalism in governance and leadership in Indian higher and technical education. This is necessary so as to make most of global opportunities. Opportunities do not last long. They are short lived. They come with risks and challenges. Achievement depends on professionalism in governance and committed leadership. Education has become a global subject. The competition is no more domestic but international. Foreign universities are knocking at our doors. Many have already entered. Indian education market is hot. Governance and leadership is the key determinant of success. Will it improve and come up to expectations? Institutes are reckoned as powerhouses producing leaders and leadership. They need to be governed and groomed well so as produce world-class leaders.

The numbers of students and the institutions have increased tremendously. Yet the gross enrolment ratio is too low in comparison with UK, USA, Indonesia, and Thailand. The numbers of courses and the subjects are advanced and have become innovative in character. Transnational collaborations and networking with similar institutions in India and abroad so also with industry are becoming common. World-class education is eagerly sought. But very few are able to offer. Living up to expectations of students and industry requires universities and colleges to have new organization structures, new systems and procedures, flexibility, international perspectives, global visions and missions. The universities and colleges are now expected to become innovative in character and giving new technology to industry. Students are expected to acquire skills for entrepreneurship, giving birth to start ups in new technology. These are the critical areas which need exploration to generate new jobs and income.

Is present governance up to the task? To cope with challenges the paper suggests adoption of professional management, which demands autonomy. Direct supervision of institution by government and by members of layman trust should be discouraged. Board of governors' model with subject experts is recommended. The paper presents deficiencies in governance and leadership in institutions in India, and suggests improvements. Conclusions are drawn so as to make education globally relevant and purposeful. If India does not improve governance in near future, the Indian economy on global plane may lag behind; the present tempo of good economic growth may not remain sustainable. Professional governance and committed leadership in universities and colleges is necessary condition for their own good health and the health of Indian economy.

Where does India Stand in Global Ranking?

India stands as low as in Olympics. Is it due to poor governance? The editorial in *Economic Times* of 21 August 2010 says, only two institutes/universities, namely IIT-Kharagpur and IISC Bangalore appear in the world's top 500.[1] In sharp contrast 34 universities from China up from 16 in one year find place in the list. Eight out of first ten are from USA. What does this speak about Indian higher education? The editor raised a doubt whether Indian universities are managed like a good academic institute or poorly managed and bureaucratically run like government departments? Are they not professionally managed? Should they be enterprising in nature? How many centres of excellence they have? How many papers they publish? Presently, universities are producing unemployable graduates. National Knowledge Commission (2007) in its report observed that poor governance and leadership is the root cause.[2] What is wanted is not taught and what is taught is not wanted. On one hand, there is unemployment of people and on the other shortage of skilled people. There is a serious mismatch. A survey was conducted on improving technical education. Ninety per cent of the respondents expressed great dissatisfaction and serious inadequacies in governance and leadership at all the levels, namely college, university, state and national. They specifically mentioned about lack of political will. The visions at national and institutional levels are too poor. Value attached to education in practice is too low, so India is behind in education.

Why thousands of students every year go abroad by spending huge sums of money? They are going from Gandhi-Nehru period. How long they will have to go? Are we sensitive to their demands? Why foreign universities are coming in India? The demand is huge. Indians have contributed to raise US universities to high level. When such brilliant people are available in India, why our universities are behind? It is because good people have to work under poor governance and inefficient outdated systems. In spite of having hard working people India falls in the category of low income economies in the world. About 25 per cent people are living below poverty line. Rewards for good education to an individual and to a nation are high, but penalties for poor education are much higher. Crime rate is increasing, Nexalism is growing, and farmers in increasing numbers are committing suicides.

Now one good thing, the government have become conscious of improving the quality. Honbl. Prime Minister had appointed National Knowledge Commission in the year 2005 and Yashpal Committee in 2008. Their recommendations are eye opener and government is in the process of aggressive reforms. The reports observed Indian institutes are not short of resources and talent, but they are short of good systems for governance and leadership. They need more inputs of proper systems. Some of them are[3],

Establishment of National Commission for Higher Education and Research

- Public private partnership
- Inviting leading professors rather than foreign universities
- Establish single discipline universities
- Autonomy and governance (subject of this paper)
- Industry institute interaction.

Indian industry thus far was propelled by foreign. Can Indian academics propel now? Knowledge is power especially technical. It is the real capital. It changes the lives of people. It converts a liability into an asset. Higher and technical education institutes are the seats of learning, which have a mandate to create, preserve and disseminate knowledge. Knowledge institutions are in driver's seat. They have achieved critical importance in development. They, as never before, have come to the centre of national economic and social endeavour.

Can India, in interdependent world, ever become a developed nation without making higher and technical education globally competitive? It is they who produce leaders in technology, leaders in industry, politics, and all other walks of life. Leaders of tomorrow are strolling today in the campus of universities and colleges.[4] As a society have we failed so far, to provide them world-class infrastructure and world-class academic culture?

Why only 30 per cent graduates are employable? Lack of good governance and lack of able leadership is mainly the cause. Can and should higher and technical education really change, in global context? Research which should go hand in hand with education is hived off to specialist institutions, namely to CSIR labs, that do not teach. Research in educational institute does double duty. Firstly, new knowledge is generated at cheap cost, and secondly it is transferred to younger generation. Linkages with industry are weak, and parallel entry from commercial practice to academics, almost is non-existent. They lack autonomy to experiment. Should autonomous model not be used in governance? Should it be made open and democratic? Is overcoming inertia a problem? How to raise funds for education? How visionary, imaginative and responsible are the boards of governance and governing councils? Is higher education going enterprising? How Board of governors can be made more effective? How to abandon mediocrity? These are some of the questions, and challenges addressed in this paper.

Autonomy and Accountability—To Achieve Global Standard

World experience tells us that the successful Higher and Technical Education institution of 21st century will be that which maintains institutional autonomy, lively faculty, independence, and vigorous academic freedom, but should enjoy strong, impartial, public governance and decisive committed institutional leadership. All winning institutions, world over, are essentially autonomous. Professors and students ought to have freedom to be innovative and creative. Autonomous status is a prerequisite to be globally competitive. Government, UGC, AICTE are encouraging institutions to be autonomous. Colleges, university, boards of management are learning to use autonomy effectively. They should do so fast. They need to take in to account international experience.

Nations are prosperous where institutes are autonomous,[5] **creativity and imagination nursed.** An autonomous institution signifies its overall ability to act by its own choices in pursuit of its chosen missions. Autonomy is a dynamic participative model of governance based on continuous evaluation of performance. The evaluation need be done at regular intervals by internal as well as external agencies. Autonomy means freedom to think and freedom to act, but freedom implies accountability and responsibility. Autonomy means self-determination, self-control and self-regulation with least interference from external sources. Autonomy implies going away from government closer to its own students, faculty and industry. Bureaucracy and politics destabilize education. For example, professors are transferred more out of whims and fancies. Policies change with the change in government. They should grant funds but not interfere. Capping imagination of institutions and students by government should be avoided. Autonomy means internal debates, discussions. Autonomy enables to make best utilization of available resources, available ideas to harvest opportunities.[6] Council of Europe Conference, 2003 said institutes have to be autonomous at the heart, to be able to meet needs of world around it. Autonomous institutions think great, beyond government, in global context.

Autonomy stimulates excellence. Starting more number of colleges and universities in India is good, but not enough. More autonomy, creativity, innovation, imagination is needed. Institutions by using autonomy over a period of years are found to become innovative and rich in terms of knowledge. Knowledge and decision is distributed throughout the organization. Creativity and innovation, trust and confidence, are the main pillars on which institutions rest. They attract brains from anywhere and everywhere. Scholars dream to study in them. The professors think great in global context. And provide guidance to government, corporations and other bodies, in respect of public policies. Autonomy enables professors to be equal to world-class professors. This is so essential to make institutions world-class. They need to use new technology to produce more with fewer resources.

An autonomous institution has an inbuilt mechanism to reform continuously. It should be allowed to function even if it fails, for failure teaches important lessons. There is a tendency to fall back on old system when autonomy does not succeed. This falling back should be avoided. These are the teething troubles. Freedom in any case should not be curbed. Government should not interfere and kill its self-improvement capacity. These autonomous institutions by virtue of self-control are a security for the economic future of India. It is a world proven model of governance. American council on Education in its report "Shifting Ground-Autonomy-Accountability and Privatization in Public Higher Education of 2004" observed that autonomous status has elevated the scholarship, and economic performance of US ahead of European counterparts.[7]

EXPERIENCE

Indian Experience. IITs were born autonomous. Experience of IITs in using autonomy has been too good. It is because of autonomy that they could shine in world. This autonomous model is recommended by several education commissions starting from Radhakrishnan Commission, then Kothari Commission in 1966, new education policy 1986. Now National Knowledge Commission 2006 has recommended. Yashpal Committee 2009 has strongly advocated. Not many colleges in India have yet become autonomous. Why? Change from affiliating to autonomous status is not easy but difficult. If an institution right from birth is autonomous like IIT it is easy. Why universities have not taken a drive to promote autonomy on these lines? Are universities an obstacle to autonomy? India needs better governance to promote innovation. Poor quality in education is not really education at all. It a result of weak and improper governance. Technology push from institutes and market pull from industry are critical to good health of economy. But technology push is missing. Market demand for technology is abundant. Academic freedom is usurped by non academics. Spin-offs from research, patent and IPR enable to get more value out of investment in universities and colleges. They increase the rate of return. Do we realize this? How many of the Indian universities have set up incubation centres, research parks, obtained patents, spin-off New Technology Based Firms (NTBF)? This is what their counterparts have been doing from years in developed countries. Japan has research companies on the periphery of universities. Why and how they are flocking round the universities? Are we using yesterday's technology to solve the problems of today? The challenge is to make a social transformation in favour of down and out people.

Governance of self-finance institutions in India, is posing a serious problem. It is a flash point of crisis. This is the central issue for discussions in State Assemblies and Parliament. Turmoil is breeding everywhere, because of rising fees in self-finance colleges. Pretty strong signals that something is not quite right are being received. Policymakers and educators need to listen to their voice. It is feared that majority of the bottom 50 per cent population are not able to send their children to college. It is hoped that the governing boards of these institutions will show wisdom will recognize their obligation to community, region and world. Avoiding exploitation of students in them is a challenge. Autonomy facilitates to provide an answer.

International Experience. The higher education institutes in USA enjoy a high degree of autonomy. Government is reluctant to interfere in their affairs. Government grants them funds but it governs them indirectly through the governing board. Institutes are far too away from government. Institutions ensure that education is affordable and qualitative. Founder president of USA Mr. Thomas Jefferson gave the principle, that world-class institutions are a pre-condition to make a nation economically and politically world-class. Formation of responsible board of governance, executive council is the important lesson we ought to learn from USA.[8]

Unique feature of UK is that government has funded the creation of Quality Assurance agencies. Government has handed over monitoring of the institutions to these QA agencies. Also funding agencies monitor them in their own ways.[9] Internal and external examiners are prescribed for each course. Every institution has a senate to control quality of education. They have prepared a code of practice. Collaboration between the institutions is prescribed.

European trends in governance,[10] this stemmed from the recognition that a higher degree of institutional autonomy would improve governance and strengthen leadership at all levels. Governments are urged to endorse the principle of institutional autonomy so as to accommodate diverse institutional missions and to include:

- Academic autonomy (curricula, programs and research)
- Financial autonomy (Lump sum budgeting)
- Organizational autonomy (the structure of the university)
- Staffing autonomy (responsibility for recruitment, salaries and promotion)

University association is committed to identifying supplementary revenue streams and promoting modes of governance that supports optimal transparency in financial management.

The 46 Bologna process countries are moving towards greater autonomy. Rates of progress are however different. The European Universities Association supports the European Commission's goal to invest at least 2 per cent of GDP in higher education. Mediocre institutes are more costly than the cost of their upgradation. Do we realize this?

The Republic of Korea,[11] increasing institutional autonomy remains a government priority. However, it is a slow process. It believes sweeping changes are neither desirable nor feasible. They are progressing step by step, in an incremental manner.

In Japan,[12] internal quality assurance system is closely linked with the external. This is the essential feature of governance system. Accreditation procedure prescribes a healthy system to "plan, do, check and action" cycle, which is the quality assurance tool. As a result of this procedure, all universities have now their own internal evaluation system. This is a good aspect of governance system of Japan.

STRATEGIC DIRECTIONS NEEDED

Following strategies to make autonomy successful are needed.

Envision creating imaginative leaders for future. Importance of academic institutions in today's volatile time of globalization is very high. It is they who are furthering human civilization to greater heights. It is the academicians who provide new knowledge, new theories, and new technology and can provide competent manpower to business and industry. They are supposed to provide learned leaders to government and to the total economy. This in turn creates wealth and comforts. Industry, society and government in return ought to provide funds to academics to make it grow. India can be richer only by use of advanced knowledge. There is no other way. It very much matters for India, what kind of leaders institutions produce. Are Indian institutes aiming at producing global leaders including those for academic institutions? Do the key people have love of upbringing of students? They have to have unlimited, fathomless love like one's own sons and daughters.

Adopt strategy to orient governance to harvest global job opportunities. Want to be globally competitive? It essentially demands change. The world under the forces of globalization is changing fast. Only those who change to innovate again and again can only educate the youths on correct lines. Students now demand world-class education. They are ready to pay for in terms of time, effort and money. But where do you find such institutions? IITs are very few. Thousands are going abroad by spending huge sums of money. Universities and colleges in India will have to be competitive by nothing less than world standard. Education now is a global subject. Foreign universities have come in India. Where do the Indian institutions fall short? Have we made a gap analysis between Indian institutes and their counterparts abroad? Why are our universities woefully unsuited to the quality demands of globalization? Why they are far too behind their counterparts in developed world? Indian men and women intellectually are too good. They have contributed in American universities and made them forerunner. In India similar people fall too short because they are under poor governance, poor systems and procedures. We need to make introspection, especially in the light of world-proven policies and practices. Do our institutions lack proper visions of new world? The present method of governance which is under the "grip of government" is age old. It needs to be changed and made competitive in global context. How can the institutions become autonomous, and have effective governing boards? This is a challenge before Indian academicians.

Good governance can reduce cost, make education qualitative and affordable. Models of governance in institutions vary from government funding and government control to self-finance and private control. In either and almost all cases universities and colleges in India are poorly managed. The world-class academic culture is totally missing. It is a challenge before the leaders in education, as to how to install good governance.

The academicians are kept away from decision makers. They cannot bring to the notice of planners, how important education is? Indian academicians are less successful in influencing the government for reforming education. This is their main weakness.[13] Role of academicians must forthwith be integrated in public policy at government, urban and rural levels.

Future of children and grandchildren is hidden in institutes today.[14] Debate is going on round the world on the subject of governance and leadership of the universities and colleges and their relationship with the government of respective countries. Experts in academics and government consider that there is an acute need and great scope to improve. Lack of proper governance is observed to be causing Lapses in education, causing the efforts of development less fruitful. The traditional government-dominated model will not suffice the complex situations of today to overcome problems. People are paying heavy price for such lapses. Millions are living below the poverty line. It is needless to say that development of India can be greatly accelerated by creating an educated citizenry. Higher and technical education is a critical input for development especially in present knowledge based economy. Increasing the capacity of higher education institutes in terms of quality and quantity is the first and foremost challenge.[15] Proper governance will be achieved by autonomy.

Adopt strategy to reduce the "grip of government". Boards of governance should have full sense of responsibility and accountability. The vice chancellor is appointed by government. Here political considerations dominate and the person selected is not necessarily the best. Moreover, the vice chancellor is under the obligation of the government. Professors are like government servants. They have no autonomy and no resources to innovate. They have to fall in line with the government policy, which is often non academic. The university acts are age old, resulting in poor governance and leadership. The system of State Governor as ex-officio chancellor of universities is age old. Now chancellorship is a specialized full time job. Part time Chancellor, howsoever competent an individual may be, is too inadequate. The problems remain inadequately analysed and they continue, cost of which is paid by students and the nation. It is a time to appoint full-time chancellor with specialization in education.

This is necessary so that institutions can determine their own strategies and take more responsibility for their own growth and prosperity besides financial sustainability. With their imagination they could dream and execute desirable activities far beyond the government thinking.

The higher and technical education today, is sensitive to global winds of change. Yet it has to be locally relevant and purposeful. The variations in parameters such as job requirements, generation of new knowledge, aspirations of students, etc. are so frequent that they could best be attended by institutions themselves. Giving them autonomy, to take care of their sensitivities and responsiveness, is essential. The role of government it is observed should therefore be restricted to regulation and supervision. The remotely located civil servants and legislature have to change their traditional role from rowing to steering, or from micro-regulation to meta-regulation, government control to government supervising.[16] For this government, although it provides financial aid, prescribes a board of governors of most qualified and competent men, for each institution who will take care of the public interest and link institutions closely to development goals of the nation.

Institutions will be successful only if the mechanism of governance at all levels, i.e. governmental, university and college levels is modernized by using scientific approaches. It should be made flexible, participative, and responsive to the aspirations of students. Government is devising policies and practices so as to make it inclusive. E-Governance is recommended.[17]

What is Good Governance?[18]

Good governance maintains connections with their counterparts elsewhere in the world. It permits mobility for professor's world over. Lack of mobility is more costly than the cost of mobility. Do we realize this? Indian higher education is almost disconnected and so it is far too behind. Professors need to be enabled to grow to the level of their counterparts abroad. Institutions cannot be big by keeping professors small.

Good governance is that which facilitates decision-making rational, informed and transparent, and leading to organizational efficiency and effectiveness. An important characteristic of good governance is that of probity, that is to say working honestly, earnestly with integrity for public good. Government should not dictate the governing body. Governing body should have to assert autonomy and accountability to the interests of all stakeholders. The governing body should unambiguously be responsible for overseeing the institute's activities, and determine the future directions. It should essentially foster an environment in which institutional mission can be achieved, enabling learners to reach to their full potential. An institution should be thinking body, not a slave of old outdated rules.

Government therefore recommends formation of board of governors for each institution.[19] Institutions have to develop new capacities for internal governance when the locus of responsibility for decisions about student examination, curriculum design, staffing, and the use of financial resources are shifted to institutional level. Composition of governing body has to be more or less the same for both the government-aided institutions and self finance institutions.

Characteristics of a good academic leader, principal/director/ vice chancellor.[20] Good institutional leader is of paramount importance for success. He ought to possess the following characteristics.

Director has to be a professor, leader, a magnificent speaker, a good writer, a good public relations officer, a man of iron health and stamina. He should have spiritual qualities. He should have honesty, integrity and good value system in favour of public good. He should be good in administration delegating adequately to others. He should be a great scholar, a social philosopher mobilizing public opinion. He should be a friend of a common man. He should bear in mind that future leaders of the world are sitting in his classrooms, and then make decisions. He has to frame the institution mission, goals. Everything else will depend on mission and goals. He should not think in smaller terms but make great dreams. He should remember that there can be no great creations without a great dream. He should be able to articulate the visions. He should be successful in creating the campus climate, recruiting the team, and providing resources to achieve the set goals. He should set an atmosphere of trust and confidence, take initiative, and build partnerships, inside and outside. He should reward achievement and reward success. At times he should take risk to break rules, in tune with time without selfish motive. He should frequently meet students, faculty, alumni, and everyone in campus. He creates leaders who will carry human civilization to greater heights. He should have high level commitment. He should be able to charge the people working with him with mental energy, ideas and give winning strategies. He should be fund raising and friend rising. He has to lead every activity in the campus.

Most of the industrial and political leaders in various countries in the world are educated in USA. US is producing leaders not only for self but the whole world. This is a proof of quality of their education. Best brains from every country dream to study in US.

LEADERS MATTER

There is a story of two armies which were fighting a battle with each other. One army had a lion as its captain, but the soldiers were sheep. The second army had a sheep as its captain but the soldiers were lions. The lion captain employees bold strategies. The other captain a sheep designs strategies like a coward and looses battle although his soldiers are lions, because the soldiers have to follow the strategies drawn by captain. It is the leader which matters most. The importance of principal in institution is very high. Shivaji had a smaller army than Aurangzeb. But his strategies were superior and so he could win in war. In an institution resources matter but the strategies to use resources matter more. An institution with lesser resources but better leader and strategies will win over another with more resources, badly used.

Institutions need imaginative and responsible BOG. Today's leaders were students yesterday. Tomorrow's professional pacesetters are today's graduate students. The future leaders of

India and the world stroll today across our college campus; future lawmakers, judges, chief engineers and CEO sit in university classrooms. The task in which institutions are engaged—the pursuit of learning—is not the passive conveyance of information; it is the passing of torch, the sharing of the flame. It is igniting the spirit of entrepreneurship and innovation. If the BOG of institutions trivialize that responsibility, if they reduce it to distributing the stale food of disarticulated information or limit it to sharing lifeless elements of technical competence, they will fail those who have entrusted them with responsibility, who have upheld their freedom, who have provided them resources, and who have supposed they were meant about doing a greater task.[21] India disparately needs BOG to create institutions which will provide new generations' creative, inclusive, inquiring, engaged and enabling leaders that will come out of the higher education institutions. Brave India of tomorrow is being created today in these temples of knowledge. Well-being of people critically depends on reforms in higher and technical education. It is this prestigious institution that must be challenged and enabled to play an increasingly influential role in preserving traditional knowledge, and rewriting the book of new knowledge. BOG members and the principal should essentially show high sense of responsibility and base their decisions on above stated principles.

Good governance and leadership comes out of using the following approaches.

Appointing Board of Governors[22]

The governing body acts as a custodian of the values, purpose and mission of the institution. Principal who is the executive head formulates them after wide circulation and consultation. He presents them to BOG in meeting for approval. An autonomous institute has a right of self-determination and self-government. BOG is unambiguously and collectively responsible for overseeing the institution's activities. Determining its future directions, and foster an environment in which the institution's mission can be achieved, allowing the potential of the learners to be maximised.

The chair of BOG is responsible for the leadership of that body and has the ultimate responsibility for its effectiveness. The chair has a particular responsibility for effective communication with stakeholders. The principal as chief executive is responsible for advice to BOG in relation to strategic direction and is accountable to BOG for effective management of the institution. There needs to be absolute clarity in the distinction between the governing function of the governing body and executive responsibility of the principal and the executive team lead by him or her. Governing function is described by the saying, "Noses in-Fingers out".

Board should conduct evaluation of departments, activities wherever it receives foul smell.

Functions of the Board of Governors

- Take all policy decisions with regard to smooth cost effective and timely implementation of the institution activities.
- Form, supervise and guide various committees required for implementation and internal evaluation, monitoring.
- Evaluate self-performance, and institution performance.
- Ensure overall faculty development, and to create academic leaders.
- Enable implementation of reforms.
- Ensure proper utilization of funds, timely submission of financial management reports, and utilization certificates.
- Preparing master plan of the institution.
- Select the director of the institute, and other personnel.
- Create an environment favourable for learning.
- Award scholarships, free ships, etc.
- Collaborate with other institutions nationally and internationally.
- Give new visions of new world to employees.
- Adopt annual statement of accounts and submit it to government.
- Create service manual.

- Adopt policies for disadvantaged people.
- Overcoming inertia in the organization.
- Fund raising for education.
- Make the institution enterprising.

Each institution will have to have its own BOG as per guidelines of UGC. The BOG will in all cases be headed by an eminent industrialist/engineering education expert.

UGC Guidelines for composition to make BOG more effective are given below

Three persons one of them to be the chairman—Educationist, industrialist or professional—Nominated by government. Persons of proven academic interest with at least PG level qualification

Two Members—faculty of the institution—nominated by principal

One Member—educationist or industrialist—nominated by principal

One Member—UGC nominee

One Member—State Government nominee

One Member—University nominee

One Member—Principal of the institution ex-officio.

Two members of the faculty on board of governors along with principal are essential. Only principal on GB is not enough. It is the professors who maintain links of the board with faculty staff and students. If they are not on board, it is likely that the board may not get true picture of the institution, and the decisions may go wrong. The board then tends to become external, which defeats the principle of autonomy. It is observed that government and principal have a tendency to avoid taking professors on board. This should be avoided for it is too damaging for maintaining good health of the institution.

Constitution of Governing Body of Private Unaided Autonomous Institution

Five Members—of Management—of trust or management as per the constitution or bye-laws, with the chairman or president/director as the chairperson

Two Members—faculty of the institution, nominated by the principal based on seniority

One Member—educationalist or industrialist, nominated by management

One Member—UGC nominee

One Member—State government nominee

One Member—University nominee

One Member—Principal of institution.

The minutes of the meeting should be published on institutions website as promptly as possible.

What do We Conclude?

"Civilization is on the brink of new industrial order. The winners in the increasingly fierce scramble for supremacy will not be those who simply make commodities faster and cheaper than the competition. They will be those who develop talent, technologies, techniques, and tools so advanced that there is no competition."[23]

- Good governance is that which takes into account global winds of change. It should give international perspectives to students and enable them to acquire global competitiveness.
- Government should not put a cap on the imagination of institutions, professors and students. They should be encouraged to think and act freely in wide variety way in global context.
- Government should put full trust and confidence in institutes both private and aided and their BOG; empower and if necessary reorient them to carry out their designated public roles without government intervention.
- Solution to improve higher education lies in mobilizing funds from several sources including abroad, and in making their effective utilization, which essentially requires autonomy. But for autonomy public and private funds are less mobilized and used less productively, besides targets missed.

- In addition, institutions should be prescribed by accreditation procedure to follow internal quality assurance system, namely, "plan, do, check, and action".
- All world-class institutions are autonomous, managed and maintained by responsible governing boards, using quality assurance techniques. BOG members should not only take honours and respects but give service to society.
- UGC/AICTE should give choice to an institution to be autonomous at its start. Today the choice is not available. Institutions starting in affiliation mode find it difficult to unlearn practices of affiliation and switch on to autonomous. Institutions born in affiliation mode are like children born handicapped. As difficult it is to remove a handicap so difficult it is to convert an institution from affiliating mode to autonomous.
- Nations are prosperous where institutions are autonomous. Successful use of autonomy will enhance the chances of India becoming a world leader. Government aided or private self-financed institutions, ought to have effective board of governors.
- The BOG should show statesmanship, high skills and knowledge in creating high quality governance and leadership. If they do not do so, they would fail those who have entrusted them the responsibility. They should remember they are producing today future leaders of India and the world. The future generations will not pardon them for the lapses, if any.
- A culture of self-regulation, self-planning and monitoring, trust and confidence must be nurtured in the institution.
- Grip of government on education should reduce. Governor of the state should not be the chancellor of universities. Chancellorship is now not a decorative post but a specialised job. The complexities are too many. He should be a full time academician. Present

system of governor as ex-officio part time chancellor is too inadequate for the purpose. It should be done away forthwith.

- State budget should increase to 2 per cent of GDP up from 0.67 per cent. Patent and IPR, spin-off companies should augment return from investment. Creating culture of innovation, which is the Guru Mantra, should not be forgotten. This remained neglected so far. Universities should envision propelling industrial growth, and corporate development.
- Good academic leaders are crucial for winning in world competition. Professors, principals, vice chancellors should be judiciously selected and appointed keeping public interest in view. This alone will secure the future of India.
- Institutions have now to be enterprising producing entrepreneurs in new technology-based areas.

What drives employment is the research and innovation. Resources in research, innovation and education are the most important growth stimulating instruments today.

NOTES

1. Editorial in *Economic Times* of August 21, 2010, "Just two institutions in the world's top 500 institutions".
2. Government of India, "National Knowledge Commission report 2006-2007".
3. Arun Nigvekar, World Bank working Paper No. 190. Governance of Technical Education in India.
4. Frank H.T. Rhodes, *Role of American University: The Creation of the Future*, Cornell University Press, 2003.
5. B.M. Naik and W.S. Kandlikar, *Higher and Technical Education—Book of Knowledge*, 2010, Gyan Publishing House.
6. Report of Europe Conference, 2003, entitled "Institutional Autonomy and Higher Education Governance".
7. American council on Education Report 2004 entitled "Shifting Ground-Autonomy-Accountability and privatization in Public Higher Education".

8. Aims McGuiness, senior Associate of National centre for Higher education Management Systems (NCHEMS) in the United States and former chair of Board of Trustees of the state colleges in Colorado. World Bank working paper No. 190.
9. Andrew Cubie, Chair of the Court of Napier University, World Bank working paper No. 19.
10. *Op. cit.*, 8.
11. *Ibid.*
12. Tsutomu Kimura, President of the National Institute of Academic Degrees and university evaluation in Japan and former president of Tokyo Institute of Technology. World Bank paper No. 190.
13. *Op. cit.*, 5.
14. World Bank working paper No. 190, "Governance of Technical Education in India, Key Issues, Principles, and Case Studies." Edited by Andreas Blom and Jannette Cheong.
15. Glen A. Jones, Patricia L. McCanney and Michael L. "Creating Knowledge, Strengthening Nations, The Changing role of Higher Education" University of Toronto Press, 2003 .
16. *Op. cit.*, 14.
17. Government of India, Yashpal Committee Report, 2009.
18. *Op. cit.*, 14.
19. Government of India, Technical Education Quality Improvement Program (TEQIP) Phase-II, "Project Implementation Plan" (PIP) December 2009, Government of India.
20. *Op. cit.*, 4.
21. *Ibid.*
22. *Op. cit.*, 19.
23. US Academy of Sciences, *Rising above the Gathering Storm*, 2007, available on Internet.

Chapter 9

Universities and Colleges can Do Better: They Need World-Class Visions to Compete on Innovation

Education charged with spirit of discovery and innovation alone can move a nation forward. Future belongs to those understand this.

ABSTRACT

The conventional wisdom in higher education which once served well is no fit for today and tomorrow. The time demands revolutionary changes to promote innovation and entrepreneurship. Institutions must act fast to reform; otherwise foreign universities are likely to take away the Indian education market.

Conventional teaching in classrooms is good, but not enough. Higher education institutions, without centres on campus for technological innovation, entrepreneurship development, patent and technology transfer, venture capital, hi-tech start ups, spin-off of companies and spin-off of technologies are incomplete, irrelevant and non-viable in modern sense. If India dreams to be a developed nation by the year 2020 the present higher education system needs to be strengthened urgently in respect of above stated centres. They have to be able to provide "Technology Push" matching with "Market Pull" and turn out graduates as leaders who are in short supply. They have to redesign their systems to generate new knowledge and new technologies ahead of others. The present departmental store approach, distributing knowledge generated elsewhere in the world is unfit for the purpose. They will have to install systems as WELL SPRINGS of new knowledge.

How can the institutions remain ahead of time? Institutions have to establish above-stated centres afresh in their campuses, essentially in partnership or in association with industry. Restructuring in the context of global changes has to be the main item on national agenda, without which the intellectual resource will continue to be wasted and opportunities missed. AICTE and UGC should have to do bench marking with the best in the world and make gap analysis. This is urgent because our institutions follow only that which these apex bodies prescribe.

The key factor behind unemployment is insufficient innovation. Shortage of people with innovation skills is a major barrier in employment generation. Universities, colleges and polytechnics which have a major influence on nation's capacity for innovation should have to resort to new strategies. They would have to install systems to generate new ideas and new technology for industry and help them to win. Indian higher education institutes must recognize the full scope of the innovation phenomenon. They should produce leaders, and captains for industry of world standards.

STATEMENT OF THE PROBLEM

On one hand, there is so much of unemployment amongst educated youths and on the other hand, there is a shortage of entrepreneurs to develop innovative enterprises. There is abundance of natural resources on one hand and shortage of finished goods and services on the other hand. Lucrative opportunities due to lack of entrepreneurs are either dying or being taken away by foreigners. There is an influx of goods from East and West countries in Indian market. Indian industry unfortunately is far too behind the world. India ranks as low as 42nd in industrial competitiveness, and 127th in Human Development Index. Government has set a goal to build India a developed nation by the year 2020. So as to accomplish this, young engineers urgently need to depart from their conventional approach and focus their attention on innovation and entrepreneurship. Higher education institutions in partnership with industry, in this cause, have a key role to play. They ought to become business oriented, with focus on spin-off of hi-tech start-ups. They ought to capitalize on emerging technology. Can they provide "Technology Push" matching with "Market Pull" on sustainable basis? The present frame of universities and colleges without innovation and entrepreneurship centres is not competitive enough to produce leaders of world-class standard. They are producing good soldiers, which is necessary but not enough. They need to produce competent captains to lead in industry and economy. To be able to become so they are going abroad every year, in increasing numbers.

Universities need to be enlarged forthwith to cover centres like technology innovation relay centre, entrepreneurship development centre, technology, incubator, business incubator, research park, venture capital foundation, technology park, patent and IPR centre, industrial services centre, technology transfer and marketing centre, corporate education centre, which are existing from last more than 50 years in counterpart institutions in developed countries. It is on account of this that those nations have prospered. IITs, IISc have recently started such centres in their campuses.

Institutions should have to initiate a movement for creation of New Technology-based Firms (NTBF) and venture capital foundations. It is a new dimension to be added to our present university and college campuses. They function as profit centres. They are not a liability on university finances, but generate wealth, which subsidizes cost of education and makes education relevant to market needs.

Prof. Terman in 1950 observed that,

> Industry so as to remain competitive globally needs access to first-class research in universities. So also the first-class researchers in universities need access to industry so as to commercialize their research findings.

There is a greater need of University Related Research Parks (URRP) in India. Parks in isolation from academic institutions being set up are good but cannot substitute URRP. These centres have to be the key players. They have to be the drivers of technological revolution.

A formal policy of technological innovation in higher education is urgently needed to drive the spirit of innovation and entrepreneurship as a far-reaching change in society, and not just to target potential entrepreneurs.

Need to Produce Leaders in Technology and Leaders in Industry

It was presumed in good old days that new technology could be discovered only abroad. Our colleges, universities and companies used to be happy to become best followers. We have been as a result constantly buying the technologies and they are selling. But now Indian talent has become conscious of its capabilities. It has become ambitious to discover new technologies ahead of others. Indians in Silicon Valley have made a mark. It is observed that students, who learn to innovate in college days, are better suited to discover unknown in service career. They are fit to lead in world market. Students who aspire to become leaders in technology and leaders in industry should have necessarily to acquire skills to generate new technologies, new products and new processes and obtain patents. It is realized that

> The key factor behind unemployment is insufficient technological innovation and entrepreneurship.

Do the institutes possess visions and missions to generate new knowledge? Have they nurtured culture to produce new technologies? Visions are in short supply and not the capabilities or the resources. We need to acquire them from world-class institutions. Low aim is a crime.

Why do thousands of students go abroad for higher education? They have been going from pre-independence period. How many more years they may have to go? Can all those who desire go? What are the things which foreign universities teach, but we do not? Unless we teach students skills of innovation, skills for generation of new technologies, skills for discovery of new knowledge, patent and IPR, our institutes will remain behind the time and the outflow of talent will continue. Their institutions are innovative in character, our institutions are conservative. Foreign universities live today as if future has arrived, we exist today as we existed in past. They teach sunrise technologies we teach sunset technologies. They produce leaders we produce followers. They lead a change we follow the change. They are engines of growth, we remain bogies. They are not afraid of change, we are. They practice creative destruction.

The challenge now is to create a knowledge-based society. It is that society in which new knowledge is not only used but also generated. The mindset of key people in UGC and AICTE needs to be reframed in favor of creating hi-tech entrepreneurship rather than to prepare youths with knowledge for employment in Multi National Corporations. Equipping universities in respect of innovation infrastructure is a crying need to achieve the desired goal.

Technological innovation is an essential precondition for growth, maintaining employment and competitiveness. An innovative person never remains unemployed on the contrary he is more in demand. He has a mission in his life, which gives him extra energy and purpose. An innovative person constantly strives to improve. He is always dissatisfied with the prevalent. He wants to create new and again new. The innovation is progressing constantly on the strengths of new ideas of such scholar persons. Can the institutions produce such innovative persons more in number? If they do so institutions will be more in demand like Oxford and Cambridge.

Innovation is Indispensable

Ideas are the real capital. Ideas are needed to succeed. They come from innovation. Idea generated is opportunity generated. Idea killed is opportunity killed.

> Knowledge memorized and stored in brains is important, but more important is the ability to discover new knowledge, new theories and new ideas.

Institutions are the legitimate places, the crucibles of experimentation, for the manufacture of ideas. It is their prime function. They have no reason to exist if they do not do so.

The importance of innovation to the country's economic future should be realized and infrastructure as stated above provided forthwith in higher education institutions. This will avoid the shortage of suitable persons for innovation and entrepreneurship, which is found to be a major barrier in employment generation.

Most of the students in colleges and polytechnics learn in a passive way. Students learn quietly what is handed over to them. They learn through transmission and are not guided to take active hand in creation of technologies. What did the famous philosopher Socrates teach his students? He taught how to raise questions. That means institutes have necessarily to ignite the creative minds of students.

The competency of work force today is measured in terms of its ability to innovate. People have to be innovative to see ahead of others the incoming opportunities.

India possesses the largest pool of youthful work force and high quality human capital. This is our competitive advantage. We ought to prepare youths for global needs.

Commercial Exploitation of Brand New Technology

Invention when exploited commercially is known as innovation. Research conducted in universities, colleges and polytechnics often results in publication of wonderful papers, but rarely results in commercial exploitation. Thesis written mostly remains on shelf. No conscious effort is made to obtain economic value from them, mainly because teaching in this direction is lacking. Students do not get opportunity to learn to convert inventions into usable goods and services. To that extent skill set of students, in spite of potential, remains deficient. This in addition reduces utility of research done and reduces the rate of return on investment.

It is a good sign that higher education in India is growing. But acquisition of skills for commercial exploitation, which is the demand of time, is lagging.

Multifaceted units in partnership with industry, like research park, innovation centre, patent and technology, transfer centre, entrepreneurship development centre, incubator, venture capital foundation, IPR centre, etc., which constitute innovation infrastructure, is found to lead to creation on enterprising atmosphere enabling students to acquire innovation skills more the commercialization of technology more is the wealth generation. In developed countries, innovation in academic institutes is a usual practice. This has generated a wave of entrepreneurship facilitating students and the whole community to be creative, tapping the market in the whole world. USA produces leaders who employ followers from countries like India. Unfortunately, this wave of creativity, leadership and outward looking culture is yet to reach the Indian shores.

A NEW VISION OF NEW WORLD

How long students should keep learning knowledge generated by others elsewhere in the world? How long they should join the army of foreign companies, serve in supporting roles and be content with that? If the necessary infrastructure is provided some of the students, if not all, would certainly become "First Movers" the institutes and students need to dream high, in tune with global competitiveness. Learning innovation enables students to consolidate their knowledge of basics. Innovation centre is more than a learning place. It gives an inspiration to students besides generating economic surplus. The role of institutions in vision development should not be under estimated.

Innovation in education institutes in India is conspicuously absent.

Students do not get global perspectives. This is a serious lacuna. The institutes without innovation are truly incomplete in modern sense. They still follow an old outdated model whose, educational and financial efficiency is too less. They live in past, while their counterparts abroad are ahead of time.

Quality of technical education and research can substantially be enhanced and returns on investment increased if innovation policy in universities colleges and polytechnics is introduced.

Joblessness and industrial slowdown is a result of lack of innovation. When shall we realize this? The situation is to innovate or die. Hence, Government of India has launched the following program.

Quality Improvement Program

For reformation of higher and technical education, Government of India has recently launched a massive program, termed as Technical Education Quality Improvement Program (TEQIP). The objectives are, to impart world-class education, to enable students to grow to the level they are capable for, so also reduce dependence on foreign technology.

From what is reported it is observed that the scheme is good, well formulated in many respects but in competitive environment it lacks a step towards "Technological Innovation". Modernization of laboratories, library, classrooms, faculty development as usual are essential but not sufficient it is necessary to think differently, think great going beyond current practice. It is necessary to design new organization structure oriented towards innovation, and enable students to acquire enterprising skills equal to, if not more than their counterparts abroad, which is the need of the hour. This is to say that institutions must provide a portal through which all the students compulsorily should have to pass through, for practice of commercial exploitation of the new knowledge that is to say new technology. They should target their efforts towards production of marketable technologies, patents, etc. The students should have to do some field surveys to identify level of technology used, productivity, and difficulties in using the latest technology.

Can Higher Education Institutes Give New Ideas, Leadership to Help Industry to Win?

Surveys conducted elsewhere in the world indicate that NTBF started by young entrepreneurs with origin in academic institutions are far more successful than those started by persons with experience in industry. Academic institutions provide a powerful engine to launch the new technology-based enterprises and thereby generate employment.

According to a new item published recently, "India slipped to 21st rank from 13th in number of scientific output." The PhDs produced in engineering are only 293 (1998) as against China 2900 and 5930 in USA. The number of graduates produced in USA are almost double than in India. Yet all get jobs or become self-employed. Still they have a shortfall. To meet the same they invite engineers from abroad. This is mainly because they produce larger number of PhDs. Who constantly explore new opportunities, everywhere and anywhere in the world.

A critical examination of the schemes of technical education in the light of global winds of change, so as to avoid mistakes is essential. If the infrastructures like entrepreneurs centre, research park, incubator, innovation centre, venture capital fund, patent and technology transfer centre, etc., in partnership with industry are not incorporated, it is feared that the whole effort of reformation will remain on traditional lines, preventing change. Massive investment being made will not yield expected results. The education policies and practices should have to come out of old ruts. They are less efficient, unproductive and outdated. You need new ideas to win in new world.

It should be remembered that any investment in present structure, present systems and procedures without introducing autonomy and improving academic culture is like investment to perpetuate and subsidize incompetence, inefficiency leading to failure.

Change is most wanted to replace worn out ideas. The resources should not be frittered away on trodden paths but should be used creatively on to proceed off the beaten paths, essentially importing academic culture and output. Developing countries in general, are hopelessly conservative, inward looking and hostile to change. Innovative societies are essentially outward looking. Individually, Indians are forward looking but society wise not. Unless we change our mindset and work to accelerate reformation process we cannot progress.

Academic Culture and Infrastructure

Unless innovative measures like academic autonomy, administrative autonomy, are introduced in higher education the additional investment in infrastructure will not pay dividends. Our own people in college, university and government unknowingly, out of inertia become obstruction to reformation. The authorities who are used to older style of working and for personal benefits do not take initiative to change. However, this should be guarded to avoid failure.

The experience of India-Canada project and World Bank project in the recent past, has taught us many lessons. Financial aid from World Bank to countries like Congo, Zambia indicates that the aid turned out to be counter productive. The men in-charge of governance were accustomed to benefits from the present system. So they did not take any initiative to change. It went towards subsidizing inefficiency, bad policies, corruption, discouraging reformation, etc.

The present case of universities and colleges, which are offering resistance to change, is a capability failure. Raising the organizational capability, making them competent and amenable to change is the key aspect which must be attended to with utmost care by aid-receiving institutions. Without which they may not be able to make most of the aid. Development of an institute cannot be forced from outside. It comes only from within. It is an endogenous growth. Organizational capability need to be developed so as to bring about change. Exposure to developed world needs to be made, time and again, to accelerate arrival of change.

Benchmarking with the Best in the World

What we observe differently in higher education institutes abroad is that they have on their campuses centres like research park, patent and technology transfer centre, entrepreneurship development centre, incubator, innovation relay centre, industrial services centre, etc., venture capital companies have opened offices in the campuses for early commercialization of technologies. Institutes have become sources of new ideas enabling companies to win. An institute functions like a light house for industry. It is these things which have increased productivity and added value to growing economy. Such institutes are functioning like a magnet attracting best of brains from anywhere and everywhere.

In the world benchmarking is considered to be a big driver for improvement.

Systems in World have Changed—Where are We? Can We Afford to be Stationary?

All these multifaceted centres provide an opportunity to students to learn beyond curriculum, as per their intrinsic motivations. They have been established especially after 1980, in 84 technical universities of Germany, in 125 research universities of USA, and in many universities abroad MIT Boston has a technology licensing office (TLO) in which about 200 people work. The author has personally visited this office. The institute earns about one hundred patents every year and earns as much as 20 per cent of its budget from the sale of technology.

Quality and relevance of education in developed countries is reported to have improved mainly because of the presence of centres in the campus. Enterprising culture is imbibed in students, which leads to spin-off of companies. Around ten companies are born every year in MIT. Institutes have become the maternity homes, where good baby care is taken and companies are consequently born without any congenital defects. This is found to be a good help to budding entrepreneurs. Our institutions are lacking in all such ideas. Can we not adopt these strategies? True that is a long journey. But it has to begin some where. Is it not that a thousand miles journey begins with a single step? The vector of learning of our students should have to be made in right direction. Otherwise their efforts, time and money goes astray.

INNOVATION—GENERATES JOBS

Cambridge Research Park, Limerick University Research Park, Harburg University Park in Germany, technology-based spin-offs from Sophia Antipolis, University Park in France, Oulu Business University Park in Finland, etc. are world famous examples which have benefited most of the students, industry and academia. The author has personally verified by visiting them. China, Taiwan have installed such parks in their institutes and thereby currently have successfully been converting brain drain into brain gain. An OECD study recently reported that

> Those nations which lead in introducing innovation tend to win jobs from those who lag.

Joblessness in India is increasing due mainly to lack of innovation. Insufficient innovative activity in India is due to shortage of people possessing innovation skills because innovation is not taught in colleges. This is cited as a key factor behind under performance of Indian economy and fast growing unemployment.

India must recognize the full scope of the innovation phenomenon without which proportion of sick industries will increase and new born companies will be handicapped at birth itself.

Can Indian academics teach innovation skills by international standards? Can they teach skills of discovery and skills to generate technologies equal to their counterparts abroad? Certainly, yes! They have the potential. Can India hope to become a developed nation without learning innovation? Should we keep on teaching sun set technologies? Can we hope to reform education without adopting innovative strategies? We cannot generate employment without NTBF. Can students acquire innovation skills without infrastructure for innovation? We essentially need a swimming pool to learn swimming.

CONCLUSION

A new enterprising society in the world is coming into being. Institutions should therefore focus their attention on reorienting students for closer integration with the world. Mobility of academicians at international levels is advocated. This has remained our serious deficiency in the past.

Education and training in universities, colleges and polytechnics have a major influence on nation's capacity for innovation. The role played by them, however, is not satisfactory. Much needs to be done. Scientific methods like in developed countries need to be introduced. Innovation policy needs to be evolved. Can they produce NTBF, and how many, is a pertinent question which they should be asked.

How much knowledge is acquired and stored in brains is important, but how well-innovative skills are learned deserves priority. India in globalization should deviate from traditional methods of learning and take a lead in sharpening the innovation potential of students. They have missed opportunities in the past because necessary infrastructure and direction for self-employment were not available. Now at least they should not miss.

If India does not become a centre for technological innovation then there is no other way to become a developed nation. If we develop systems in colleges to produce new knowledge and new technology, then there is a fair chance to convert brain drain into brain gain.

The knowledge infrastructure proposed in this paper is a profit centre. It generates wealth much in excess of consumption. It is found to subsidize education and research, besides improving the quality and relevance. It should therefore be installed forthwith in each university, college without any delay. Government should play its central role.

If India desires to become a technological superpower, then higher education institutions must have to throw away the old shackles, and install new innovation and entrepreneurship culture to create NTBF. This is no more an option but compulsion.

Resources are not in short supply, but the visions. Capacity to implement visions matters. Universities must generate leaders and brand new ideas to enable industry to win.

Imagine, all colleges and universities are suddenly closed. No student, no professor, no laboratory. What saving or harm would this do? Education is not a luxury; it is a necessity, especially for the less knowledgeable in developing countries like India.

REFERENCES

Bowden, Rob, *Globalization, Impact on Our Lives*, Rain Tree Chicago Publication.

Government of India, National Knowledge Commission Report, 2006-07.

Green paper of European Union on Innovation and Technological Transfer Enterprise Unit, EUFO, 2295-2920 Luxumberg.

Jones, Glen A. Patricia L. McCarney and Michael L. Skolinik, *Creating Knowledge Strengthening Nations, The Challenging Role of Education*, University of Torronto Press, 2002.

Naik, B.M., *Higher and Technical Education—Book of Knowledge*, Gyan Publishing House, 2010.

Rising above the gathering storm, report National Academy of Sciences, US, 2007.

Turnatzky, Lous G., *Innovation U-New Practices Enabling Cultures.*

Chapter 10

Public and Private Universities Together can Provide an Answer to Education in India

So as to win in competitive world it is now necessary to build a learning society consisting of learning organizations and learning individuals.

Private universities, although new to India, exist in the US from hundreds of years. Almost half of the 2500 US universities are private. They are managed and maintained either by the church, industry, or philanthropic organizations. The standard of education in them and the quality of research output vis-à-vis that of the state-controlled universities is superior. The best university like MIT Boston is private. The US has progressed well and due share of credit goes to private universities. Many important inventions and innovations have taken place in them. Human civilization would not have advanced so much, if there were no private universities. Today, private universities in the world earn a large proportion of patents and IPR. Following article explain the need and importance of establishing private universities in India.

ENTRY OF FOREIGN UNIVERSITIES

Universities from foreign countries like UK, USA, Australia are entering India in a big way. People do have a craze for foreign degrees. Special counseling sessions by foreign universities are being held in metro cities. The proposal of private universities being discussed and debated in India needs to be examined under the influence of arrival of foreign universities. India would have to strengthen its higher education system, both private and government, so as to face aggression. Foreign universities are making an entry so as to capture education market, which is so abundantly available in India. In such a case, education will be much more expensive. Students would have to pay much more, than both government universities and private universities. Already thousands of students are going abroad each year by spending big amount. It is now for Indians to consider whether to have foreign universities which are much more costly or private, although costlier than government universities. India has signed an agreement in WTO, according to which from 1 January 2005 foreign universities are permitted to come in, so also Indian universities can go out. When India has made university sector open to private foreign universities, how it can stop it for those of Indian origin?

Why Private Universities?

India needs private universities to strengthen its own education. This will be achieved through competition to government universities. Private universities can bring new life and blood through competition, which government university cannot.

Government universities have rendered very valuable service so far. All universities in India are state funded and hence state controlled. They enjoy monopoly. Students have no option. Their performance, by global standard, is however far below. Neither the students nor the employers are happy. They are over centralized, bureaucratic, and monopolistic, thwarting and impending ideas of students and professors. They kill the innovative talent of students and faculty. They care only for their bosses, ignoring the needs of students and industry. They are far too behind their counterparts in the developed world. It is because of their poor performance that many students go abroad for higher education. They are using outdated structure of affiliating colleges. They are giving admissions, and degrees but not latest knowledge. Therefore, they appear cheaper but truly are not. The limitations of government universities lay in their government structure. They are managed and maintained by people who are not qualified for the purpose. If India wants to become a champion in higher education, it must create competition in institutions. There cannot be a champion without competition. Monopoly of present universities must come to an end. That will be the beginning of improvement. Mere presence of a competitor can force an incumbent to lower prices and improve services.

> Private universities can bring competition and initiate new innovative projects—to make most of world wide opportunities. Private universities are more enterprising by nature.

The organizations/innovations like research parks, innovation centres, incubators, campus companies, venture capital companies, etc., which exist from almost 50 years in universities in advanced countries have not yet reached the Indian universities, which offer only irrelevant courses. Consequently, the educated unemployed are growing. There are six lakhs in Maharashtra alone. The competition in Indian economy is far too low mainly because of mediocrity. The students are still required to go to UK and US for higher studies. How long they will have to keep going? They are going from Gandhi-Nehru period. How long we should fill the coffers of foreign universities? The answer lies in setting up private universities, and bringing competition to the state-controlled universities, private universities are cut for entrepreneurship. India will miss opportunities in patents and starting of New Technology-based firms, if private universities are not started or delayed. We do not have innovative mechanisms so far mainly because we do not have private universities.

> Private universities are more responsive to market. They cater efficiently to the rising demands in terms of quality and quantity. State universities need to be supplemented by private universities.

Because state universities have limited resources, they need to be supported by private. In the newly emerging knowledge society, the need and importance of efficiency in higher education needs no emphasis. The proportion of students taking to higher education in India is only 6 per cent but it is rising fast at the rate of 12 per cent per year. In the US, this proportion is more than 50 per cent, Korea has 37 per cent and Thailand 12 per cent. In the fast-paced globalization, if India has to compete, the only option is to augment its private universities. This is the only way to get a competitive advantage. State universities are subordinate to government. They often play the tune of political masters, who keep changing.

Private Universities can Take Long-range View of Education

Because their management does not depend on government, they take long-range view. The government, which is elected for a short period, does not pay the required attention to higher education, which essentially demands long-range planning. The Vice Chancellors most of the times are appointed on political considerations. They bring politics in universities and the scholarship is driven out. Research is given a back seat. Private universities, if installed, will break the monopoly of the present universities, which is so essential for progress.

Who will provide remedies to remove the weaknesses in state universities? Only private universities can come to its rescue. They can bring improved methods of work and capital investment from the world over especially from NRIs. Any delay in such timely intervention would take away our huge education market to foreign universities. Autonomy to colleges is prescribed by National Education Commission way back in 1986. But it is not yet implemented. The government is not willing to part with the powers and pass them to colleges.

Private Universities can Avoid Political Intervention

They keep pushing forward their academic missions and visions regardless of the political party that comes to power. The Vice Chancellor is not appointed by the government but by the university board. With a humanistic aim, they admit meritorious students from anywhere in the world. They bring about a cultural exchange between the nations and enrich the human civilization. Most of the private universities abroad are reported to be making more productive utilization of resources. They get donations, so much so that every year they start new research projects and new courses. Almost only 50 per cent of the university budget is met out of student fees. The rest is met out of donations and patent IPR royalties.

The fees prescribed by US universities are much higher. It is because they maintain a high standard of laboratories, library and education. They do not get financial aid from the government. The students get loans from the banks and scholarships from philanthropic organizations. In India too loans are now available.

Private Universities can Make Private College Scheme More Successful

In India, there are private self-finance colleges affiliated to state-controlled universities. This is a case of partial privatization; the final responsibility of quality rests with the university. Colleges many times tend to play mischief and follow unethical means to encourage students to copy in examinations and even buying degrees like the episode of the Nagpur, as it may affect reputation so much that the university stands the risk of closure.

However, a fear prevails that the private universities may indulge in malpractice and sale of degrees. This has not happened in the US or anywhere else. The system of controlling academic standards of the university, world over, has now changed to the scientific method of accreditation adopted nationally and internationally besides ISO.

Private Initiative can Make Research and Education More Productive

As per the Bush Commissions Report, 1945, "Science—The Endless Frontier", US universities have been strengthened for research. They are primarily knowledge-generation centres, where students learn by researching. In this system, quality of education is found to be the best, so also the research aspect. Cost wise, research subsidizes education and education subsidies research. Institutes are granted status of university only if they have a proven ability of knowledge generation and not merely teaching. India will have to install such systems for innovation. There are associated risks, like in any good project, but the gains are tremendous.

Private Universities Inherently are more Enthusiastic and Co-operative to Industries. Private Universities are Friendlier with Industry

Private universities if started bond between industry and institutes will become thick. Flow of technology will take place to industry and national productivity will increase. The expected synergistic relationship between the two will happen. Brainpower of Indian students will be used in India to solve Indian problems. Patent culture is more likely to pick up.

Private Universities are Good to Promote Export and Reduce Import

We have been buying technology and goods from foreign countries and they are selling from many years. Now the situation is proposed to be reversed. This cannot happen without starting of private universities. There are greater risks in not starting private universities. Indian universities can reach out to foreign, only if they are private.

Private Universities Take Away Poverty from Poor

They can bring vibrancy to rural areas. Some people are making hue and cry that the private universities will educate only rich. And gap between rich and poor will widen. Poor and deserving students need not hesitate to take loans for paying fees. They will get proper education like in foreign; worth the fees government has liberally started education loan schemes. This is the way for poor to become rich. When students go in private universities many seats will become free for poor people in government universities. Is this not a benefit for the poor?

Private universities have many other sources of income, e.g. earnings from patents, donations, consultancy, and research projects. Many campus jobs become available to students. The turnover in campus goes several times more, bringing income, scholarships to students. The students from poor family background are in fact better attended in private universities.

To win in global competition and to fulfill rising aspirations of the people, India cannot afford to ignore the proven model of private universities.

Private Universities are more Successful in Producing Leaders

India is rich in resources yet we get goods from foreign countries. We have abundance of manpower. Yet, the wanted cutting edge technologists are not available. There is a huge population but enterprising leaders are not available. Our conventional universities are producing followers. They bring technologies from abroad and teach here as traders. They do not have wellsprings of new knowledge, new technology and patents. They are like departmental stores or relay centres. India needs private universities to create leaders, who create new theories, new technologies patents and IPR.

If India does not Start Private Universities, will it Cause any Damage?

Certainly yes, it will. Many students will miss opportunity to take higher education. The overall intellectual capability of India in world comparison will remain low. The existing universities due to lack of competition will not improve. More and more students will go abroad for higher education. It will be a big drain on financial resources, besides brains. Universities abroad will flourish, and Indian universities will sink. Money from people in India instead of coming to our universities will flow out. Poverty in India will tend to increase. There will be plentiful manpower in India but unemployable. India's position in world instead of improving is likely to deteriorate. India is destined to miss vast opportunities if starting of private universities is delayed. The employment and income generation in India will get a setback. The present rising wave in software will also be adversely affected. If the above damage is to be avoided, it is urgently necessary to start private universities. It is no more an option but compulsion. There are almost no risks in starting private universities. There are much greater risks in not starting private universities.

India Needs to Promote Private Universities to Excel in World

It is believed, the world over, that universities are international organizations. Although they get grants from government, yet what to teach and how to teach is not the business of government but that of the university. Universities should render academic advice to government and not the other way round. Private universities in industrially-advanced countries were the first to give Phillip to scholarship. Nations like USA and Japan came forward to start private universities. It is these private universities, and not the state universities which have become a moving force, of their economies.

Starting Private Colleges is Good but not Enough. It is Essential to Start Private Universities

Government universities are not able even to declare the results of examination for three months. Now in WTO regime monopoly enjoyed by the universities in India and elsewhere in the world is being, abandoned. They are being exposed to competition not only domestic but also international. This is the beginning of worldwide improvement. Internationalization of higher education is taking place. This is too good for the younger generation. Private universities from abroad and from India in this will play important role, which should be viewed as a positive sign. Private universities alone can take India on top of the world. This is the only way. Private universities in USA have taken their universities ahead of European universities, so are the findings of a evaluation report. In India too, private universities will take us ahead of our counterparts elsewhere in the world.

PRESENT STATUS

Maharashtra Government has issued the Ordinance No. XXII of 2004 on 16 August to provide for establishment of self-financed universities in the state, to regulate their working and functions and for matters connected therewith or incidental there to. The bill is yet to be presented in state assembly. The select committee is examining it.

The private university bill was presented in Parliament in August 1995. It was passed by Lok Sabha but unfortunately rejected by Rajya Sabha. The Supreme Court has already given green signal.

Supreme Court in the case of Chhattisgarh has given stay in the matter. The Government of India is re-examining the proposal. This is with a view of better implementation.

Private university is a worldwide trend with high merits. However, it has to be implemented carefully. Otherwise, a good scheme is likely to go in disrepute.

Universities, in India, unfortunately are tending to become pawns in the hands of bureaucracy. Universities tend to become salves of the government. It is only on account of this that there are many ills in higher education. More is expected from universities, which they are not able to give. Because most of the times bottlenecks are at the top like appointment of Vice Chancellor is not on fair considerations. The common man is unhappy. Blame for ills in higher education is passed on to teachers wrongly. Appointment of a non-academician like Divisional Commissioner or Police Commissioner as VC is against the fundamental principles of management. Such persons are experts in their fields but do not and cannot understand the pulse of academics. What will happen in match if selection of cricket team is done by government officers and ministers instead of cricket control board?

Private universities which do not have interference from government, provide a cure to the problems in higher education. They attach more value to academics. This explains the urgency of starting private universities. The implementation however is not that simple. Discovery and innovation skills are the distinguishing features of university organizations from other government department. But government treats higher education like any other government department. Consequently, the nation is being left behind in brain race. These are the things stopped forthwith.

CONCLUSION

Prime Minister Manmohan Singh in his speech on 15 August 2004 said,

> Higher education should not be the prisoner of either bureaucracy or ideology; it must develop on the foundations of professional excellence and intellectual integrity.

These are the words of wisdom, which need to be remembered and acted upon by the educationists and education administrators.

Bureaucracy is hi-jacking the interests of higher education. This is not desirable, in public interest. Dr. Radha Krishnan as Chairman of UGC in 1948-49 wrote:

> We must resist, in the interest of our democracy, the trend towards the governmental domination of the educational process.

University system, in public interest, need to be pulled out of monopoly, and bureaucracy. It is necessary to expose it to competition locally and internationally. Setting up of private universities will restrict entry of foreign universities, which is essential in public interest. It will mark the beginning of a new era.

Creating knowledge-based society in India demands a transnational effort. India has adopted the route to create the most dynamic and competitive knowledge-based economy.

REFERENCES

Dubhashi, P.R., "Privatization of Higher Education", *University News,* 30 June 1997, Vol. 135, No. 26.

Higher Education in Crisis, *Economic Times Editorial*, 23 December 2004.

Loksatta, 25 November 2004.

Loksatta, 21 July 2004.

Loksatta, 26 April 2001.

Naik, B.M., "Positive Aspects of Privatization", *The Hindu*, 7 Nov. 2001.

———. Private Universities, Sakal 3 Feb. 2004 in Marathi.

Tutkane, M.A., University Education: Reflection Or Pathfinder of Society, *University News,* 42 [46] November 15-21, 2004.

Chapter 11

Total Quality Management (TQM)

> The tension of the bow, the strain put by string on its opposite ends gives the arrow force to carry firmly to a mark. Teaching and research are the two ends of the same bow. Neither has much force without the other.

Total Quality Management (TQM) approach emphasizes quality assurance, by providing quality inputs. It has made a change in performance of organizations around the world. TQM enables to develop self-assessment culture, so essential to be progressive on sustained basis. Quality improvement involves the statistical tools, consumer research, goal setting, teamwork, problem solving, Human Resource Management, bench marking and strategic planning. The paper reviews different aspects of quality assurance, steps involved in implementation and organizational framework.

NEED AND IMPORTANCE

As many as 1,64,000 students in the year 2012 went to USA, UK, Australia, New Zealand, Germany, for higher education. The trend year after year is increasing. It is because education in India, of the quality in foreign, is simply not available. Each student has to spend around ₹ 15-25 lakhs per year. Yet, they are going. Why? We need to make introspection and build our institutions qualitative and competitive by world standards.

This is essential to avoid brain drain and to achieve the dream of becoming a developed nation by 2020. India can fulfill the rising aspirations of younger generation, if and only if, it leads in quality, in research, innovation, IPR, patenting, and hi-tech start ups, etc.

Both the students and industry have become quality conscious. They are willing to pay necessary cost. People expect more, but universities are not able to give. They put blame on shortage of finances. Truly, available finances are being spent unproductively. Many institutions have five star infrastructures but the academic culture is obsolete. For example, the capacity utilization of installed facility in most of the institutions is too low. Most of them open in the morning at 10 and close at 5 in the evening. The counterpart institutions in developed countries open at 8 in the morning and close at 11 in the night. The libraries, in particular remain open twenty-four hours, round the year. Indian institutions are spending money, effort and time but fruitlessly. It is because there is almost a complete lack of scientific approach in quality management, which is the theme of this article.

TQM approach emphasizes quality assurance, by providing quality inputs. It has made a change in performance of organizations around the world. Japanese economy became a powerhouse by using Total Quality Management. Dr. Deming one of the pioneers is practically worshiped in Japan. World best institutions are using TQM and by virtue of which they have reached high standing. It is necessary for the governing boards of universities and colleges to prescribe TQM. They should provide visible unwavering support for implementation. Alignment of all the people in the organization to world-class visions and missions is necessary. The curricula need to be made matching with the requirement of tomorrow and day after.

There are professors and staff who like to contribute in a full way to improve. But there are poor systems and compelling circumstances, which prevent them from reaching their full potential. What kind of circumstances? TQM identifies them. It is for policymakers sitting in AICTE/UGC, with out any delay, to initiate steps for installation of quality assurance cell.

Accreditation will become more meaningful only if the cell for quality, in each college, is set up.

IMPERATIVES OF TQM

Quality can be improved by external agencies like AICTE/UGC through inspections. It has, however, to be supplemented by internal efforts, within the institution. It is here that quality assurance plays a key role. Having resources, enthusiasm, and commonsense is good but adopting scientific quality assurance method is essential, without it howsoever hard the people in college may work will not get the results.

The students in both private and public institutes deserve the best possible quality, so as to fulfill the national dream of becoming a superpower. It is the duty and professional responsibility of governing boards, trustees to provide best possible education. Are they responsible, accountable, and effective?

Professors and administrators have to be competent by international standards. They ought to have professional commitment and an obligation to employ world best practices. They ought to have freedom to think and freedom to act. Do they have authorities matching with responsibilities?

The imperative stems from competition prevailing in education. Best students and best faculty can be attracted only if the institute is professionally managed. The institutes can remain on top only when they use TQM.

Institutes have to be accountable to government and society. TQM enables them to become more accountable.

The cost of ignoring the quality assurance is too high. It is in big terms like letting India down in world brain race, resulting in low standard of living and poverty. The institutions tend to lose best teachers, best students, and reputation. Why not many students from outside dream to study in India?

TQM can't be purchased. It has to be practiced internally step by step and developed by conscious efforts. This cannot happen overnight. It does not provide instant success. It will throw up new difficulties and challenges. It is a slow process, but the benefits are long term. TQM enables to develop self-assessment culture, so essential to be progressive on sustained basis.

PRINCIPLES OF QUALITY MANAGEMENT

Quality assurance believes in "prevention is better than cure". Eating good food is essential for good health. "Garbage in garbage out" is the popular saying. With this logic, the method prescribes control on inputs. Traditional Quality Control concept of inspection at the end is obsolete. It is the lack of application of scientific systems that hold back quality and not so much the shortage of resources.

Design and working of systems is at the roots. Institutions where systems are good, people tend to work efficiently. Bad systems are found to cripple the innovative people and innovative ideas.

Quality comes with systems improvement. It is the systems which matter.

Systems improvement is not a one shot affair. It is an unending journey.

It requires a deliberate and persistent attempt in a systematic way.

Quality does not come by chance or by accident.

People are not the problems but the systems.

Quality is every one's job, from top to bottom.

Quality is continuous improvement [Kaisen], i.e. working slowly and steadily, like tortoise that won the race.

Quality comes when the leaders are passionate.

Quality comes through strategy of better Human Resource Development.

Quality is empowering professors and staff.

Quality is fear reduction in the minds of employees.

Quality is recognition and reward.

Quality comes through better teamwork.

Quality is measurement of input, output by using statistical methods.

Quality is systematic problem solving.

Quality comes through opinion surveys for understanding customer needs by statistical methods.

Quality comes through benchmarking, i.e. by comparison preferably with world best. What the counterpart institutions else where in the world are doing, and how are they doing? What do the teachers in best institutions do? Are they passionate about teaching and research?

Quality comes when every one does work in correct way, right in the first instance. It requires hard work, but essentially smart work.

Quality is meeting or exceeding the customer needs. If you do not satisfy the customers, some one else will. If institutions do not offer better education, students will go somewhere else.

Inspection does not improve quality. It hurts.

Quality improvement involves the statistical tools, consumer research, goal setting, teamwork, problem solving, HRM, and strategic planning.

Quality goes beyond accreditation. Accrediting agencies, program reviews, standing committees, local inspection committees, and control-minded governing boards and well-intension task force all alone by themselves will never be able to improve quality. Most of these traditional quality improvement mechanisms view quality from inspection perspective, which is defeated scientifically.

Inspections do not result in decrease of the number of defects. In fact, they increase.

Accreditation measures quality, like the thermometer.

Impressing pre-requisites of quality on the minds of people, government and people's representatives is necessary. If quality is important it must be well articulated, so that legislators make it obligatory.

Organizational Framework for Implementation

It requires creation of a cell in the institution.

It requires a team of leaders to develop vision.

It requires office of quality assurance.

It requires implementation team.

It requires internal and external networking.

It requires advisory team.

It requires support from top.

It requires planning.

It requires design of questionnaire and feedback from customers, students, industry, and alumni.

The word total in TQM stands for, total number of systems, total number of persons, activities, customers, stakeholders, and inputs and outputs.

Satisfy all the customers and quality follows

Some of the customers are listed below:

Students

Faculty

Alumni

Industry

Staff

Government

Society, etc.

Aim of the institute should be to satisfy each and every customer without an exception. The institute has to respond to multi-customer environment. Developing happy customers is a sign of quality. TQM leads to making the institute preferred.

The leadership of an organization must, by word and deeds convey the message that customer satisfaction, through a process of continually improving quality is the responsibility of every member of the organization. Inappropriate systems create problems, regardless of person or persons. Therefore, systems should be attended with utmost care. Incentives should be given to remove deficiencies.

Remove the barriers that rob the people of credit/pride of their work. Do not ignore any one, for ignoring is demoralizing. Make sure that expectations are clear and well understood. This creates a positive environment. The expectations must become tangible and ubiquitous. It is impossible to feel ignored if some one is paying attention.

Quality circle is a mechanism to involve all from bottom to top. Small groups of people analyzed and evolve solutions to current problems.

Solving problems in such a way that they do not continue to occur is the essence of TQM. Reacting to crisis, known as "fire-fighting approach" is not good.

A little praise goes a long way for most of the people, to keep them prideful. Individuals are like flowers, which need watering regularly, without which they wither. Efficient people become mediocre without encouragement and by abandonment. Mediocre people become efficient by appreciation. If maintained prideful, they deliver quality.

There were two stonecutters. One was emotionally involved in building a temple. He was found doing a fine job. The other stonecutter was rather sour, disgruntled. He was also involved in building the temple. But he was not doing his job as fine as the other. He was seen unhappy because he did not know the noble cause for which he was working. People need to be motivated time and again for the good cause they are working.

Systematic approach to quality management is necessary. This is given by TQM. Institutions need a new approach to managing human and fiscal resources. Quality management is not one-shot affair but an ongoing journey.

Increased funding will not improve quality, if we do not allocate resources wisely. Using them wisely demands TQM. If we do not use funds to promote distinctiveness, and if we are not able to create customer satisfaction, the investment is unproductive.

DIMENSIONS OF SERVICE QUALITY

A CCESS: Maintaining customer-driven office hours is desirable. Providing efficient telephone, e-mail service provides easy access. Effective communication with customers is important.

Keeping Customer Informed: Explaining in writing what services will be provided by the institution, what are the costs and visions of the institution in long range and short range. Assuring the customer of the intentions of the organization is essential.

Competence: The institution should spell out and justify how it is competent, having the necessary skills and knowledge. It should demonstrate its excellence in its teaching job through statistics of discoveries and examination results. Appropriate indicators should explain the research capabilities.

Courtesy: Politeness treating students with dignity and honor. Extending equal treatment to all students, staff and faculty is desirable.

Credibility: Honesty, trust worthiness, having fair policies in recruitment of deserving candidates.

Reliability: Consistency of performance and dependability, getting rid of incompetent employees, reducing billing errors.

Responsiveness: Returning phone calls, replying letters, resolving complaints on time are the usual weaknesses.

Security: Freedom from risk, danger, doubt, assuring physical safety, protecting individual's privacy.

Tangibles: Physical evidence of service, maintaining campus grounds, acquiring appropriate technology deserves greater attention.

Customer Focus: It is essential to treat each student as a separate entity. Providing individual attention and developing means to listen obtaining feedback at regular intervals is essential. Institutions must change their attitudes in favor of customers.

There can be no culture of quality without consistent and persistent distributed leadership like departments, faculty and staff throughout the organization.

Autonomy is Desirable

An institute needs considerable degree of autonomy, and flexibility so that it has the freedom to teach and freedom to research, without political or any other kind of interference, so that creativity and imagination are encouraged, and so that resources including the time and energy of faculty, staff, and students are used effectively. The institute also needs the involvement of state as a force for meeting the public needs, as a force for change, and as a force for accountability. The problem therefore is not to eliminate the state's role but to perfect it.

As a leader do you hear the customers?

Do you issue only circulars or obtain feedback?

Do you meet employees formally and also informally?

Do you conduct customer surveys, to assess how satisfied they are?

Do you simply talk on quality or engage in deeds?

Are the curricula fit for tomorrow and day after?

Do you change the minds of employees with new ideas every time you meet?

Do the principal and other institutional leaders continuously mentor the team members?

VISION STATEMENT

Vision statement ought to be stimulating, unifying, guiding, and distinctive. It is the foundation on which the "house of quality" is built.

What is the unifying distinctive vision? It is a vision, which touches the hearts of people inviting their emotional involvement. It provides organizational rallying force. It evokes a meaning with reference to the institution proper. It allows an institution to enjoy a unique position in the higher education environment.

Vision statement communicates key values for today as well as for the future. Vision statement provides a sense of purpose, for which the institution exists.

Vision statement of a typical world-class institute, says

It needs to be recognized internationally.

The institute wants to be the world best place to study and work.

It intends each student to learn at least one additional language, to have three months experience in foreign country, show tolerance towards culture, beliefs and faiths of others.

The institute wants faculty to have international experience and to increase international research projects by 50 per cent in coming five years, and to involve students in each of them.

The institute wants to know, what clients ten years from now expect, and to excel their expectations.

The institutes want to solve problems and meet challenges by a team, regardless of their level of jobs.

Institute aims at producing leaders in industry, pioneers in technology.

It intends to produce start-ups in high technology. Raise the target from 20 to 40 in coming two years.

The institute today obtains 150 patents every year. It intends to raise the target to 200 in coming year.

It wants to discover newer technologies for the welfare of human kind.

It intends to expand its net to countries in Africa, and China.

Existing vision statements in most of the institutes in India are meaningless, because connecting links between vision and operating systems are missing.

The top people must articulate quality in speeches, and weave if with public relations. The top management should make their institute unique by becoming outstanding.

Every one needs to connect his duties and responsibilities with visions and missions.

SOLVING PROBLEMS

Each principal's/president's office is a magnet, which attracts problems. The buck stops there.

Solving problems is not the answer to improving the quality. The solution lies in understanding and continuously improving the processes that give rise to problems.

Take processes in hand for improvement first which are easy. One should attempt difficult processes in the course of time. Do not attempt all at a time.

The 85:15 Rule

It is believed that 85 per cent what goes wrong in an institution is due to poor systems. Only 15 per cent fault is attributable to individuals.

The process is incomplete without closing the loop, known as feedback loop.

The responsibility for quality in higher education does not lie at the top alone but with everyone in the organization.

Empowering people within the organization to improve quality is essential. If you do not empower people to improve quality, you can loose both the customer and employee.

If you do not empower people, you encourage and reward inefficient.

If you do not empower people, you will become inundated with unnecessary bureaucrats and manuals.

The organization becomes a collection of under achievables.

Quality management needs to be viewed from others point of view who receive higher education services, and not from the viewpoint of those who provide.

Make a five-year quality improvement plan.

Motivation alone is not enough to generate change.

It essentially requires academic freedom to maintain a distance from a whole host of evils, both real and imaginary.

The implementation team will prepare a quality manual.

Quality policy, quality procedure, quality audit be conducted every year.

STEPS INVOLVED IN IMPLEMENTATION OF TQM

Conduct awareness programs.

Make a survey of expectations of the customers, and assess how satisfied they are, through well-designed questionnaire.

Discuss the results of survey openly.

Prepare vision statement with the involvement of all.

Identify the processes, and systems in the institutions and outside.

The systems are for example.

Internal systems for:

Admission,

Teaching theory and practical,

Examination,

Practical training, recruitment of faculty and staff,

Promotions,

Pension benefits,

Dealing with unions,

Finance and account system,

Purchase system,

Campus maintenance,

Hostel admission and maintenance, etc.

External systems:

Interaction with industry,

Interaction with international institutes,

Industry,

Research,

Exploitation research findings,

Links with university,

Links with government,

Fund raising, etc.

Each process needs thorough examination:

Questions need to be raised,

How well is existing process doing?,

Why does the process exist?,

How does it compare with the processes else where?,

How it compares with world best?,

Who benefits from the process?,

Does the customer benefit?,

What are the inputs and outputs?,

What is their quality?,

What are unfulfilled expectations?,

What incentives are needed?,

Do you celebrate success at each step?,

What are opportunities and strengths?,

What are the threats and weaknesses?,

Have you prepared vision statement in joint meetings?,

Have you conducted interviews with the people who are benchmarks?

Each system has

(a) Inputs

(b) Processes and

(c) Outputs

For improving the system one has to make analysis, benchmarking, and use of "Planning-Development-Control-Action" [PDCA] cycle, on continuing basis for each of inputs, process, and outputs. Histograms, flow charts, pie chart, and other statistical methods are strongly suggested. Decisions should not be based on intuition but necessarily on statistics. To summarize, the future of our children and grandchildren is bright only if the institutions are professionally managed by using TQM.

TQM is essential for survival and growth. If they do not do so forthwith, the governance of education in India will be labeled outdated non-professional and inefficient. Indian education may go in the hands of foreign universities. Implementation of quality management systems should be done preferably with the help of a consultant. This is to ensure success.

Professors and staff should be trained and empowered in use of TQM.

TQM is made compulsory in England for all organizations, which draw financial aid from government. Should this not be a hint for India?

TQM enhances capacity utilization. Cost per unit of output is reduced, with increase in quality. Economic rate of return from investments is increased.

Indian academic community should take an initiative.

There is none from India in the 100 world best universities. Why? Is it because we ignore TQM?

MIT, Wisconsin, and Oxford, Cambridge all are using TQM, and so they are world-class.

Many institutions in India are spending money far in excess but due to lack of TQM use they do not excel.

Implementation of TQM does not require money; it results in saving.

The members of legislatures, governing boards should immediately take a drive to use TQM.

The responsibility for using TQM lies with the policymakers sitting in the governing boards, accreditation agencies, AICTE and UGC.

REFERENCES

Aruchami, M., Quality Imperatives in Higher Education, *University News*, Vol. 42, No. 05 February 02-08, 2004.

Mohanty, R.P. and Lakhe, R.R., *Handbook of Total Quality Management*, Jaico Publishing House, 2004.

Prema, P., Quality Assurance in Professional Training of Teacher Educators: Challenges and Strategies, *University News*, Vol. 42, No. 32, August 09-15, 2004.

Sails, Edward, Does TQM have a Role in Education. *The Journal of Engineering Education*, October 2005, Vol. XIX, No. 2.

Verma, Romesh, Quality and Relevance in Education, *University News*, Vol. 42, No. 10, March 08-14, 2004.

Vrat, Prem, Quality System for Excellence in Engineering Education, *University News*, Vol. 43, No. 39, September 26-October 02, 2005.

Chapter 12

Research Park is a Proven Model in the World, for Promoting Industrialization. Can India Afford to Ignore?

Today success in the global marketplace means creating and applying new knowledge—which is to say new technology—faster than one's competitors. World winners will be those who develop talent, technologies, techniques and tools so advanced that there is no competition.

ABSTRACT

Which government does not want to generate hi-tech employment, high pay international jobs, spur industrial growth, and make education globally competitive? Then it must install research/technology parks, incubators, patent and IPR to facilitate commercial exploitation of sunrise technologies. Classroom teaching is good but not enough. Industries, world over, are seen flocking round the advanced knowledge centres to obtain brand new ideas for global competitiveness. Institutes must have original knowledge springs like well water springs. They must have a mechanism to convert intellectual strength in to usable goods and services. Role of higher education has emerged central to industrial and economic development, in creating India's future. Association with industry, venture capital firms, international agencies who succeeded in this cause is essential.

The paper prescribes "dream big" for universities and colleges. They should aim at technology generation, technology diffusion, which is achieving high significance in enabling a nation to win. The paper emphasizes adoption of new organizational inventions like research park, technology park, which when implemented will contribute to India's international competitiveness. The institutions should have now to look beyond the traditional lines of teaching and learning and adapt to corporate development, and help industry to win. They should have to restructure themselves to become fountain heads of new knowledge and new technology. They should deserve the status of "Light House" for industry. People demand world-class education. How can this be done? Synergy between industry and academics in this cause is vital. Parks play a middleman's role in this. They have enhanced the scholarship of universities. They jointly can give economic and political stability to India. Will industry institute interaction become a national priority? The paper recommends reforms in the light of experience elsewhere in the world.

INTRODUCTION

World experience tells us that now the economic development is knowledge/technology driven. The limiting factor for growth and prosperity of a nation is not oil, nor land, nor minerals but the scientific and technological capability of people. Industrialized nations by virtue of technological superiority are found capturing the world market and emerging as epicentre of interdependent world. Industrialized nations through knowledge especially of emerging technologies are amassing wealth. 80 per cent of world's wealth is possessed by G-8 countries. World Bank observed that wealth is flowing today from developing to developed countries because of level difference in technology. Besides, advanced nations yield economic and political powers. Solow, the Nobel Laureate observed that the GNP of USA doubled between 1909 and 1949, and that 85 per cent of the growth was attributable to technology change.[1]

Those nations, organizations and individuals exploiting the latest technology are likely to win others may work hard, may have essential resources to draw on, but will lag behind without technological capability and adaptability.

Scientific Infrastructure "Research Park" and its Relevance to India

True that India is late starter in engineering and technology and so it lagged behind. However, after independence, it has made a laudable progress. But it has yet to go a long way. It is today distinctly a technology follower. The technology development plans of most of the companies in India are propelled by foreign collaborators. Universities and academic institutions are too weak in research, and innovation. They have remained reflection centres teaching that knowledge which comes to them from abroad. They do not have "well springs" of new knowledge. Besides, they have remained away from industry. There are systems and procedures for import of technology, but there are no systems developed for technology generation and transmission from institutions within the country to industry.

Industry institute partnership world over is observed to be critical to success. The world proven model of Silicon Valley was initiated by Prof. Terman of Stanford University. Research Triangle Park in North Carolina was initiated by Prof. Luther Hodge of Duke University. MaRS innovation district in Toronto, is evolved in partnership with Toronto University, by Prof. Evans. This model for technological and industrial development has been adopted now in many east-west countries. The role of government in so doing has been central. The universities and other higher education institutes in the respective regions have undoubtedly been the leaders of this change. The underlying principle given by Prof. Terman being that—

> Industry so as to remain competitive globally needs access to first-class research in universities. So also the first-class researchers in universities need access to industry so as to commercialize their research findings.[2]

Thousands of research parks are now installed in Japan, Taiwan, China, UK and elsewhere in the world. They are found to provide a high-class infrastructure in the vicinity of higher education institutes where qualified scientists, engineers and entrepreneurs can professionally grow. Research parks have come to be known as the maternity homes for safe birth of hi-tech industries. It provides a fertile ground for creation of New

Technology-Based Firms (NTBF). It has proved to be effective in tapping the valuable resource of new knowledge for the growth of professions and productivity. It is an engine of development reducing lead time between invention and commercialization, giving new direction to human civilization. India so far has been trying to catch up technology race from behind rather than riding the crest. If it adopts research park scheme, it will be able to ride. It will move new knowledge and new technology continually to economy like blood supply to our body. The economy will thereby have more knowledge/technology intensive business. India must recognize the role of new technologies and universities responsible for generating them. Research scientists and engineers if attracted to good infrastructure of research parks they will not migrate to other countries. New knowledge industries keep coming around universities.[3]

Where do Indian institutions stand in technology generation and diffusion? How many engineering colleges and universities offering education at graduate and research levels have corporate development as a vision and mission to carry out technology transfer to industry? Department of S&T, Government of India has installed more than twelve parks in universities. They are doing very well. But they are too few for a big country like India. Doing research is good. But what use it is if not exploited commercially? Many institutions have now reached a stage where establishment of innovative endeavors like Research Park, technology incubator, patent and IPR centre, entrepreneurship development centre can prove immensely useful to them, to industry as well as to students passing out of these institutions. It is now not enough to produce just engineers and technologists but it is essential to produce leaders in technology and leaders in industry that too by international standard. To win in world economy it is now necessary to produce technology pioneers, for which innovative infrastructure like research parks are absolutely necessary. Education charged with the spirit of discovery and innovation alone can move a nation forward. Future belongs to those who understand this. The purpose of this article is therefore to prescribe innovation, creativity and commercial exploitation of research which are the present-day deficiencies of Indian economy. This will necessitate installing units as stated above as integral components of institutions. Industries, venture capital companies and institutes must come together to set up such parks. The "Stand Alone" policies of industry and education must be done away with. This is today's Guru Mantra.

Reforms Needed to Create Future

Knowledge is power. It changes lives of people. It converts a liability in to an asset. The world, due to rapid advances in science and technology, is changing fast. Change is accelerated by globalization, privatization, and liberalization. Survival of fittest in competitive world is tending to become the law. People have to cope with high velocity environment on local and global planes. Institutes of technical education, under these stormy changes, have not to perform the way they performed in the past. They have to depart from old style to enable the people to assimilate emerging, technological advances and use them so as to win jobs and earn income in competition at world level. They have to facilitate increase in scientific and technological capability of people. It is they who produce scientific and research personnel to do discoveries. Institutes must have to be adaptive, constantly changing, and using world-class strategies. Courses, curriculum and methods of teaching must have to change with times. Their visions and missions, policies and practices, systems and procedures must have now to be constantly changing to fulfill local as well as global needs. World experience says institutes ought to provide economic stimulus for regional development. Even political development of nations depends on capacity of institutions in what and how they teach.[4]

Where do the Indian institutes stand in world list? They are far too low, like India in Olympics. They are progressing. Yet, thousands of students are going for higher education abroad, to be humiliated? Why? The education in India is yet not aligned to the needs of globalization. No longer well-being of a nation and its future destiny are constrained by its geography, population, natural resources. Knowledge especially of science and technology has become the prime mover.[5] Science and technology represent the new driving force. Economic prosperity, energy supplies, manufacturing capacity, health, public safety, military security, political stability and environmental quality all these and more will depend on knowledge owned and possessed by the people, women and men in the community. Scientific knowledge with usage does not deplete but multiplies. This is the unique beauty of knowledge resource. India will be strengthened by learning to compete in S&T in this flat world.

Education must be Compatible to Globalization[6]

Technical education ought to be qualitative and cost competitive not only by local standards but by international. Many opportunities and challenges are arising in the areas of research, innovation, manufacturing, sales, etc. on global plane. The borders of education are expanding ocean like. How to prepare people to make most of them? Do the policymakers have to be outward looking? Do they have to take in to account the global dynamics in respect of technology, industry, economics, etc.? Yes, certainly they have to. It is essential, without which design of system will be imperfect. People can harvest opportunities ably only if they are well aware of what is on horizon and how to prepare in advance? They can make most of the situation if they are educated and technically trained and not without it. On the whole to win in world economy, university education must have to be compatible to globalization.

Education must be world-class to enable people to win in interdependent world.[7] People are ready to pay for in terms of time, effort, and money. But universities and colleges in India are not able to give. Why? This needs examination in depth. Their frame of work is old, outdated, primitive, and dysfunctional. They lack in creation of new knowledge, discoveries, and creative endeavors which are now the integral components of modern institutes elsewhere in the world. They lack in organizational capability. They lack in global visions and missions. That is why Indian institutes do not stand high in world list, and thousands of students every year go abroad. From experience elsewhere in the world, it can be said that higher education has to be necessarily coupled with research and innovation. Multifaceted research facilities like technology incubation, patent and IPR, start ups entrepreneurship, research park have become now the integral components. They are observed to have a deeper impact on quality of education. Quality in institutes is now critical and related to improving economic and political security of India. Do we realize this?

Institutions must now Change their Orbit[8]

They must jump up to creating hi-tech enterprises, hi-tech world-class entrepreneurs, producing not just engineers but more of MTech and PhDs. Institutes must take active hand in corporate development, by virtue of research become a "light house" for industry. The centre of gravity of operations must have to shift from UG to advanced education like PG, PhD and post-doctoral. This is what National Knowledge Commission 2006-07 has recommended. Without them India cannot hope to become a superpower, and achieve its declared dream. Without research, innovation, technology transfer Indian institutes may keep on producing engineers but they will be just followers and not leaders. They will not be able to create new India which people dream. Will India create a brand name in innovation? Without it India will lag behind in brain race.

Attempts for reforms are being made in India through Technical Education Quality Improvement Program (TEQIP). Techniques of industrial management like Total Quality Management (TQM) are being implemented. Leaders in industry are being appointed as chairman and members of Board of governors. These efforts are good but not enough. Hi-breeding by way of transnational collaboration is necessary. Role of academicians in reformation is crucial. The authors say leadership skills on the part of academicians to establish and run institutes in world-class manner need urgently to be developed. It is ultimately the academicians alone who can change the scene in institutes. First-class professors need to be recruited and deputed to world best institutes and enabled to grow to the international standard. Professors and researchers need to be respected more. Science and technology need to be accorded more budgets, comparable to those in developed countries. The establishment of new institutions like new universities, new IITs, IIMs, as declared by government has to be designed and implemented not in a routine manner but in a world-class manner. These institutes must be designed with the involvement of world best professors, regardless from which country they come. We did this in IITs and so they shine.

Education must be Enterprising Oriented to Producing Entrepreneurs like Narayan Murthy, Bill Gates[9]

An institute exists basically for two purposes. First, it exists to educate people, to make them more competent to do jobs using the state of the art technology. Secondly, it exists to conduct research, innovation and use their findings in various vocations and professions. The purpose of education is to instill knowledge in those who undergo education. The purpose of research is to discover to create new knowledge, new theories, new technologies, etc. so as to raise human civilization to greater heights. Institutes are also expected to train professionals to do professional practices more efficiently, to do consultation, technology transfer, assist students in career planning and contribute to broader social agenda among other things. They must promote entrepreneurship.

The role models of students should have to shift to becoming world best entrepreneurs. But these are not the things; they were expected to do in the past. These are now the new additions in their roles. Modern institutions unlike in the past have now to target to build a learning society consisting of learning organizations and continuously learning individuals. They have to play different roles in a variety of ways. All institutes however may not do all that. They may choose to do what fits in their visions and missions, and fits in their respective resource availability.

Education should reach to excellence which comes through research and innovation institutes which engage themselves simultaneously both in research and teaching are found to show excellence and hence are preferred by scholars. It is this kind of institution which tends to excel in competition and attains the world-class status. People want world-class education. But where do we find world-class education? It is available in only a few institutions like IITs. Many universities and colleges are not able to give. Students are going abroad by spending huge sums of money. According to one estimate, the total drain on foreign exchange, every year is equivalent to the cost of establishment of 20 IITs. The purpose of education in changing global context must therefore be understood by people who matter most to bring about changes. Only those who realize this win.

Teaching and research ought to go together.[10] An investment of rupee one in research in an educational institute does double duty. Firstly, it produces research output in the form of new knowledge, new technology, contributing to human civilization. It enhances economic competitiveness. The students at younger age are more agile and productive in research. Catch them young, becomes possible. Secondly, it results in elevating the educational standard of students and thereby quick dissipation of the findings of research to society, making it competitive. It is thus giving double profit. Research funding in an education institute is adding greatly to human capital making them innovative lifelong. Developed nations follow this strategy and hence they are found to be more progressive. India should therefore learn to invest with priority in research in institutes of technical education. There is lot of potential lying idle in youths in these institutes. Will India succeed to utilize it, remains to be seen?

Research Subsidizes Education, and Education Subsidizes Research[11]

A modern institute is a place where teachers simultaneously do research, and where researchers do teaching. It is observed that in these institutions teachers teach the latest and researchers discover unknown faster and better. The new sunrise knowledge, which they discover, flows automatically to classrooms. They tend to teach tomorrow's knowledge today. They remain ahead of time. Professors conduct research with the help of students at a cheaper cost and in lesser time. Students acquire research and an innovation skill which they use lifelong, is the prime gain. It is the best economic proposal for any nation. Teaching and research are thus found to be complementary to each other. Hence, they must go together. Students learn to cultivate habit to dream high and possess tenacity to fulfill the dream. In the absence of research in an educational institution, professors tend to teach sunset technologies, i.e. yesterdays knowledge today, throwing the new generation behind time.

This however does not mean that teaching institutions and teaching professors are not necessary. They also have a place in society. There are jobs which do not require research skills. Working knowledge is required to handle in marketing, purchase and manufacturing. They are quite large in number. Teaching institutions do important job of providing people for them. Such institutions and professors in them however need continuous updating. They must have to undergo retraining at the hands of researching professors.

Nations with higher knowledge level are found economically more secure. Emphasis on technical education in developing countries to elevate technology level therefore achieves high importance.

Are researching professors passionate to teach? Students ought to learn not only the known knowledge and known professional practices but learn to discover unknown. They ought to elevate professional practices constantly to newer heights. The professors and students rightly form a wider community of close knit researchers; build a team to become think-tanks for the society. Thus, an institution fulfils both teaching and research functions in a most efficient manner. It is this intimate connection—the idea that professors bring cutting-edge knowledge and expertise to the classroom that makes the institution relevant and purposeful. Institutions which are involved in only teaching remain teaching shops teaching 'parrot like' that which is obsolete, irrelevant and comes to them from other researchers mostly in foreign. They have therefore no first-hand experience and hence lack force in teaching. Researching professors are found highly passionate to test and teach new knowledge to students. Institutions are thus the testing grounds, of forthcoming technologies and generations.

Teaching and Research have no Force without being Tied Together

There is a school of thought that those who pay more attention to research tend to neglect teaching. They believe students are put to disadvantage. However, this is a myth. How much time a professor should devote to research and how much to teaching is an art. This has to be left to the judgment of individual professor. It is observed on the whole that students prefer to have instruction at the hands of researching professors. All world-class institutions excel simply because professors in them are research oriented. They have excellent bond with students. They function in an autonomous manner. In such institutions, there is always a tension between teaching and research. The tension is like the tension in rope of a bow only on account of which arrow moves forward with force. Education gets force on account of this tension.

Modern Institutes should be Multifaceted[12]

Technical education institutes have no longer to be simple. They have to be reformed much beyond classroom teaching and learning. They have to be necessarily multifaceted complex organizations in part driven by technology and in part mirroring other organizations in the world. Increasingly, they have to cater to people's demands such as research skills, i.e. generation of new knowledge, technology innovation, patenting and IPR, lifelong education, technology incubation, technology transfer, entrepreneurship, start up companies, venture capital, etc. It is these aspects whose presence in campus is adding to institute's reputation. They create and add tremendous value in learning environment. Students at UG, PG, and doctoral levels get thereby inspired to dream high, learn even that which is beyond curriculum and learn to be innovative and creative to take paths not trodden by their predecessors. Research, patent and IPR, entrepreneurship, etc. enable to get more value out of investments in an institution. They increase the financial rate of return. Institutes become more viable. They succeed in attracting more and more funds.

The paper emphasizes the urgent need to establish on priority basis the units like research park, technology incubator patent and IPR centre, entrepreneurship development centre, technology transfer centre, venture capital fund, innovation centre, etc. on the campus. This is to set a tone of discovery, innovation, creativity, spin-offs, new technology-based firms, create technology pioneers, etc. in economy. Without this the paper argues that India, in spite of its potential will lag behind.

Attracting best talent in PG, PhD matters. A nation cannot win economic war with only soldiers like BTech degree holders. Captains and Generals with MTech, PhD degree are needed. In India not many scholars however are found to be attracted to postgraduation and doctorate courses. Why? An analysis will indicate that due to poor infrastructure and poor knowledge availability at institutes, value addition being made through these courses is less than the value addition made by working in industry. Besides, the students have also to forego the salary income. The institutions are deficient in respect of multifaceted activities. Many students in competition prefer to go to universities abroad. Indian institutes to that extent are losing talent, and hence lagging behind. They need to be made attractive enough in comparison with their counterparts abroad. Also they must have to offer what industry cannot in terms of research, innovation, etc. Without innovation infrastructure, institutes will not be able to produce captains needed to win in world economy. Achievement-oriented missions in Indian institutes need urgently to be practically built on big scale. Capability building is a big challenge to reach to world-class standards. Institutes ought to be empowered with autonomy to do all that and to award degrees of BTech, MTech, and PhD.

Number of PhDs awarded by an institution has become a differentiating factor of one nation from the other. It is now the critical measure for economic development. By virtue of this they alone tend to become a 'light house' for industry and to bring prosperity to the nation. The purpose of an institution thus goes far beyond and extends to nation building and building humanity. Many institutions in the world attract scholars from anywhere and everywhere in the world. This is the strategy worth emulation.

Do we give research grant to professors at the time of appointment?[13] If yes, it will attract better talent in professorship to increase university value. Education is not necessarily synonymous with teaching. One can acquire knowledge by reading, researching, experimenting, discussions, etc. Being taught in a classroom is only one way of learning. Similarly, new knowledge can be developed through the simple act of thinking like Gautama Buddha. An institute is one place in society where inquisitive minds assemble to brainstorm, leading to breakthroughs yielding enormous benefits to society. It is a place where a student motivated by questions like why and how can find answers. An institute to be excellent has necessarily thus to be multifaceted. It must grant funds for research right at the time of appointment. Many institutions in the world are doing and this is the best way to become world-class.

Should Institutions be Autonomous and Transnational in Character?

Yes, without which they will not be able to bring about changes. The mandate to an institution is to preserve, discover and carry knowledge from one generation to the next. This mandate cannot be fulfilled without financial resources and grant of autonomy. It is for the government to allocate adequate funds out of public exchequer, yet grant autonomy, i.e. liberty to think and liberty to act and not intervene in its internal matters. It is obviously because government is least qualified in academics, it cannot steer the direction and hence it should not interfere. Public private partnerships are being evolved to make most of knowledge and financial resources available in any society for the cause of technical education. Transnational partnerships for both research and education are also growing. They must grow so as to tap and bring together good work being done everywhere and anywhere in the world. Experience tells us that transnational research linkages are vital to effective teaching. It creates favorable environment for achieving excellence. Nations are prosperous where institutions are autonomous and transnational in character, multifaceted and free to conduct teaching and research in a multiple way. Institutes should keep control of their destiny in their own hands; hence they should necessarily be autonomous. If control goes elsewhere it will then not be able to do justice to its vision and mission.[14]

Make Governance and Leadership Fit for New Visions

Improving governance and leadership of institutions so as to install research park is essential. The old style of working and thinking does not suit. Bringing corporate principles of management in academic institutions is a trend. It is good but not enough.

How does an institute differ from an industry? Can industrial management practices work well in academics?

Management of a small institute worth the name is much more difficult than management of a big factory, so said Pandit Jawaharlal Nehru in 1959 on the occasion of laying the foundation stone of IIT Mumbai.

Institutes are meant to produce leaders, leaders for the nation and leaders for the world. This is what American universities are doing. Many leaders in many countries have received education in USA. Today's leaders were students yesterday. Some of the students of today are going to be the leaders of tomorrow. An institute deals with human beings who create future engineers to run factories. An industry on the other hand deals with machines and materials for profit. They produce goods and services, which is much different from producing leaders. An institute attempts to unfold the capabilities lying dormant within the students. Professors are research scientists working for a much broader aim like developing human civilization. Factory managers on the other hand are in service of factory management. Industries do processing on non-living materials. There is thus a vast difference between the two. Skills needed in factory management and institution management is much different.[15]

Management Strategies Need Modifications to Fit New Visions[16]

Factory methods and strategies for improvement like TQM do not apply as they are to academic institutions. They need to be modified so as to suit and achieve the humanistic and scientific excellence of an institute. The spirit of academics should not be lost while implementing TQM. The quality of education leading to excellence does not have external referent like in industry. In globalization links between the institutions with the government of nation state are weakening, although they provide funds. Links are strengthened with bodies which work for humanity. Institutes are more in the service of humanity in general. Personnel from industry who are associated with academic institutions in their management should have to bear theory of education in mind.

The strategies employed for successful working of a factory therefore do not necessarily apply to all activities in an institution. Institutes are not for profit like factories. That is why they are registered not under companies act but under charitable trusts and society's act. However, of late institutes for profit are on horizon. They are under debate and discussion.

There is a school of thought that institutes must remain institutes and industries must remain industries. Each has a separate reason to exist. There are some common purposes for which they may have to come closer. Industries need to have a continuous flow of competent manpower, new knowledge and new technology so as to remain competitive globally. It is the institutions which are legitimately meant to supply. Industries have R&D cells. All the research which the industry needs cannot however be done all alone by itself. Some research of fundamental nature for public good has to be necessarily done in institutes. Professors need freedom to think and freedom to act much more than in industry. They do research not alone in private interest but also in public interest. They need more mobility and sharing of research experience across the world. To be a successful leader in industry is one thing. To be a successful leader in an academic institution is quite another. The skills needed, knowledge and mind set needed for each is much different. However, there are commonalities.

Industries cannot do all the long-range research they need to be competitive by themselves. They essentially need support of universities. To illustrate

> The invention of Geographical Positioning System [GPS] was initiated in Cambridge University by a UG student named Kleppner under the guidance of his professor. This invention today is found to have a high impact in automobile sector. The impact came after a period of 50 years. Universities do not take a short-range view like an industry. Return on investment in academics is not immediately apparent. Economic analysis indicates that

the returns from research to the institute are about 20 per cent, to the nation 50 per cent, and much greater to global society. The impact of research done in institute is on a much larger plane from which many industries world over draw benefits. This is not the case in isolation but there are innumerable cases of them. Larger public interest has to be kept in view in coming of industry and institute together. Industries are benefitted most by conducting research in universities. They must cash on research in universities and support them financially.

What can We Conclude?

Waves of technology are sweeping the world. Now is time for India to dream big and take a jump start in creation of new technology. Do we want Indian brands of technology? Or do we want to follow the foreign brands like in the past? Indian brands require creation of hi-tech enterprises, technology and business incubators, entrepreneurship, research parks, patent and IPR, venture capital fund, continuing education centres, etc. Enterprising institutes have a deeper impact on improving the quality of education making it more relevant and purposeful. Scope of PG, doctoral and post-doctoral courses must be widened. Institutes ought to expand and look beyond conventional horizons to what their counterparts elsewhere in the world are doing.

Indian universities and colleges must have to study the strategies, visions and missions adopted by world best. Internationalization should become the trend. Can we create world-class centres of excellence? This will decide India's future.

The Indian economy can flourish only if there is a culture within the country which is favorable to innovation and technology transfer. Is finance for innovation available? The priority given to S&T in national budget, although increasing, is still far from adequate. Research, education, and industry are isolated from each other, which constrain their growth. Venture capital is not available for innovation in universities and there is a fear for failure. How many patents are obtained every year by each university/college? How many NTBFs are born in university?

How many pioneer technologies are developed? These are the pertinent questions now to be asked.

India dreams to become a technology power in the world which could be made possible by adopting world best policies and practices and not without them. The sermons of National Knowledge Commission must forthwith be heard and implemented.

Institutions must be governed, managed and maintained by following world proven academic principles. Permitting mobility of professors and establishing transnational collaborations between the institutions is essential. Professors should be enabled to rise to international standard for which suitable schemes must be designed.

"The success in international competition depends now on turning intellectual strength in to marketable commodities".

NOTES

1. Abheek Barman, "Fund a lab and grow", *Economic Times*, 2 May 1997.
2. The role of science parks in the promotion of innovation and transfer of technology, Proceedings of the Science Parks Association, Annual Conference 6-7 April 1989.
3. "Great minds meet at MaRS Centre—Taking Canadian innovation to world"—University of Toronto Research Park "MaRS" in Toronto—Canada Research Park.
4. Frank H.T. Rhodes, *The Role of American University: The Creation of the Future*, Cornell University Press.
5. Rising Above the Gathering Storm Report Published by National Academy of Sciences US, 2007.
6. National Knowledge Commission report 2006-2007.
7. Rob Bowden, *Globalization: The Impact on Our Lives*, Rain Tree Chicago Publication.
8. *Creating Knowledge, Strengthening Nations—The Changing Role of Higher Education*, Edited by Glen A. Jones, Patricia L. McCarney, and Michael L. Skolnik—University of Toronto Press.
9. B.M. Naik, 2004, Technological Innovation in Educational Institutes, *The Indian Journal of Technical Education*, Vol. 27, No. 2, pp. 59-61.

10. Innovation and Technology Transfer, News Letter of the Institution of Engineers [India] 1998.
11. Robert E. Goheen, *The Human Nature of a University*, Princeton University Press, 1969.
12. B.M. Naik, *Global Visions and Missions in Technical Education*, 23 Meher Nagar Garkheda, Aurangabad, India, 2008.
13. Charles M. Beach, Robbin W. Boadway, R. Marvin Mclnnis (ed.), *Higher Education in Canada*, John Deutsch Institute for the Study of Economic Policy, Queens University.
14. University of Ontario—Research and development Park at Sarina Lambton campus and London campus-Canada-website.
15. Neil Tudiver, *Universities for Sale*, Canadian Association of University Teachers.
16. *Op. cit.*, Ref. 4.

Chapter 13

Revamping of Higher and Technical Education Going to Higher Orbit

If the reforms do not happen in time Narayan Murthy said, India would lose out on global scenario.

ABSTRACT

Where does India stand in the world list in higher education? Why thousands of students every year go abroad? Have we failed as a society to provide adequate opportunities to our youth to be educated in world-class manner? Have we failed in creating a vibrant educational ecosystem that supports cutting-edge research? How are their institutes different from Indian? What do they teach which we do not? Where do we go wrong? Teaching profession in India is a grim affair. Whereas it is prestigious in foreign. We have too much of rote learning. They have more of innovation, creativity. All teachers abroad hold doctorate degree, whereas in India very few. Why coaching industry in India is booming? Nalanda and Taxshila were the first universities of the world, where scholars used to come from abroad. Now why a shift in culture has taken place and our scholar students going abroad? Is it due to inadequate value attached to discovery of new knowledge, new theories? It is essential at this juncture of time to make introspection and learn from the world experience in science and engineering education. The future of youths depends on knowledge, rather than resources. Status of India in world, in leadership, income level, and well-being of people depends on its scientific and technological capability. India, to cope with challenges will have to enlarge the scope of institutions to cover research, innovation, creativity, generation of theories, technology creation, patent and IPR, creation of new technology-based firms, etc. What value we attach to above in budgeting? How can we bring back the past glory of Nalanda?

Students studying today in universities are tomorrow's leaders, in politics, industry, academics, etc. They sit in Parliament, board room, write books, become creative thinkers, and drive the society to progress. For India to win in world economy they have to be competitive by world standards. To be able to have world-class leaders tomorrow we have to have world-class professors and world-class institutes today. They have to learn not only known knowledge but learn to discover unknown.

The article presents in brief, the gap analysis in respect of visions and missions; policies and practices; organization structures, systems and procedures in India and their counterpart institutions in developed countries. They are critical to the success. IITs were set up under foreign collaboration. Their visions missions, policies and practices are molded on foreign lines. Hence, they could shine. The paper observes that rest of the Indian higher education is far too behind. India will have to capitalize on emerging technology to fulfill people's needs. Institutions will have to have wellsprings of new knowledge like in developed countries and not remain mere reflection centres. The gap analysis presented here makes an attempt to find answers to the questions raised above.

ENVISION CREATING LEADERS

Importance of academic institutions in today's volatile time is very high. It is the institutions which are furthering human civilization to greater heights. It is the academicians who provide new knowledge, new theories new technology and competent manpower to industry, leaders to government and leaders to the total economy. This in turn creates wealth and comforts. Industry, society and government in return ought to provide funds to academics to make it grow. India and for that matter any nation can be richer only by use of advanced knowledge. There is no other way. What kind of leaders our institutes produce matter.

This is a time characterized by change. The world under the forces of globalization is changing fast. Institutions would have also to change. Only those who change to innovate and again innovate tend to educate the youths on correct lines. Students now demand world-class education. Institutions in India will have to be competitive by nothing less than world-class so as to remain in service. Otherwise foreign universities will come here and capture major share of education market, and our students like in the past will keep going abroad.

People in India are as intelligent and hard working as else where in the world. However, today their efforts do not bring fruits as much as their counterparts. We work six days a week as against five days in foreign. Yet per capita income is around only 1000 dollars where as that of USA is 30,000. It is 30 times more. They work less and earn more. Twenty-five per cent people in India, live below the poverty line. It is mainly because of the lack of new visions of new world. It is due to lack of dedicated effort to realize the vision. We lack vision of research based education, relevant to the current needs. It is the people's development, development of men and women who constitute the society which matters more.

The systems employed in India in education and all other walks of life are less efficient than those in developed countries. Indians when they migrate abroad they are found to contribute far more. It is the systems efficiency which enables people to contribute more. We are spending resources and efforts on education but because of outdated systems output is less. Indian students study so much with less relevance. Foreign students study so little but with high relevance. This makes them more competitive. Our visions and missions, policies and practices, systems and procedures need examination in the light of world proven policies and practices. They need substantial improvement. Hence is the importance of gap analysis.

IDENTIFICATION OF GAPS, AND THEIR ANALYSIS

The paper presents only critical gaps which demand immediate attention. They are presented with a constructive criticism.

Creativity, Discovery, Innovativeness is the Character of Institutes Abroad. Is it so in India?

I was reading an article written by an American author in the journal, *Fortune*. The writer was addressing the question, "Can India ever compete with US in software business?" To answer the question, he made an analysis of higher education in both countries, and recorded that Indian system is rote learning that is to say mechanical, stereo type based on memorization and not creative thinking. Students are taught sunset knowledge. Institutions in India do not produce new knowledge, new theories. Students are not learning innovation and hence they do not know how to discover unknown. They are reflection centres teaching that knowledge which comes to them from developed countries. It does not focus on creativity, discovery and innovation. He came to the conclusion that Indian institutions can produce at best followers in technology but not leaders. On the other hand, thrust of US universities is on producing leaders, discoverers, creators, who obtain patents and intellectual property. It is US which are pumping new technology most in the world market. Eighty-five per cent of IPR is held by Americans. He said student's education in universities and colleges is an enabler to competitiveness of software industry. A nation creating followers can never compete with a nation creating leaders, unless in future it improves. Universities in India need to incorporate creativity in syllabi and aim to produce leaders.

Another study from Duke University was examining if there is a threat from India to US competitiveness. It observed that today the quality of Indian engineering schools is by and large poor. The number of MTech and PhDs who are crucial to technological innovation are too few and so India is far too behind in innovation. It concludes by saying that India on account of poor higher education does not pose a challenge to US competitiveness in near future.

Universities abroad have been upgraded as birthplaces, [maternity homes], of New Technology-based Firms. How many of our universities do this?

MIT Boston is giving birth to as many as 50 companies every year. Microsoft was born in Harvard. There are more than 3000 companies which owe their origin to MIT. Australian universities (Fang Zaho),[1] each one is giving birth to 40 companies every year. Chinese universities of late are also doing the same. Why Indian universities cannot? How many companies are born in Indian universities? They can do this. But they need to have this vision. Where do our institutes stand in comparison with their counterparts? In the recent past IIT Mumbai has set up a technology incubator, Business incubator. It has started spinning off hi-tech enterprises. Employment and income generation depends on New Technology-based Firms. It is these companies which provide new life and blood to industries and keep them technologically up to date. This gap needs to be filled up with priority. Indian Universities need to take a drive to adopt new visions as their counterparts to install a mechanism for spinning off companies. It is reported that IISC Bangalore has recently made collaboration with MIT Boston in this respect.

Institutes Abroad Display Patents for Sale in Industrial Exhibitions

Do we do that? Patents are unknown to institutions in India. It is good to do research but it is essential to make commercial exploitation of the findings of research. This makes research financially more viable, and attracts more funds. Today, the economic returns obtained from research done in India are far too few. This has been our weakness, and so actual funding for research does not grow.

A few years back I happened to visit Handover industrial exhibition. There was a pavilion meant for universities and colleges. It was most crowded by the visitors. Students were explaining the new researches, emerging technologies like, patents and IPR to visitors. Universities had come from world over to display. Visitors wanted to know the technologies of tomorrow. In India how many institutions have obtained patents and participated in industrial exhibition? Students do research for PhD, MTech. Thesis remains in library. It is published in journals and is being harvested by foreigners for obtaining patents. We do not exploit research done commercially. Even the traditional knowledge like Haldi, Turmeric, Ayurvedic medicines, wheat, etc. are converted in to patents by USA. We need to build this culture in our education. If the young students learn this they follow in future career. If they do not learn they do not practice. Attempts by Technology Information and Assessment Council (TIFAC), New Delhi, a Government of India body, are being made to popularize patent, IPR. It has yet to reach universities and colleges. We need to protect our research findings before publication by patenting and convert it in money. Research is a wealth generating mechanism provided it is converted in to patents, IPR. When shall we realize this? (Naik 2004).[2]

Institutions in India today are distinctly a technology follower. They do not lead; do not give birth to new technology. They are by and large inward looking, restricting to classrooms and not going beyond. They lack the world vision. They are not enabled to think and act in this direction, the situation needs correction.

We need to install patent IPR centres in each institute and display patents in exhibitions. Industry is keen on knowing emerging technology. Institutes should aim at that. Visions of our institutions need to be enlarged, to go beyond to what their counterparts else where in the world are doing.

Institutions Abroad are in Driver's Seat. Indian Institutions are followers like Bogies of a Train

A friend of mine 25 years back went to USA. He studied MS, PhD and then started a company in Silicon Valley. He returned to India after a gap of 25 years, we received him on the airport at Mumbai. He was curious to know about the progress made by India. We were driving by car to Pune. He was happy to see the new high way, as good as in USA. When we came to Pune I was telling him now we have entered Pune. He was not able to see any signs of his time on roads. He would not believe that this is Pune. He said how Pune can change so much, beyond recognition.

We came on Deccan Gymkhana, yet he was not ready to believe that this is Pune. Then we came on Laxmi road. He did not see a single bicycle, which at his time used to be crowded. Then we came on railway station. He did not see a single horse tanga. He refused to accept that it was Pune. Then we brought him to the college where he studied. Immediately he exclaimed, now I cannot refuse. He said whole city has changed but his college has not. He said in USA cities change because of institutions. In India, institutions are followers of change.

Institutions in India, instead of becoming an engine have become bogies. This he said is an unfortunate situation. Legitimately, institutions should have to initiate changes in society. Institutions need to have attitude to shape the development. Only those cities are well developed where universities are having such visions.

Institutes abroad have innovative character. They produce far more captains and Generals (MTech, PhDs); we produce more soldiers, (BEs.) Teaching Assistantship and Research Assistantship in India are almost absent.

I have visited more than two dozen universities in Germany, China, UK, US. I found that they are in the pursuit of discovery, research and innovation.[3] Their centre of gravity is on post-graduation and Doctoral studies. They produce far more graduates of advanced degrees. They produce more captains and generals. We produce more of soldiers. They produce around 7720 PhDs (2006) whereas in India around only 5000 are registered for PhD, many of them are in service lecturers from little known colleges. There are no schemes like teaching assistantship and research assistantship in many universities, to attract the fresh scholars. This is a serious shortcoming of our education.

It is on account of advanced courses offered in the institute that the quality of UG becomes superior. They teach sunrise knowledge and sunrise technology. According to the report of G. Bush Commission, namely "Science the Endless Frontier", research is the main function of university and teaching is a by-product. Teaching without research leads to irrelevance, and obsolescence. In India, this is the status.

Many universities in India teach sunset technologies to students. Institutions are behind the time. According to Mckinsey report published recently only 30 per cent of the engineering graduates are employable. Government has now proposed, "Finishing Schools" in IITs and NITs to educate half-baked graduates coming out of universities. From NASSCOM to CII, every body is crying hoarse about the quality of our technical manpower.

Education to policymakers to make policies enabling institutes to become innovative like abroad is necessary. Policymakers should enable the professors to be innovative and produce more of MTech and PhDs that is to say captains and generals. This is a major point of difference between Indian institutes and their counterparts abroad.

Size of Institutions Abroad is Large and Hence Economical. In India it is Pigmy, Uneconomical

National University Singapore has 350 acres of land but it has 1900 professors and 32,000 students. MIT Boston has about 500 acres of land and 40,000 students with 3000 professors. Georgia Tech University has 20,000 students and 1000 professors. It offers 130 different courses. Karlsruhe University in Germany has 30,000 students and 2000 professors. Our universities by and large are pigmy in size. They have big land of the order of 1000 acres but students and professors are far too few. Pankaj Jalote[4] in one of his articles has advocated scaling up the strength of students in IITs from 4,000 to 10,000. Courses offered are stereotyped besides too low in number. Most of the universities like Pune, Mumbai in their campuses have too few students and faculty. Aurangabad University for example has 500 acres of land, has 1000 students and has only 100 faculty strength. The size of our institutes is uneconomic. They are over capitalized in terms of land and buildings. Universities abroad open at 8 in the morning and remain open up to midnight. We open at 10 in the morning and close at 5 pm. There is a big difference in libraries. They are far too behind. Capacity utilization of installed facility in India is too small. Private colleges in engineering are like small "pan shops" with out PG and PhD education. There are no wellsprings of knowledge in the institutions. They depend on borrowed knowledge. The scope of our institutions needs improvement. They need to see what is happening elsewhere in the world and do benchmarking.

They have Built Visions for Patent IPR Culture for the Year 2015. Have We?

How many of our universities and colleges have patent culture? MIT Boston every year obtains around 100 patents. The institute has a Technological Licensing Office with 200 people working in it. There is a trend of commercialization of new technology in almost every university. It is a source of income to the professors, students and the institute. Many universities in Germany, UK have patent departments. In fact, their performance is measured in terms of how many patents are obtained and the revenue earned. They have Technology Incubators, Business Incubators, research parks and Venture Capital Firms available in campus. Students develop skills of innovation and patenting in them. This is our serious weakness. This is one of the important reasons why Indian students go abroad. We need necessarily to learn from international experience abroad.

They Give High Priority to Education in National Budget. What Priority We Give?

Professor's profession is very important, but the profession is not made attractive. Education is not accorded the priority it deserves in national budget. It does not get budget as their counterparts. India spends around 3 per cent only where as developed countries spend around 10 per cent of GDP. Budget allocation to R&D in India is only 0.8 per cent of GDP whereas in China it is 1.5 per cent. Papers published and patents obtained in China are ten times larger. Less number of people and that too poorly are therefore educated. This adversely affects the quality of leadership in all walks of life. Technological content in economy is far too low. It is to be realized that it is education which makes a man competitive. Without education man is less than an animal. It is like training a cook to prepare food. A trained cook uses less material yet prepares tasty food. Untrained man is unfit to live a worthy life. Nobel Laureate Dr. Amartya Sen recommended increasing budget on education. The then Finance Minister Mr. Yashwant Sinha asked him what should be the first priority in budget. He replied education. Then he asked what should be the second priority? He again replied, education. Then he asked, what should be the third priority? He replied again education. Should the government care for his advice?

Policymakers in India are not Galvanized with New Ideas

Foreign universities galvanize their leaders from time to time with new ideas. Do we? Strategies employed in India are far too behind the world. The strategies have almost no strength to take the nation forward. Research subsidizes education and education subsidizes research. Research and education are complementary to each other. This world proven fundamental strategy is not adhered to. Strategies adopted in India are not strong enough in world comparison.

There is a story of two armies which were fighting a battle with each other. One army had a lion as its captain, but the soldiers were sheep. The second army had a sheep as its captain and lions as soldiers. The lion captain employees bold strategies. The other captain, a sheep designs strategies like a coward and loses even though his soldiers are lions, because the soldiers have to follow the strategies drawn by captain. It is the strategies which enable the army to win.

Situation of India is something like sheep as captain. We have a strong base of intellectuals, and academicians but strategies which are drawn by leaders in bureaucracy and leaders in politics are weak. Academic leadership as a result at national/state/ institution levels is crippled. Students of today are tomorrow's leaders. To have good leaders tomorrow we have to have good institutions today. Shivaji had much smaller army than Aurengzeb but still he could win, because he employed better and bold strategies like a lion.

There is a greater need to shed the mental weakness in academicians. They need to be enabled to grow at par with their counterparts abroad.

Brain Power is Nursed Abroad. It is Wasted in India

Brain power is said to be more powerful than any other power, like money power, political power, electrical power, etc. Demand for knowledgeable people in globalize world is sky rocketing. SEZs and industrial development plans demand people with skills like research, innovation, entrepreneurship, patenting and IPR. Nations which understand the dynamics of world market and match it with institutions will win. Others may work hard, spend resources but will lag behind in brain race. Those who take strategies in favor of nursing brain power are only to win.

We have to recognize the importance and work with knowledge, IPR rather than muscle. Salaries of only a few in industry are sky rocketing. Many on the other hand are jobless. They have brains but under nourished. The dichotomy can be resolved only by upgrading the institutions.

Academic freedom is the legal right of students and professors abroad. In India professors are servants without any academic freedom. They have to teach what is given in university syllabus. They cannot teach based on personal research. Students have no choice than to learn what is handed over to them.

Institutions also do not have academic freedom. This is proved from IIM-A case. They have become puppets in the hands of government. Independent free thinking and decision making is not allowed. CAFETERIA approach courses are not run, although badly needed. Industries are varied in nature and so are their manpower needs. Courses ought to be unique. Standardized stereotyped courses are giving birth to mediocrity. Hence, coaching classes industry is booming.

Academicians are being exploited by governing boards. The students and public at large are also being exploited. Academicians, however, ought to work in only public interest. Some times the government, institute and industry are too selfish damaging interest of public at large. Academicians therefore ought not to work to further in the foul interest of institute, industry or government. They must behave fully in a professional manner. For this they have to be autonomous by law, although they receive salary from institute, and from government or industry. World experience tells us that nations grow best only when academicians can function in autonomous manner.

Academicians generate sunrise knowledge and educate people to use. They essentially should not have to go too close to education barons, industry or to government. They should have academic freedom to be able to play their legitimate professional role including that of a critic. Academicians have to work in larger public interest, for maintaining a healthy national economy. They should not have to bend before education barons, industry or government. They work in the pursuit of new knowledge.

Indian economy is a low-income economy mainly because of lack of application of new knowledge. All institutions and professors should forthwith be made autonomous. Parliament and State Assembly should pass laws in national interest empowering professors for the cause of education.

Universities, institutions and private colleges have become the prisoners in the hands of government. Non-educational principles and strategies of government are guiding the people in universities and colleges. In fact, it should be the other way round. Higher education institutes have become slaves of whims and fancies of government. They change every five years when new party comes to power.

The scheme of contract appointment of lecturers on fixed salary of ₹ 12,000 is introduced in Maharashtra State. UGC and AICTE have objected. It has no backing of any academic body but only of bureaucracy. Mediocre are getting in. Although cheap, quality of education is deteriorated. Can the entry of professionals in teaching be protected? How can we produce globally competent leader engineers?

Government is not best qualified to govern education. Government should make only legislation for which it is meant. Long-range policies and practices in education in India need be made by professionals considering the trends in world.

Research is Main Focus Abroad. In India it is Lacking

Research is given back seat in higher education. Professors have no research grant. Institutes and universities have become teaching shops. Professors and students have no budget for research. Professors teach sunset knowledge coming from abroad. They have no research skills. They learn parrot like that which was taught to them ten years before. Neither the teachers nor students are trained to learn to discover what is unknown. Unfortunately, teaching and research have been segregated from each other. This leads to weakening of both. This is not the way to build a nation. They therefore remain followers. Research must become the core function of an institution.

Institutions are Governed in India by those who have Low Value for Academics

Privatization of education is good provided it is governed by those who have value for academics. In most of the cases, it is the politicians who do not understand it, and sit on the governing board. Today, education barons have usurped the powers of academicians. Professors have become humble servants.[5] They have no freedom to think and freedom to act. They have no budget for research. While money earned in colleges is siphoned for political purposes. This is too damaging for the future of children and grand children. That is one of the main reasons why brain drain from India is rampant.

Education barons have brought unethical commercial trends in education. Government is a party to it. Thinkers have no place in education. Nobler aims of education are thrown to winds. Bottoms 50 per cent of population, because fees are high, do not have access to higher education. Upper 50 per cent population is mediocre but wealthy and so gets access to higher education. India with such policies will stand to lose in brain race in long range.[6] The fabric of Indian culture is likely to be damaged. At a time when the level of education needed for productive employment is increasing, opportunity to go to college to bottom half population is decreasing. The common man is getting a feeling of betrayal, causing resentment which may lead to discontent, instability, even riots, which may be very costly. The present policies are an aid to Nexalite movement. Education institutes cannot and should not be run on commercial lines like General Motors. Public interest is being sacrificed by both government and industry. When shall we realize this?

There is no affiliating system abroad. In India it is rampant. It has killed the innovation capacity of students. Chancellor of universities should not be Governor. He should be an academician. Policies are at fault.

Inbreeding in higher education is taking place. University Acts are obsolete. Governor of a state who is not an academician but a politician is at helm of affairs, as the chancellor of universities. Chairman of UGC, Chairman of AICTE are academicians. How come chancellor of universities is a politician? This is not so abroad.

The chancellor of universities is the appointing authority for Vice Chancellors. He does appointments mostly on political considerations. Most of the VCs are misfits. He inducts politics in universities. The situation perpetuates down below. This has resulted in politicization of higher education. Blame is wrongly passed on to professors. Policymakers and the chancellors are truly at fault. The situation demands immediate change. We need to adopt international visions to improve.

Unless the change is brought in chancellor's post as suggested above, the affiliating system may not go. There are no affiliated colleges in developed countries. Every college from its beginning is autonomous.

There is More Number of Technical Universities Abroad. India has very Few

Almost half of universities in US are technical. Germany has more than 84 technical universities.[7] So is the case in Japan. It is observed that those nations which have more of technical universities have capitalized technology more effectively.[8] India has more multi-faculty universities, which is an outdated model. In these universities, technical discipline does not get a deal it deserves. Hence, it lags behind the world. AICTE has recommended establishment of exclusive technical universities. However, in most of the states there is only one technical university and many colleges are affiliated to it. It creates monopoly, bureaucracy. Efforts, investment done by colleges, students as a result do not get fruits they deserve. Agriculture universities which were set up in sixties developed new varieties of seeds, which have resulted in increased food production. Technical universities should not be only examination bodies awarding degrees but should generate new technologies and improve industrial production.[9] Future of children is linked up with creation of technical universities.

CONCLUSION

Good ideas are available not only in India but also abroad. We should not close our eyes and ears to them. We should not miss to benefit from them. Foreign collaborations are necessary. It is too costly not to interact with the counterparts elsewhere in the world. Mobility of professors to world best universities at any cost must be planned in a big way on priority. This is the only way to build good leaders and to take India on world map.[10]

We lack visions and not the resources. We lack interaction with our counterparts elsewhere in the world. We lack dedicated efforts. Institutions, universities need to show new visions of new world which inspire students to become leaders on global level. Institutions ought to shift their culture in favour of creativity, IPR and discovery. India's growth rate can be sustainable only if academic institutions adopt innovative character. Visions drive the national economies forward.[11]

In this time of knowledge society it is the intellectual capital that matters. People work with hands, but it is the brain behind which gives inspiration. Government should have to attach more value in national budget to create and use new knowledge.

The paper has identified only a few gaps, which are critical and need to be attended to forthwith. Without which higher education will not be up to the mark and fulfill the growing aspirations of people. Opportunities do not last longer. They do not wait. Achieving the declared dream of India to become a developed country by the year 2020 depends on how ably and urgently we initiate steps to make up the gaps.

We must not forget to recognize the importance of IPR. Creation of favourable environment for the same should be our top priority.

Rapid upgradation of higher education institutes and universities in the light of experiences in the world should urgently be taken up. There is nothing more urgent for India at this juncture of time than reviving higher education.

> Research Park leads to teaching valid knowledge. It gives quick returns at enhanced rate on investment. It gives strength to industrial development.

NOTES

1. Fang Zaho, Academic Entrepreneurship, Case study of Australian universities, Published in *International Journal of Entrepreneurship and Innovation*, pp. 91-97, IP Publishing Ltd., Vol. 5, No. 2, 2 May 2004.
2. B.M. Naik, Needed—Innovation and Entrepreneurship in Higher Education Institutes, Published in *Indian Journal of Technical Education*, January-March 2004, Vol. 27, No. 1, pp. 27-32.
3. Green paper of European Union on Innovation and technological transfer Enterprise Unit DG, EUFO, 2295-2920 Luxemburg.
4. Pankaj Jalote, "An Opportunity to Scale Up the IITs," *Economic Times*, 26 April 2007.
5. B.M. Naik, Privatization of Technical Education, Identification of Risk factors, and their Management-making Education affordable, *Journal on Engineering and Technology*, i-manager Publications, Vol. 1, No. 2.
6. James J. Duderstadt, "A university for twenty first century". The University of Michigan Press.
7. Derek Bok, Universities in the Market Place, The Commercialization of Higher Education, Princeton University Press, Princeton New Jersey.
8. Clark Kerr and Marion L. Gade, Association of College Boards of Universities of America. "The Guardians, Boards of Trustees of American universities and Colleges, What They Do and How Well they Do It."
9. William G. Bowen and Derek Bok, Princeton university press, "The shape of the river, long-term consequences of considering race in college and university admissions."
10. B.M. Naik, "New Vistas in Technical Education", Vivek Publication, Aurangabad.
11. V. Raghunathan, "India Needs More Quality PhDs", published in *Economic Times*.

Chapter 14

Role and Responsibility of Board of Governors (BOG)/ Board of Trustees in Ensuring Educational Quality in Colleges and Universities

Today success in the global marketplace means creating and applying new knowledge which is to say new technology-faster than one's competitors. World winners will be those who enable professors to reach to international standard, to generate new knowledge, new technologies, techniques and tools so advanced that there is no competition.

ABSTRACT

The paper presents in brief need and importance of effective, imaginative and responsible governing boards in colleges and universities, so as to ensure educational quality. Board of Governor (BOG) should engage fruitfully with the principal/vice chancellor and activities in college/university. Government has now prescribed creation of effective boards for both government and private colleges/universities and outlined their functions, duties and responsibilities (NPIU 2012). Quality of education in colleges is observed to be as good as the imagination and engagement of board with institutions. Discussions are made on their role and responsibility for effective governance. Conclusions are drawn so as to make colleges and universities innovative, creative, and qualitative by world standards.

INTRODUCTION

Why Indian universities and colleges do not figure in top one hundred? Why thousands of students every year go abroad? Students demand world-class education. They are ready to pay for. But not many colleges are able to offer. During the year 2011-12 as many as 1,04,000 students went to USA. Many more have gone to UK, Germany, and Australia. They have been going from Gandhi-Nehru period. How long should they have to go? Is education in India not up to student's expectations? Why foreign universities are coming? Is it not because there is a huge unmet demand? Why coaching classes are booming? Why formal education is decaying? Why industrial goods from east-west countries are flooding? India is not short of either talent or resources. But poor governance and poor leadership is the root cause, so observed the National Knowledge Commission (NKC) 2006. Do institutions lack ambition and commitment to rank high in world list? Do they fall short of resources or visions? In the era of globalization, India needs world-class professionals, to manage its professional affairs ably at national and international levels. Government is therefore planning to adopt globally-proven policies and practices, systems and procedures. Periodic feedback from students and alumni to reform education is a regular practice in foreign. Why it is not yet in India? Higher education now is facing global competition. Do we have world-class leadership in education? Can we create? What are the internal and external threats? What is the governing boards doing? If BOGs do not act, India will lose in brain race. It will trail behind the developed world, like in the past.

It is on the background of these questions that BOG and trustees must respond and come in action, make introspection and find out what is critical to quality, which when done quality will improve. Universities and colleges abroad have installed research parks, technology incubators, and patent and IPR centres.

These are the units which facilitate engagement of industry with colleges. Have we done this? This is the role and responsibility of BOG to expand horizons from classroom teaching to innovation, generation of new knowledge, new theories and new technologies. Knowledge is infinite. Students should learn to discover, innovate. Colleges have invested in buildings, equipment but not much in research. It is mainly the lack of research which is holding back quality. Can installation of quality assurance cells provide an aid? Is it possible to create a culture of self-discipline and self-assessment? Do the institutions care to increase their influence and outreach beyond classroom? What is the use of BOG if it does not ensure educational quality? If members of BOG come together with common commitment for change, change to world-class level is certainly possible. Creation of the future of children and grandchildren depends on how BOGs perform today. The article is an attempt of brainstorming to diagnose the problems and possibly evolve solutions. BOG has to learn how to be effective, from its counterparts elsewhere in the world. Will the BOG play its legitimate role effectively? This decides the future of institutions.

In view of above government with the assistance of World Bank has started Technical Education Quality Improvement Program (TEQIP) and 200 colleges country wide are being up graded to world-class level by investing around 5000 crore rupees. Academic culture is being improved. So as to achieve the mission, TEQIP has made it obligatory to these colleges, both in government and private, to appoint BOGs. As a consequence, for the first time in Indian Government has relaxed its direct supervision on government colleges and is indirectly supervising them through BOGs consisting of able professionals. Education will become world-class if and only if the boards perform effectively.

NEED AND IMPORTANCE

Innovative, accountable and effective BOG is the need of the hour. Many Indian universities and colleges have all the resources at hand. They spend money more than necessary, but in return they do not gain quality. Why? Studies show they do not have proper visions, missions and commitment to excel. Indian universities lack systems for quality assurance, quality policy, quality manual, quality planning and monitoring cells, and mechanism for periodic internal and external review. They lack methods and not the resources. They lack force in their action. The paper presents in brief, need and importance of effective board of governors for ensuring educational quality, in both private and public sectors. Effective BOG with ambition to rank high in world list is found to navigate the college to prosperity. Working hard by principal alone is good but not enough.

Good board selects and appoints good principal and good faculty. Good board attracts world-class professors and merit students from anywhere and everywhere, in the world. BOG together with the principal sits in driver's seat. They both jointly with faculty and staff are responsible for educational quality. It is observed that quality of education is as good as the imagination, visions and commitment of the board for the cause of education. If the board is excellent, the quality of education is most likely to be excellent and vice-versa. BOG needs however to envision new goals from time to time to cope with emerging opportunities and challenges in globalized world.

BOG is the chief fund raiser, raising funds with imagination from national and international sources. So far, colleges have neglected alumni as a source of money and ideas. Involvement of alumni to ensure quality education is essential to make institutions world-class. Board needs to engage appropriately with the principal, activities in college and alumni. BOGs are increasingly being appointed in more and more colleges private and public, which is good but it is better if board is consisting of visionary, imaginative, and responsible professionals. Nobel Laureates, Bhatnagar award winning scientists, industrialists and fellows from Indian Academy of Engineers (INAE), distinguished professors if appointed on board, they will make a big difference. Great leaders matter. World experience tells us that BOG of an institution serves the nation better in inculcating human and ethical values if it is protected by legislation from political and bureaucratic interference. Board chair should be as far as possible an eminent industrialist, educationist, committed to the cause of education. Successful boards have a culture of periodic scientific self-evaluation of college and all authorities including board itself. The paper provides a base for brain-storming. It is high time that

BOGs are created and activated to become an effective force in enhancing quality of education to world-class level.

Landscape of higher and technical education in the world is changing fast. Knowledge is becoming the driving force of world economy, obviously so knowledge institutions like colleges and universities are achieving significantly high importance (NKC, 2006). Providing good governance to them for improving quality and relevance of education has become of paramount importance. Good governance and distributed leadership is important for their own health and the health of Indian economy. It is the prime responsibility of the head of the institution, together with BOG. An institution in spite of all the resources at hand without good board may falter and lead to autocracy and disrepute.

Which government does not want to generate hi-tech employment, high pay international jobs, spur industrial growth, and make education globally competitive? Then it must install research/technology parks, incubators, patent and IPR to facilitate commercial exploitation of sunrise technologies. Classroom teaching is good but not enough. Industries, world over, are seen flocking round the advanced knowledge centres to obtain brand new ideas for global competitiveness. Institutes must have original knowledge springs like well water springs. They must have a mechanism to convert intellectual strength in to usable goods and services. Role of higher education has emerged central to industrial and economic development, in creating India's future. Industry is now research driven. Association with industry, venture capital firms, international agencies who succeeded in this cause is essential. Will BOG facilitate to build bridges?

Education does not grow where high-end research is absent. The paper prescribes "dream big" for BOG of universities and colleges. They should aim high at technology generation, technology diffusion, which is achieving high significance in enabling a nation to win. The paper emphasizes adoption of new organizational inventions like research park, technology park, which when implemented will contribute to India's international competitiveness. The institutions should have now to look beyond the traditional lines of teaching and learning and adapt to corporate development, and help industry to win. They should have to restructure themselves to become fountain heads of new knowledge and new technology. They should deserve the status of "Light House" for industry. Synergy between industry and academics in this cause is vital. Parks play a middleman's role in this. They have enhanced the scholarship of universities/ colleges elsewhere in the world. They jointly can give economic and political stability to India. Will industry-institute interaction become a national priority? The paper recommends especially these roles for BOG for reforms in the light of experience elsewhere in the world.

BOG to an institution is like navigator to a ship sailing in sea, charting the course by long-range planning, and using techniques of strategic planning, while the head of the institution is like a captain facing day-to-day operational problems. Both the BOG and the principal together are the key players to serve the educational interests of society. If navigation is proper the ship sails smoothly in intended direction. Good BOG ensures quality of education ensures economic security to India and avoids technological obsolescence.

Role and Responsibilities of Board

Boards of aided and government colleges and universities are appointed by following the prescribed procedures. They have wide powers within a budget approved by legislature. In private colleges and private universities, the boards are self-appointed as per UGC/AICTE guidelines. In both cases, board is the authority for all decisions, within the powers delegated to them, though in practice many responsibilities are delegated to others.

The members of the governing board represent the public interest in a broad sense and are responsible for the appointment of principal/director. Secondly, it is responsible for framing the institution's visions and missions, the oversight of its programs, its financial health and the good order of the campus. Successful boards create a collective ambition, collective passion, shared vision of growth and prosperity to bind all the people faculty, staff and students together. Each year it is the board which gives authority to the head of the institution to award degrees, subject to the recommendation of the faculty. It is the board that approves all new construction, new programs, and new ventures. The board approves appointments of all professors and staff. It is accountable for well-being of the institution. Functions of BOG as outlined by UGC are given in Annexure A.

The principal/director is the link between the board and the campus. The principal is responsible for all administrative arrangements for developing budget, admissions, examination, etc. and overall effectiveness of the institution. Board and principal both delegate substantial responsibility to the faculty. Vigorous governance by faculty lies at the heart. The faculty, in one sense are the institution. They determine who should be admitted, what should be taught and who should graduate. Faculty governance and responsibility remains at the core. The three, namely BOG, principal and faculty ought to clarify each other's roles, develop trust and confidence and exercise able leadership. Differences in opinion some times are however, inevitable. Leadership at each level plays a vital role to bridge.

Effective governance of the board. Governing boards must delegate some appropriate and well-defined authority to other responsible groups with the understanding that decisions made by them may sometimes be subject to board review and that board may not delegate its ultimate authority to subordinates. The responsibility of the board is to govern and not to manage. There needs to be an absolute clarity and the distinction between the governing function of the governing board and executive responsibility of the principal and the executive team led by him or her. Governing function is described by the saying, "Noses in-Fingers out" (Rhodes, 2001). This is the tested advice to board members. Whenever and wherever there is foul smell in an institution board is expected to go to its roots, diagnose the cause and evolve solution to stop further rot. It may take help of internal or external agency to evaluate and correct. Good BOG should not tolerate the rot for a long time. Good BOG finds solution for every problem.

The most important single responsibility of the board is the selection, appointment, periodic performance review and continuing support to principal and faculty. The most effective boards are those that have developed a board code of conduct and self-assessment practice of their own performance.

The institution is expected to provide salary, professional support, facilities, equipment and protection to academic freedom to professoriate, while the reciprocal obligations of the faculty member are not explicitly spelt out. To make faculty governance effective in the college "Socratic oath" is given in Annexure B, a practice from Cornell University. It is found to ensure creation of self-driven, self-monitored, self-actuating faculty for the cause of education and research.

Effective governance requires creating collective ambition, shared goals, dreams corresponding to counterpart institutions abroad, and that is the responsibility of the principal. Without strong and dedicated leadership of principal no system of campus governance can be effective. He should have the characteristics, given in Annexure C. He must bear in mind that tomorrow's leaders, who are movers and shakers of the world, sit today in his classrooms and he should dedicate his efforts in that direction.

Principal and board should not make small little plans. They should dream big, think great and make an attempt to be world-class. They must articulate institute's vision time and again to faculty, staff and students. There can be no great creation without a great dream. The vision drives the goals and creates a collective ambition, which is a great power. Principal should every time tone the debates and discussions with the dreams cherished by college. Principal has to create trust and confidence, encourage initiative, build teams, partnerships, rewarding achievements, and celebrate successes in campus. Good principal and a good professor are never "off duty". We know Newton invented the law of gravity while relaxing under a tree. Archimedes invented the principle while taking bath. Professor/principal's mind is always at work. Principal is a good leader if he succeeds in creating good leaders in his college at various levels. He need not try to be a good manager but try to be a good leader. He needs to prepare good agenda and notes for board meetings and drive them to conclusion. Family of the principal/professor in his busy schedule is most likely to be neglected. It deserves special support from board.

How visionary, responsible and imaginative BOG is, decides educational quality. The chair of BOG is responsible for the leadership of that body and has the ultimate responsibility for its effectiveness. The principal as chief executive is responsible for strategic direction and is accountable to BOG for effective management of the institution.

In autonomy principal is required to manage the college by following democratic methods. He should consciously avoid becoming autocratic.

Indian education is responding positively for global winds of change. Much foreign collaboration is being made both in private and public sectors. Students have craze for foreign degree.

The governing body acts as a custodian of the values, purpose and mission of the institution. Principal is the executive head who formulates them after wide circulation and consultation. He presents them to BOG in meeting for approval. BOG is unambiguously and collectively responsible for overseeing the institution's overall activities, determining its future directions, and fosters an environment in which the institution's mission can be achieved (AGB, 2011).

The most cherished values are integrity, impartiality, excellence, transparency, civility and self-actuating. These are the essential requirements for the effective pursuit of knowledge. Without respect for these values there can be no college/university worthy of name. In fact, those countries and institutions where these values have been neglected or suppressed, universities have become places of turmoil, with no worthwhile quality education.

Appointing responsible visionary BOG is the lesson we ought to learn from USA. Many US universities and colleges have appointed Nobel Laureates on board, and mainly so they rank high in world list. MIT Boston has six Nobel Laureates on board. Indian professors in USA have contributed to raise the performance of US universities to world number one. Brilliant dedicated professors here in India however falter, because they have to work under poor governance (World Bank).

Good governance will come to colleges if there are good BOGs. Absence of effective BOGs has led to mediocrity.

Absence of board or mediocre board is very costly, costlier than the cost involved in appointing a good BOG member even from abroad. Ineffective boards lead to autocracy and mediocrity. Good boards follow democracy and scholarship. Effective boards adopt world proven policies and practices, systems and procedures. They seek to achieve world standard in educational quality. They seek new strategies compatible to globalization. They bring professionalism which is so essential for quality in education.

Familiarization and concern of the trustees and BOGs to quality aspects to reach to world-class on continuing basis is the crying need of the hour.

There is a great scope in India to improve. Lack of quality education is reported to have led to 70 per cent unemployable graduates, so says NASSCOM. Effective BOG is expected to reduce this percentage if not eliminate. However, the principal should have to show good initiative to make most of the capacities of board members for the cause of education. Mediocrity is more costly than the cost of upgradation.

Good Governance. An important characteristic of good governance is that of probity, that is to say working honestly, earnestly in a transparent manner with integrity for public good (Kadam). Governing body should have to assert and be accountable to the interests of all stakeholders. BOG of an institution should be thinking body, sensitive to world dynamics, preparing students for globalized world. A good BOG scientifically evaluates its own performance from time to time. It is a great fund raiser, from alumni, national and international sources, so the institution gets financial strength to implement plans for future.

Successful BOG is that which arranges written feedback from students, faculty, staff, alumni on quality of education, and makes strength, weakness, opportunities and threats (SWOT) analysis from time to time. This is a powerful tool to know where the institute stands today, and where it tends to go. The results of SWOT analysis must be made known to all stakeholders.

AICTE has prescribed appointment BOG to new colleges starting from the year 2011-12. Educational institutions are non-profit organizations. They are registered with charity commissioner under the Society's Act. The trustees usually come from various walks of life. They may or may not have expertise in education. In the era of globalization, trustees all alone by themselves may not be able to give good governance to the institution. So AICTE Government of India from 2011-12 for newly starting self-finance institutions have made it obligatory to appoint a board of governors consisting of experts from various fields. The UGC and AICTE have outlined the composition, duties and responsibilities and their functions. Each institution will have to have its own BOG as per guidelines of UGC. The BOG will in all cases be headed by an eminent industrialist or distinguished educationist. Educationists are observed to bring, deeper insights in education.

Good BOG is spearheaded to excellence. BOG needs to be liberated from political influence (World Bank) the institution which is managed and maintained by government is also now required by government to appoint BOG. Until and unless it does so it is not eligible to receive financial grant from government. About 300 institutions which are selected under Technical Education Quality Improvement Program (TEQIP) have now under the prescriptions of AICTE appointed BOG (TEQIP, 2010). Government for the first time has relaxed its direct control on these institutions and is controlling them indirectly through BOG. These selected institutions have been granted autonomy. Autonomy in its real spirit will take some time to come. Fund raising, mobilizing alumni support and building synergy with industry and increasing outreach to global society, good governance achieving excellence, etc. are becoming new visions and missions. BOGs are created in these colleges, but some of them are highly influenced by politicians and bureaucrats. Governments elsewhere in the world are accepting the notion that institutions serve their nations better if BOGs are protected by proper legislation from political interventions. Government should make a note of winds of change in the world, and insulate institutions from disturbing forces.

Appropriate engagement of the board with the principal and educational activities in an institution is not an option but compulsion (World Bank). Board members are expected to demonstrate their sense of responsibility and commitment to society. Board by their charter of duties and responsibilities should oversee and shoulder the responsibility for quality of education and its relevance to the needs of society. Board members should not just attend meetings and remain decorative figures. They should not leave the matters totally to the principal and professors. Of course, they must respect the professorial community, and their legitimate rights. They should share efforts, maintain dialogue with them to put the college they serve in higher orbit. The journey to good governance is a long-drawn process and passes through several stages. Commitment of the trustees and board members to the cause of education however should remain at the heart.

Some suggestions for engagement of board with college are as under.

1. It should persuade government and banks to give cheap loans to students.
2. It should attempt to obtain endowments and scholarships from private sector.
3. It should attract and retain best faculty.
4. It should integrate high-end research with education.
5. It should follow efficient methods in examination, curriculum design, etc.
6. It should persuade faculty to obtain and effectively use autonomy.
7. It should attempt to build an atmosphere of trust and confidence in college.

Quality does not come merely by pumping more money and appointing more men but by introducing innovative methods. True feedback from students can help in this regard. Students, however, do not want to be detected, they are afraid, for obvious reasons they do not open mouth against the faculty. Secrecy for identity therefore needs to be maintained. Only BOG can remove their fears. Suggestion box in entrance of college may be put. Take a resolution in board meeting to take feedback from students, with or without signature. Feedback enables college to reach to the top. To reach to top is easy, but to remain there for long is difficult. Innovative methods to reach and remain on top are necessary at all the times.

Institutions have to develop higher capacities for internal governance. When the locus of responsibility for decisions about student examination, curriculum design, staffing, and the use of financial resources are shifted to institutional level. Composition of governing body has to be such that they become effective in achieving the mission (Naik, 2011). Appointment of quality cell, preparation of quality manual, and strategic plan is found to be useful. Often there is a tendency of conflicts between the groups in BOG, which should be consciously avoided.

How effectively the institutions respond to global opportunities and challenges matters. How the governance of colleges and universities can be improved to come up to the task? How to keep all the stakeholders happy? How to make BOG effective in performing their functions? How they can give creative solutions? How to increase the rank of the college/university, and make education qualitative and cost competitive are some of the questions? Where is the weak link? And how to make it strong needs exploration. It is the board which will undertake (Glen, 2003).

The paper has attempted to address these questions and raised some more like, how the boards of colleges and universities can do their best to ensure educational quality? What policies and procedures they should adopt to make institution innovative?

Should BOG assess its own performance from time to time? Will this leverage for reformation? BOG can demonstrate their commitment to society? How to raise funds for college? How to stage effective and meaningful board meetings?

What is the use of that board which does not ensure educational quality? The paper makes a humble attempt to throw light on key aspects which govern educational quality. It presented in brief, big ideas that are transforming higher education, the world over, and the role of BOG together with principals and other institution leaders. How can the trusts and BOG discharge their functions more effectively is outlined? The article has attempted to provide a think pad for trustees and members of the BOG.

India has a tradition of good gurus to educate the children. Gurus have dedication, and commitment but they need good BOGs. It is high time that the BOGs are activated.

Some Difficulties and Possible Solutions

Some difficulties on the way during implementation are bound to arise. We should not get panicky on account of them and feel frustrated. By imagination and intelligent working many of them are possible to be solved. Colleges do not get nomination of experts from AICTE and university in time. Industrialists when appointed on board do not take seriously. These are some of the common observations and cause of hold ups experienced in functioning of the boards. However, by proper persuasion they may be reduced.

From experience it is suggested that new members of BOG should be added to induct fresh/young faces and newer ideas. Using video conferencing if expert is not able to physically attend the meeting should be practiced. Linking web-based ERP of institute to BOG members so that they can monitor the activities from their own office/residence through Internet may be practiced. With these technological advances BOG members are possible to be chosen even from foreign countries. These solutions can make the boards more effective in improving educational quality.

It would be better if some boards and their chairman make good use of their offices to influence government to correct certain state policy decisions in favour of improving quality, prepare some strategic programs for faculty up gradation sponsor some strategic research projects, etc. The effective functioning of the boards will undoubtedly go a long way to make education globally competitive.

CONCLUSION

Who is responsible and accountable for raising the educational standard? From the discussions above it can be concluded that BOG of which principal is secretary is the answer. BOG chair should not remain inert. It should have ambition to take institution to greater heights. If he does not have ambition, in spite of potential the institutions will not grow. Low ambition is a crime. Board should take full responsibility and be accountable. Transformation in education will take place to world-class standard only if boards perform effectively.

Why are world-class institutions necessary? They are found to produce world-class leaders, leaders in technology, leaders in industry and all other walks of life. We need them to win in brain race, otherwise India will trail behind the world. World experience tells us that nations have developed because of world-class education. Indian higher and technical education is presently grappling with several internal and external threats, it has many weaknesses. Who can remove them? Only effective BOG can.

If BOG members make a common commitment to change, change to world-class level is undoubtedly possible. Global opportunities are abundant which need to be harnessed, using our existing strengths. We do not have to import them. They are well within us. We have to use them. The task is huge. Only those boards who work with optimism and "can do" approach are likely to succeed. India to win in global competition requires imaginative BOGs to make institutions world-class (Naik, 2010).

Do the institutions produce today job givers or job takers? Should the board prescribe and insist on periodic review? A strategy for internal and external periodic review and scientific evaluation of all authorities from top to bottom is desirable in each college/university to know where the institution stands today and where it is tending to go. This is unpleasant task but essential. This reform does not require money but it requires will. Future of our children and grandchildren depends on what boards practically do today. Future will not pardon the present generation for lapses, if any.

Should BOGs learn from their counterparts abroad? New BOGs and those which exist for years may have to learn, as to how to be effective from their counterparts elsewhere in the world. They should have to articulate and pressurise trustees/ government on one side for more resources, and pressurise for better systems on the other side to principal and faculty to upgrade standard and relevance.

Are students learning what they need in 21st century to thrive? BOG once created should not remain passive, but become active and become a motivating force, and a mentor to principal, faculty and staff. Board should engage appropriately with principal and activities in college, keeping in view the educational needs.

What is the next big thing for boards to do? Many institutions are spending money far in excess but without gain in quality. It is because they do not have quality assurance cell. BOG should initiate steps to install the quality monitoring cell. In fact, installation of cell provides a lasting solution. Today, it is observed that arrangements for meeting and cleanliness in campus, etc. are staged only during the period of visit of accreditation committee. As soon as the visit is over the institution falls back to original status. The institution will remain neat and clean all the time.

There is a tremendous strength in collective wisdom and collective ambition of faculty and alumni. Colleges should harness alumni strength without delay. No institution can provide all the services needed all alone by it. It must be backed by ideas, experiences and feedback from alumni. They are learned and experienced ambassadors of college.

Do boards need to update? Without that they tend to become obsolete. Joint meetings, group discussions and conferences should be held for members of BOG time and again to focus on current public issues in education, at national and international levels.

Invest in creating leaders. Modernization of BOG on continuing basis is the most important aspect for ensuring educational quality. Then and then only institutions will respond ably to global opportunities and challenges.

Attract innovators. Award winning scientists, leader industrialists if appointed on board will they take the institution ahead of time? If we do not appoint good imaginative BOGs, our colleges may produce mediocre graduates and we may lose in world brain race. India may then continue to lag behind the developed world.

What do you foresee in future? What crucial topics should figure on BOG agenda? Those nations, organizations and individuals exploiting the latest technology are likely to win others may work hard, may have all the resources to draw on, but will lag behind without technological capability and adaptability.

Expanding horizons of the universities and colleges to integrate research parks, technology incubators, patent and IPR centres should now be the first and foremost item on agenda. Developing human resources especially professors as leaders to plan and implement above stated units should be given high priority.

Knowledge-driven economy has led to competition for excellence, nationally and internationally. Enabling professors reaching to world-class level now is not an option but compulsion. So as to win in global competition, effective BOG at the top supported by good principal and good professors is the only answer. No institution, no nation can be bigger than the knowledge level of its professors.

ANNEXURE A

Functions of the Board of Governors

- Take all policy decisions with regard to smooth cost effective and timely implementation of the institution activities.
- Form, supervise and guide various committees required for implementation and internal evaluation, monitoring.
- Evaluate periodically self-performance, faculty and staff performance and institution performance, by obtaining feedback from students.
- Ensure overall faculty development, and to create future leaders.

- Enable implementation of reforms.
- Ensure proper utilization of funds, timely submission of financial management reports, and utilization certificates.
- Preparing master plan of the institution.
- Select the director of the institute, and other personnel.
- Create an environment favourable for learning.
- Award scholarships, free ships, etc.
- Collaborate with other institutions nationally and internationally.
- Give new visions of new world to employees.
- Adopt annual statement of accounts and submit it to government.
- Create quality policy, quality manual.
- Adopt policies for disadvantaged people.
- Overcoming inertia in the organization.
- Fund raising for education.
- Make the institution enterprising.

ANNEXURE B

Socratic Oath to Improve Faculty Governance

The oath is prescribed for all those newly appointed and all those already in profession.

It should be a public ceremony, a formal inaugural event to be held at the beginning of each academic year (Rhodes, 2001).

Oath

I shall devote myself to the advancement and extension of knowledge, recognizing that I have an obligation to my students, to my discipline, to my professional colleagues, to my college/university, and to the public.

I embark on teaching as a moral vocation. I recognize research and scholarship as a public need and accept professional service as a social obligation. In pursuing my responsibilities, I will devote to both teaching and research the same sustained, imaginative, and rigorous attention. I will pursue new knowledge and creative activities in a scrupulous manner that befits the highest professional standards in my field. And I will play my full part in service to the larger community. In undertaking these tasks I recognize that teaching, research, and public service are the fundamental responsibilities. I understand that every faculty member of university, ably shoulders the responsibilities, and that teaching lies at the heart of the mission of the university.

Towards this end, I accept the trust that of transmission of knowledge with accuracy, fairness balance, and integrity are exemplified in the way my subject is presented and arguments are handled. I will present my subject, whatever it may be, with rigour but also in a liberal spirit, "illustrating the general within the particular" with a breadth of outlook and a humane concern for its foundations, context, relationships and implications.

I will respect the integrity of the relationship between professor and student, in both personal and intellectual terms, so that hucksterism or improper advocacies are as unthinkable as abuse or harassment. I will be scrupulous in preparation for class, discussion, laboratory or other exercises and supervise the same scrupulous preparation of any student teaching assistants who might assist me. I will be objective, rigorous and fair in student evaluation, and will be available for student conferences, office hours, lab sessions and other formal contacts outside the lecture room.

Finally, I will participate in the life of the university community, cooperating with my colleagues in educational endeavours and participate in campus wide activities. And, as I develop in my own career, I will encourage, help, and mentor my colleagues, especially those newly appointed, to become effective teachers and successful scholars.

The vow, which I freely take, I will keep, recognising that the privilege of academic freedom that is entrusted to me carries with it the obligation of professional responsibility in honour and serve my students, my discipline, my profession my colleagues, my university, and the larger society.

ANNEXURE C

Essentials of the Principal of an Institute, and Professors

A person to be able to become successful has to be a good leader, go getter, a magnificent speaker, a great writer, a good public relations man, a man of iron health, and stamina, married to a virtuous wife, having peace at home. He has to be a great individual, with great spiritual qualities, an experienced administrator, but able to delegate, and a great scholar, a social philosopher, raising pertinent questions to faculty and staff, in national interest. He should have first-hand touch with students in all branches. He should be converting negative energy of people in to positive.

He has to be more encouraging, inspiring to faculty, staff, and students, but less controlling them. He should be enabler, to make people at all levels to grow. He should give first priority in his duties and responsibilities to "People's Problems". If people grow, the institution grows. He should have to think great, dream big, have passion, tolerance and commitment to implement ideas. He would have to treat all professors, without cast creed, sex and religion equally. He should have to contribute to uplift every down and out man in organization to greater heights.

Merely giving salary every month to employees, although essential is not enough. He has to give joy of work, joy of learning to everyone, student or employee. He has essentially to create a learning organization with learning individuals. Learning organizations change with time. He has to be not imposing but discussing and debating. Disputation is the core of an academic institution. Dogmatic approach in dealing has to be discouraged. He has to create and continuously elevate his knowledge organization to successively greater heights. Enable professors to grow to international standards, benchmarking with world best.

He has to forgive people, students for any mistake. Needless to say that he has to have high integrity, honesty. He has to be impartial in his dealings with all.

Above all a leader has to be humane, deserve to have followers (Rhodes, 2001).

REFERENCES

Association of Governing Boards, [AGB] 2011, USA, September-October newsletter.

Glen A. Jones, Patricia L. McCanney and Michael L. "Creating Knowledge, 2003, Strengthening Nations, The Changing Role of Higher Education", University of Toronto.

Kadam, Lalwani, Jadhav 2010, "Perspectives on Governance of Higher Education", Bharati Vidyapeeth Pune National Knowledge Commission [NKC], 2006, Government of India.

NPIU-2012 World Bank supported initiative "Good Practice Guide for Governing Bodies".

National Knowledge Commission—NKC (2006).

Naik, B.M. and W.S. Kandlikar 2010, *Higher and Technical Education—Book of Knowledge*. Gyan Publishing House, Delhi.

Naik, B.M. 2011, Indian colleges and universities need good governance and leadership for the future of children and grand children. *Journal of Indian Technical Education*, Vol. 34, No. 2, April-June 2011, pp. 37-47.

Rhodes, Frank, 2001, The Role of American University: The creation of future, Cornell University Press.

Technical Education Quality Implementation Program [TEQIP], 2009, PIP Department of Higher Education, Government of India.

World Bank working paper N. 190, "Governance of Technical Education in India, Key Issues, Principles, and Case Studies." Edited by Andreas Blom and Jannette Cheong.

Chapter 15

Role of Alumni and Their Associations in Ensuring Educational Quality

Coming together is a beginning, keeping together is a progress, and working together is a success.

ALUMNI ARE THE AMBASSADORS OF COLLEGE AND A GREAT FORCE TO FURTHER EDUCATION

So much is demanded from college by society that the college, howsoever well endowed in terms of men, money, materials and technology, it cannot do justice all alone by itself. Internal faculty, staff contribute to teaching and lab experiments to ensure educational quality. This is good but not enough. External support from alumni to obtain truthful feedback on courses, to promote entrepreneurship, fund raising, etc. is needed. Alumni are a great force of brand new ideas, imagination and funds. Colleges must take their supports, who are their ambassadors in society and industry. The alumni and their association should have to fully back their alma mater in this respect. There is no substitute, or alternative to what the alumni can do for college.

Alumni association is required to be a registered society. It is an independent body, having separate rules for the conduct of activities. It is financially independent of college having separate bank account, separate office bearers with chairman preferably from amongst alumni. The association can undertake activities independently or jointly with college. The head of the institution sits as a member on the governing body of the association. This is necessary to have proper bond. To be able to become a world-class institute alumni and college have to be working in synergy, putting each other's strength together. Institutes become world-class only when alumni contribute their ideas to institution development. In India, awareness is developed and a wave is set in motion to activate alumni associations, for contributing to elevate the performance of institutions. Indian institutes today do not stand in world list partly because so far alumni force was not involved in institution development. Now they have woken up. Practically, every college is keen on using alumni strength. Alumni of world best institutions like MIT are doing this and partly so they have become world-class. The author is sure that alumni of colleges in India will not lag behind. They will contribute with their full might and play their role effectively to make their Alma mater world-class. It is hoped that in every college/university they will work together, to expand the horizons, go beyond teaching in classrooms, to creativity, imagination and innovation. Institutes achieve world-class status only when alumni contribute their ideas and give valuable feedback to institute development.

Alumni elsewhere have Contributed Immensely. They will Contribute in India too

Effective engagement of college with alumni is essential to ensure faster and qualitative development. No institution has ever grown to world-class level without alumni support. Alumni support is essential for growth and prosperity of a college and university. Alumni who are the ambassadors of college give valuable and trusted feedback along with newer ideas needed from time to time. What does an ambassador of a country do in foreign land? He represents his country to build programs of cultural exchange, he builds bridges of human relations between the two nations. He facilitates exchange of ideas, facilitates commerce and trade. Similarly, alumni who know the alma mater and the industry where they work can direct best to shape what the college can and should do to meet professional needs. Matching the college programs like teaching, research, innovation and technology transfer to meet market needs can best be understood and done by none other than alumni. Absence of support from alumni is too expensive. It is found to result in mismatch between the demand and supply.

Alma mater is very near and dear to alumni. An aluminous feels very proud of his college. He is willing to contribute with his full might to add value in the alma mater, and provide the budding engineers professional information needed in working life. If an institution wants to be innovative in character it should not miss to draw support from its alumni, who are like children to parents. Growth of college and growth of alumni should in fact synergise. The success of a college is measured not only in terms of passing of students, but in terms of what is the character and standing of alumni in society. College should also contribute to make the alumni big in their professional life. The organizations for which the alumni work have needs of upgrading skills of themselves, of employees, for research and innovation, for which the college can best contribute with proper understanding. The college and its alumni can function as one family to achieve excellence mutually. Usually, it is a practice to arrange alumni meet, every year, in convenient location. It is then a joyful event. They usually organise cultural activities.

STUDENTS WANT WORLD-CLASS EDUCATION

They are ready to pay for in terms of time, effort and money. But where it is available? Not many colleges and universities in India are able to give. They are going abroad by spending huge sums of money. Foreign universities are coming. Bill of foreign universities is pending in Parliament. Why are they coming? Is it not because there is a huge unmet demand? A study by NASSCOM observed that only 30 per cent graduates are employable. Finishing schools are being run to make up the deficiencies. Coming of foreign universities is an opportunity or threat? It is both. Do they bring professors from abroad? They will bring at the most only leaders. But they will certainly bring proven systems and procedures, policies and practices. They will bring new visions of new world to universities. They will make use of contacts of alumni, expertise, and financial support from alumni. These are the good proven policies and practices followed by world best institutions. Can and should we not emulate them on our own to our advantage?

Alumni make collective ambition, come together and hold shared visions, to take alma mater to greater heights. College needs to have courses matching with market needs. They have to be changing according market forces. They have essentially to be compatible to opportunities and challenges of globalization. The courses have to be innovative, creative and taking students to excellence. Precisely, for this the colleges are required to be autonomous. Then only they can adapt changes quickly without any time lag to global demands. Who can give market orientation and truthful feedback best way? It is only the alumni. Hence, the role of alumni association in an institution is of significant importance.

What have the Alumni done so far in India and Abroad for their Alma Mater?

Alumni of IITs have contributed immensely in terms donations, technology development and raising the reputation. IIT Mumbai has set up a Technology Incubation Centre in partnership with alumni, management education centre in Kharagpur. College of Engineering, Pune is currently putting up an entrepreneurship Development Centre with an estimated cost of millions. Wisconsin Alumni Research Foundation (WARF) of USA has established and running a research park from several years. It is obtaining patents, commercialising them, earning money to plough back for research in university. It employs hundreds of people. WARF is giving scholarships to students and research funds to PhD scholars.

Alumni associations of US universities have made a significant contribution to elevate the performance of US universities to world number one. Eight out of first ten universities are from USA. Alumni association have taken a lead in this respect and enriched US education. Now it attracts brains from world over. Best of scholars from everywhere and anywhere in world aspire to study in US. US became a technology power partly because of the role and contribution of alumni in universities. American universities have become world-class, how? Initially, they were behind German, Italian, and UK universities. They made best utilization of Alumni associations in university development. They had collective ambition and devotion for the cause of education. National Knowledge Commission reports of 2006-07 have strongly recommended activating and creating alumni associations in our colleges and universities. Technical Education Quality Improvement Program (TEQIP) is prescribing and measuring performance in terms of how active the association is?

What the Alumni can and should Do?

First and foremost thing alumni should do is to make a collective ambition, a shared vision, a collective passion. Where there is a will, there is a way. Passion by faculty alone, by director alone, staff and students alone to make institute world-class is good but not enough. External backing of collective wisdom from alumni is crucial. There is a tremendous strength, energy in collective wisdom and collective ambition. This energy exists in each alumni association. We do not have to import. We have only to tap and use it. The association has to dream big, think great, come together for a nobler mission. If there was no collective vision, would the man have ever reached moon and Mars? It is possible only through imagination of many alumni and their systematic working. Making institution world-class is the best way for rapid progress of India, and to ensure bright future for children and grandchildren. Alumni and alumni associations can play a crucial role in making India a developed nation.

Chapter 16

Universities and Colleges Need to Provide Industry-oriented Research and Innovation Skills to Students, Besides Basics to Ensure Educational Quality

World experience tells us that unless a professor is involved in industry-oriented research he has very little current and relevant knowledge to teach. He tends to teach sunset knowledge incompatible to global opportunities. Classroom teaching gets a force, depth, and sharp edge if professors are engaged in research and innovation. They become imaginative, remain ahead of time, and update their own capacities to be equal to their counterparts abroad, which are needed to capitalize on technology ahead of others. How long industry can be run on borrowed technology? Visions and missions of colleges should essentially include corporate development to make industry and economy win in globalized world. This alone will make education relevant and purposeful.

If all the professors of college decide and make effort in this direction undoubtedly quality of education will be superb.

ABSTRACT

Research is not a fancy affair. It is the seed corn for the harvest of benefit. Benefits from research far outweigh the costs. Research fuels education and makes it quality and cost competitive. Research gives joy and sense of achievement. It provides economic security to a nation and confidence to students. It enhances the rate of return on investment made in colleges and improves campus placement. It enriches the human civilization.[1]

The paper outlines in brief, need and importance of scientific research in universities and colleges in partnership with industry and delineates their role and responsibility. If India does not introduce R&D in universities and colleges in a big way the author says, higher and technical education in India is less likely to competitive by world standards. People then in spite of potential will lag behind. Those who can afford will continue to go abroad to receive higher education. Research is a profit-making activity and not a financial liability. Research creates wealth, enables college and professors to earn money besides credit. It creates joyful atmosphere in an institution, and improves the quality of education. It goes also far beyond to improve competitiveness of industry. A student learns best by researching. He learns to create brand new technology which gives him competitive edge in global marketplace. World experience tells us that progress of human civilization depends on research. Yet, why many colleges and industry in India are not research minded? Why industry hesitates to sponsor research, in colleges? Why colleges do not have research infrastructure? The mindset of key people both in industry and institute perhaps, is behind time, very few have burning desire to be equal to their counterparts abroad. Full scope of research and innovation in India, and their deeper purposes are less understood, resulting in low priority in state budget. India is spending only 0.45 per cent of GDP on research when others are spending 4-5 per cent.[2] India to become technological power, which it dreams of, ought to spend more on research in colleges and universities, otherwise the dream may not come true.

Presently, the syllabi are oriented to learning known knowledge and a practice presuming that knowledge is finite. Truly, knowledge is infinite and students essentially need to learn not only known knowledge but also to discover what is unknown. Education without learning skills for research and innovation remains incomplete and irrelevant in modern sense. So the Indian institutes do not rank anywhere in the world list. Many students not satisfied with Indian education go abroad.

The interaction between institutes and industry for research is too weak, adversely affecting competitiveness and growth of both.

The paper illustrates with examples how research in universities and colleges in UK, USA have benefitted their economies and raised their nations to greater heights. It presents the models of interaction to build synergy between the two. Research leads to industrial development and employment generation. The paper argues that the industry and institutes need to recognise full scope of innovation phenomenon. Innovation capacity of India and its economic progress depends greatly on students acquiring innovation skills. Next generation top professional leaders, to be globally competent, essentially require possessing research and innovation skills. Vision of India to become a developed nation by 2020 depends on value it attaches to industry oriented research.

LOW AIM IS A CRIME

"Passion for research" is crucial. It must be the campus character. This is the way to win in world economy.

Geographical Positioning System (GPS) was invented in Cambridge University, birth of Genetic engineering took place in Stanford University, the discovery of DNA was done in Cambridge, Inventions in electronics in Karlsruhe University, Germany. Many inventions took place in universities and colleges elsewhere in the world. Not only inventions but companies are born based on research in MIT Boston, Microsoft was born with the initiative of Bill Gates in Harvard. Yahoos, Google, CISCO were born in Stanford University. 3000 new technology-based firms owe their origin to MIT.[3] Universities and colleges have now become the birthplace of hi-tech firms. Inventions are found to inspire students to excel. Stanford University created Silicon Valley. Modern universities and colleges, world over, are doing not only teaching in classrooms but going beyond to research and enlarging out reach. Impact of university research on human civilization is far and wide. Can Indian universities and colleges not do this? It is the need of the time that colleges and universities in India make a spear headed attempt in research not all alone but in partnership with industry.

There is a story told of Michael Faraday. Faraday had demonstrated his discovery, of electromagnetic induction on which the dynamo depends, to Prime Minister Benjamin who asked what use it was. Faraday replied, "As much use as a new born babe". Years later, another British Prime Minister, Margaret Thatcher, admitted that Faraday's invention had generated huge wealth for UK more than the entire capital represented by the London Stock Exchange. This is to say that research is financially very much rewarding than normally imagined.[4]

Nowadays many innovations are taking place in Indian institutes too. Recently, students and professors of JNEC College in Aurangabad have designed in 2011, a racing car with new shape, tested aerodynamically. It is awarded first prize in national competition in Chennai by "Society of Auto Engineers, India".[5] Awareness for research in Indian youths and "Can do spirit" is growing. This is a positive change.

True that India is late starter in engineering education and research. It took momentum only after independence. It was presumed till then that new technology could be discovered only abroad. Our colleges were initially designed to teach technology coming from foreign and not designed for generating indigenous. People were happy to become followers in technology. India has been as a result constantly buying and foreign countries selling.

But now engineering colleges have gained adequate experience. They have made laudable progress. The Indian talent has become conscious of its capabilities. People have become ambitious to discover ahead of others. Indians in Silicon Valley have made a mark. President Obama considers India an intellectual threat and publicly telling Americans to compete. It is observed that students who learn innovation in college days are better suited to discover unknown in service career. Education is observed to be the mother of innovation. Students who aspire to become leaders in technology and leaders in industry should have necessarily to be innovative in character, acquire skills and vision to generate new technologies new products, and new processes and obtain patents.

Thousands of students, in search of quality every year are going abroad spending huge sums of money. PG and PhD is our serious shortcoming, which urgently needs to be converted in to strength. Due to lack of infrastructure for research and development technical education in India is far too behind the world. The universities do not rank high. It cannot come at par with the world unless and until drive for research and innovation is taken in colleges/universities forthwith. Industry and academia should jointly participate and achieve synergy.

Implications of Global Shifts on Strategic Planning

Universities and colleges are assuming key role in global economic systems, where new knowledge and highly skilled people are perceived as fuel for economic and social development. Colleges which are the sources of knowledge have become a dominant economic force. People look at them as suppliers of new knowledge as well as suppliers of national and international leaders. They are expected to nurture today leaders for tomorrow. Good universities and colleges have become a prerequisite for a nation to win in competitive world. Universities in India however are observed to be far too behind their counterparts in developed world. They are observed to be inward looking and not having adequate interaction with the world outside. They do not have connections, with their counterparts abroad. They do not have vision to help industry to win in global market. They teach irrelevant knowledge from shelf, mostly yesterday's knowledge today, coming from abroad.

Professors have almost no experience in industry, research and innovation. Very few institutes like IITs, NITs are engaged in research. So their standard is high, hence preferred. However, by world standard they too are behind especially in making commercial exploitation of the findings of research. Vast majority of the colleges do not have infrastructure and technical capability to conduct research and innovation. They are not knowledge generators but distributors of knowledge coming from abroad. So there is no force in their teaching. They lack depth and relevance. Colleges therefore are mostly producing graduates as technology followers and not leaders. Graduates get employment like soldiers at best in multinationals. But they are expected to produce captains to lead in industry on national and global planes. Primarily, it is on account of lack of research and innovation in colleges that the quality of education by global standards is poor. There is less of creativity. So investment in fix property gives more returns than industry. Global economy is undergoing significant structural changes. Is India prepared to match and go with the world? What are the long-term implications?

A study by US academy of sciences (2007) reported that only 13 per cent engineering graduates in India are employable in MNCs,[6] the rest have to make up deficiency by attending finishing schools at extra cost and time. There is a huge energy in youths, they are brilliant, yet too few become technology pioneers, and technology leaders on global plane, because that is not what present institutes are teaching students to become. The visions and missions mentioned on college brochures remain jargons. Commitment to implement is lacking.

The paper presents in brief, Indian and international experience. AICTE, UGC, and Technical Education Quality Improvement Program [TEQIP] are now prescribing creation of research ambience in campus and providing financial support. TEQIP in association with World Bank is putting around ₹ 4000 crore in 300 well-performing engineering colleges. It is well realized that research in S&T has become very important for economic health, so also for national defence. Industry is expected to take a long-range view and actively participate with colleges in research. Industry cannot achieve peak performance by being stand alone. Industrial development today is research driven. The paper recommends ways to build synergy between the two.

Research and Innovation Generate Financial Surplus. They Provide Economic Security

Experience in the world tells us that benefits from research outweigh the costs far more. Studies indicate that the rate of return (ROR) on investments in research is around 25 per cent to college, and 60 per cent to public, against ROR of 15-20 per cent of a normal commercial project.[7] Besides, students acquire research and innovation skills, which they use lifelong.

Research provides insurance from obsolescence. It provides economic and technological security. It takes the nation ahead of others, which is so essential in competitive world. Colleges can serve the people better, if they add research in their framework. Research does not consume resources but generates surplus. The dividends from investments in research to the college and to India are extraordinary. Now engineering colleges have acquired proficiency in teaching. It is right time for them to switch over to research and development. At least better performing colleges should dream big, think great to become research based. It may be mentioned that American universities and colleges have high commitment for research, and so the economy of America and its universities rank high in the world. There are around 130 research universities in US who produce most of the research output and PhDs. Best of brains from world over aspire to study and migrate to USA. Thomas Jefferson the founder President gave philosophy that, if America wants to be a leader in the world it must first succeed to lead in higher education. Bush Commission's report 1945, gave yet another philosophy that "Research should be the main product of universities, and education as its by-product." It strengthened the research in universities which made USA a forerunner.[8]

Education Ought to Focus on Creativity. This can Come about by Integration of Education with Research and Industry

In order to become a significant economic power in this century, it is essential for India to restructure its engineering education without future loss of time and integrate the same with indigenous research. Though a large number of engineers and technicians come out of engineering colleges every year, yet the scientific and technological achievements of India bear no relation to the vast number of S&T personnel.[9] The quality as well as relevance of education by world standards, is missing. We are distinctly a technology follower nation. Now so much is expected from colleges that all alone colleges cannot give. Alumni are their ambassadors with field experience scattered all over. Alumni should back up and colleges should use their strengths. This is essential to achieve creativity in amongst youths.

It is seen that basic premise of technology changes four to five times during the service career of a teacher. A teacher cannot teach the latest developments in the field of his specialization unless he is exposed to latest developments. Engineering colleges today like their counterparts abroad are meant to provide not only competent engineers but also newer technologies to industry. Unless a professor is active in research, he has very little current and relevant knowledge to teach. It is seen on one hand that many engineers are unemployed and on the other hand engineers with specialized skills are not available. There is a mismatch. What is wanted is not taught and what is taught is not wanted. So as to improve industrial competitiveness at this critical juncture of time it is essential for India to integrate education with research and industry.

Industry knows now that it cannot do all the research it needs by itself, even if they have R&D centres. Industries cannot be globally competitive without research output from universities and colleges. It is much cheaper besides it brings fresh and unfamiliar viewpoints needed to achieve breakthrough. So they whole heartedly ought to sponsor and participate with colleges. They are aware that industry and institutes are interdependent. They cannot remain stand alone entities. SSI and SMEs cannot afford to have R&D centres. They realise that synergy between industry and institute for the cause of research and education needs to be built for mutual gains. Research in isolation remains critically unexamined and untested, unchallenged without disputation. It is believed that private knowledge is knowledge lost. The conclusions of research must be openly discussed and debated in scientific and industrial community. Hence is the importance of research in public university. It is well realised that the power of research is demonstrated not only by the single-isolated innovation but by the ability to create new technology-based industries, some of them becoming the most economic power drivers.

Expectations from colleges are high. They all alone cannot fulfil. Alumni should have to come forward to participate and contribute in terms of ideas, and money.

Research and education are complimentary to each other. Research subsidises education and education subsidises research.[10] Most important it makes learning joyful and creative. Learners become achievement oriented. Teaching and research are found to be inseparable and mutually supportive to each other. Every professor is to be viewed as a scientist; he should be given fund for research at the time of his appointment. Professor should be encouraged to build a research team consisting of junior and senior students along with lab assistants. The culture of institution must have to change in favour of research. It needs to be induced amongst the students and staff. Their performance should be measured in terms of what new they have discovered and patented and not how much they have memorized. They should make the college a source of new knowledge, new theories, and new technologies. Regions, cities, and nations develop faster where the institutions lead in knowledge and technology. No society, region or nation prospers without good research output. Research earns more money, more endowments, name and fame for colleges. They attract endowments and funds for research. Thereby they lower down the cost of education and tuition. Education then becomes qualitative and cost competitive. Bond between industry and institute becomes stronger. With advancement in technology awareness in Indian industry for research is growing.

Experience of Silicon Valley, Research Triangle Park in North Carolina, route 95 in Boston, Bengaluru, etc. indicate that knowledge institutions have now become key players for the regional development. They have moved from periphery to the centre of development. People's development especially in science and technology matters most. Indian colleges should therefore think strategically and start research and innovation centres in their campuses and become deserving to provide world-class education in cutting-edge technology to youngsters. Education with research and innovation spirit alone can move a nation forward.

SYSTEMS MATTER

Theory of education says, if there is no significant research in college then there is no significant quality in education.[11] Quality of education does not grow where research is absent. Research and education are like two ends of a bow. The arrow does not move forward unless the two ends of the bow are tightly tied together by a string. Neither end has a force without the support of other. An institution binds the two ends together, namely education and research to provide quality education. What we notice in universities abroad is that there are many research companies located on the periphery of colleges. They draw ideas from research conducted by professors and students in college. Students work in these companies on research projects. Company researchers teach in colleges. There is give and take between the two. Quality of both research and education goes up, and the cost to a nation is minimum. What they experience is that peak performance in industry cannot be reached without the support from institutes and vice-versa.

The conventional wisdom in technical education, of only teaching orientation, which once served well, is no more fit for today and tomorrow. The time demands revolutionary changes to promote quality through technological research, innovation and entrepreneurship. Institutes must act fast to reform otherwise foreign universities are likely to get hold and dominate Indian education market. Indian professors have contributed immensely in universities in USA. Why they are not able to contribute in India? Our systems and procedures are obstructing their performance. Our universities have rigid, inflexible, outdated rules and regulations, we need to adopt well-proven systems and procedures from developed countries. Some colleges are planning to be in top 20 in world list. Many have the potential, but they ought to use proper policies and practices, systems and procedures. It is not a matter of just putting more money or appointing more men on the job. It is more a matter of using current and appropriate systems in research and innovation.

Colleges with centres of excellence provide superior education. Western schools now believe that colleges without centres of excellence on campus for technological research and innovation, entrepreneurship development, patent and IPR, technology transfer, venture capital, hi-tech start ups, spin-off of technologies and spin-off of New Technology-Based Firms are incomplete, irrelevant, and non-viable in modern sense.[12] If India dreams to be a developed nation in near future, the present technical education system needs to be strengthened in respect of above-stated centres. They have to be integrated in college and enabled to provide "Technology Push" matching with "Market Pull".

They have to redesign their systems to generate new knowledge and new technology ahead of others. The present departmental store approach of distributing knowledge generated elsewhere in the world is unfit for the purpose. They will have to install systems as "Well Springs" of new knowledge.

Institutions have to set up such centres afresh in their campuses, essentially in partnership with alumni, and industry. Restructuring in the context of global changes has to be the main item on national agenda, without which the intellectual resource will continue to be wasted and opportunities missed. AICTE and UGC will have to do benchmarking with the systems in counterpart institutions in the developed world and make gap analysis. This is urgent because our institutions follow only that which these apex bodies prescribe.

Shortage of Research and Innovation Skills is a Major Barrier in Employment Generation

The key factor behind unemployment is insufficient research and insufficient innovation. Shortage of people with innovation skills is a major barrier in professional development.[13] Universities and colleges have a major influence on India's capacity for innovation. Colleges therefore should have to resort to these new strategies to induct research and innovation skills in economy. They would have to adopt corporate development as a vision and mission. They should provide new technology and new ideas to industry to keep them competitive in world market. They are like heart to our body which continuously pumps new fresh blood to keep the body alive. Indian higher education must recognize the full scope of research and innovation phenomenon. They can produce captains and leaders of world-class standard and enable Indian industry win in world only if above-mentioned strategies are adopted.

RESEARCH AND INNOVATION GENERATE JOBS

Those nations which introduce research and innovation are found to win jobs in competition from those who lag. Can Indian professors teach innovation skills by international standards? Can they teach skills of discovery and skills to generate new technologies equal to their counterparts? How long we keep on teaching sun set technologies? We essentially need a swimming pool to learn swimming, meaning thereby we need research infrastructure to be innovative.

Why do thousands of students every year go abroad? They have been going from Gandhi-Nehru period. How many more years they will have to go? Unless and until we install research and innovation culture we remain behind the time, and outflow of talent will continue.

Research and Innovation are Indispensable

Ideas are the real capital. Ideas are needed to succeed. Idea generated is opportunity generated. Research and innovation are known sources of idea generation.[14] Knowledge memorised in brains is important, but more important is the ability to discover new knowledge, new theory and evolve brand new idea. Colleges are the legitimate places to create idea people. It is their prime function. They have no reason to exist if they do not do so. The importance of research and innovation for future of children and grandchildren needs to be realised in right perspective, and infrastructure created in colleges. This will avoid the shortage of people with innovation and enterprising skills, which is found to be a major barrier to growth and prosperity.

Most of the students today learn in a passive way. Students learn quietly what is handed over to them. They are not guided to take active hand in creation of new technologies. What did the famous philosopher Socrates teach his students? He taught them to ask pertinent questions. He ignited their minds for change. The competency of people is measured today in terms of their ability to innovate. People are needed who look ahead of time and prepare for incoming opportunities. Large youthful population is the competitive advantage of India. We ought to enable them to be innovative for meeting global needs, as prescribed by Socrates philosophy.[15]

Commercial Exploitation of Research Findings is Our Weakness. Can We Make it Strength?

Invention when exploited commercially is known as innovation. Research conducted in colleges for UG, PG, and PhD often results in publication. This is good, but better it is if exploited commercially. Unfortunately, theses remain on shelf in library. No conscious effort is made to obtain economic value from them, mainly because vision and commitment in this direction is lacking. Students today do not get opportunity to learn to convert inventions in to usable goods and services. Quality of research improves when it results in commercial use. To this extent skill set of students remain deficient, in spite of potential. This reduces utility of research done and reduces the rate of return on investment. What use is of research which has potential of exploitation but not exploited. Wealth of a nation is vested today in doctoral research done by scholars. Japan produces 28 PhDs per million population, USA 30, and India only 0.45. Technical Education Quality Improvement program in its document (2011) have estimated the shortage of MTech and PhD in thousands. Our universities and colleges must take a special drive in this direction.

It is a good sign that technical education in India is expanding. But acquisition of skills for commercial exploitation which is the demand of time is lacking. Non-availability of finance for innovation is the major barrier in commercialization of new technology. National Knowledge Commission Report (2006-07), to make India competitive, has prescribed conduct of research, innovation and creativity in colleges. It said multifaceted units like research park, innovation centre, incubation centre, patent centre, entrepreneurship centre, and venture capital should become the integral parts of colleges innovation. They constitute the infrastructure for research and create much desired enterprising culture enabling students to acquire research and innovation skills. Colleges then become like magnets to attract brains from everywhere and anywhere. This makes the community to think to tap the world market. Unfortunately, this wave of creativity is yet to reach the Indian shores. Innovation in Indian education is conspicuously absent. Students do not get perspectives. This is a serious lacuna. It can be rectified only by research orientation to education in colleges. Research and innovation policy if adopted by colleges they will acquire innovative character enhance their name and increase their yearly income. When shall we realize this?

Surveys conducted elsewhere in the world indicate that New Technology-based Firms (NTBF) started by young research students with origin in colleges are more successful than those started without association with colleges.[16] Colleges provide a powerful engine to launch the NTBF and thereby generate income and employment. How many First Mover Entrepreneurs we have produced? Education policies and practices have to come out of old ruts. They are less productive, less efficient and outdated. You need new ideas to win in new world. Change is most wanted to replace worn out ideas. The college resources should not be frittered away on worn out paths but should be used creatively. Colleges are in general hostile to change. They have inertia. They tend to maintain status quo. We must become outward looking, centripetal in outlook, and change our mindset to accelerate reformation process, without which we will not be able to go with the world.

Colleges abroad are innovative in character, ours are conservative. They teach sunrise technologies we teach sun set. They produce leaders we produce followers, they lead a change, we follow change, they are engines of growth we remain bogies. They are not afraid of change we are. Foreign institutes live today as if future has arrived. We live in the past. The challenge today, is to create knowledge-based society. It is that society which uses not only new knowledge but generates on continuing basis. Adoption of new vision of research and innovation is a must to create knowledge-based society.[17]

FOREIGN EXPERIENCE

MIT Boston is a private research university. It obtains around one hundred patents every year. In addition, it gives birth to 30-40 new technology firms. A scientific study conducted on impact of MIT indicates that around 4000 companies owe their origin to MIT.[18] It has become a cradle of entrepreneurs. Twenty per cent of the yearly budget of the institute is met out of sale of patents. The institute has created employment of high income for millions. Australian and Chinese universities are also ahead in this respect. Where are we stand? Many institutes in India have included research and innovation in their visions and missions. But they are just jargons. Only a few like IIT Mumbai, IIT Kharagpur have just made a beginning in turning out companies and obtaining patents. Indian colleges ought to attach more value for research and provide funds. Hi-tech campus companies, on the periphery of institutes in backward areas must be envisioned. All universities in USA, taken together obtain around 1000 patents. Indian universities earn less than 100.[19]

Research-based Technopreneurs of Silicon Valley

The birth and perpetual success of Silicon Valley is attributed to technical entrepreneurs, who draw continuous support, inspiration and technological ideas from research conducted in universities. Silicon Valley has progressed remarkably well not because they are wealthy entrepreneurs but because they are technopreneurs. They have been deriving technological power from first-class research and innovation conducted by professors and students in universities. Silicon Valley has provided access to professor's research output in industry. Industry is now more technology driven. A new phenomenon is observed that new industrial complexes in the world are flocking around knowledge and technology centres. Patents, intellectual property have become more important assets along with land, buildings, money, etc. What drives industrial development is the research and innovation. Resources in research, innovation and education are the most important growth stimulating instruments today. Technical universities in Germany, 84 of them, since 1984 have patent and technology transfer offices. This has increased the outreach of the universities. Steinbeis centre is yet another scheme to take new technology rapidly to industry. European Union has designed and implemented the scheme of technology relay centre in member countries.

Prof. Terman of Stanford University in 1950 gave the philosophy that, "Industry to be globally competitive need access to first-class research in universities, so also first-class research in universities need access to industry for its commercial exploitation". This led to the creation of Silicon Valley. The model is being used all over the world.[20]

Towards end, I remember a story of people from two different nations. Plates were kept in two different halls full with variety of sweets and other attractive eatables. A common condition was put on citizens of both of the nations that they can eat as much as they like but without folding hands at elbows. People of one nation say A, in one hall tried hard to eat but could not take the spoons to mouth, because they were not allowed to bend hands at elbows. They went home hungry without eating food. People of other nation say B were wiser. They could eat the food bellyful. How? They ate by feeding each other without folding hands at elbows. They had no difficulty, whatsoever. They went home fully satisfied. Industry and institutes should have to envision feed each other, and not attempting to eat by self. People of which nation are wiser?

CONCLUSION

The paper has illustrated with examples how Japan by integrating research with education and industry has moved the nation forward. How research universities and professors in USA have created technopreneurs in Silicon Valley, how Germany has maintained its leadership by research, patenting and technology transfer. India to be competitive globally must have to integrate research with education and industry. Education charged with spirit of discovery and innovation alone can move India forward.

Colleges have a major influence on improving innovation potential of India. They are reckoned as mother of innovation. If colleges do not create centres of excellence then there is no other way for India to be a developed nation.

A new enterprising society in the changing world is coming in to being. Colleges are called upon to produce not copy-cat graduates but graduates with higher imagination to lead and take active hand in creating the knowledge society fit for today and tomorrow.

The government should forthwith appoint a commission for innovation at centre and state levels to give a boost to research and innovation, so as to explore people's full potential.

We need to remember "Where once nations measured their strength by armies and arsenals, in the world of future knowledge matter most". Institutes of higher learning ought to teach to invent and find unknown. India and China are progressing because of investment for economic growth and not because of investment in defence, so said Hillary Clinton former foreign minister of USA.

How long industry can be run on imported or borrowed technology? Education policy should facilitate professors, researchers, to transform themselves in to entrepreneurs, equipping them to set up and run their own high tech enterprises. This is what universities in USA have done to create Silicon Valley. Can we not do that?

Quality of education can be transformed to world-class standard only by introducing research in colleges. Colleges must have to become "Light House" for industry. Productivity of various professions and vocations will rise. Common man will stand to gain. Indian economy will become more competitive.

On the whole impact of research on life of individuals and on society can be huge. Human civilization is advancing on the basis of research. It is here in colleges and universities that they are discussed, debated and openly tested by opposing groups.

India's future is too important to be left in the hands of government alone, for the task is too big for government alone. Besides world over often government is too apathetic, non-responsive and insensitive to people's research needs. It needs genius of India citizens, and academicians to meet them. Private industry should have to come forward and join hands with academics.

Professors and institutions should be asked periodically what new technology they have discovered and how many patents obtained.

Research, Innovation and Creativity is Today's Guru Mantra

If India does not create research-based universities and colleges, if industry does not synergies with academia, the colleges will be providing mediocre graduates far too low by international standard to run its national and international affairs. Indian people in spite of potential are then destined to lag behind in world brain race. Do we recognize this danger?

NOTES

1. H.T. Rhodes, Role of American university—The creation of the future published by Cornell University Press 2003.
2. Rising above the Gathering Storm, published by Academy of Sciences, USA, 2007.
3. Fang Zaho, Academic Entrepreneurship, Case Study of Australian Universities, *International Journal of Entrepreneurship and Innovation*, pp. 1-97. IP Publishing Ltd., Vol. 5, No. 2, 2004.
4. *Op. cit.*, Ref. 1.
5. News Item, *Lokmat*, Aurangabad 5 July 2011.
6. *Op. cit.*, Ref. 2.
7. *Op. cit.*, Ref. 1.
8. Bush Commissions Report, 1945, US Academy of Sciences.
9. *Economic Times*, Editorial, 2.1.2005.
10. B.M. Naik, *Global Visions and Missions in Technical Education*, Annpurna Publication, 2008.
11. *Op. cit.*, Ref. 1.
12. B.M. Naik, Needed Innovation & Entrepreneurship in higher education institutes, *The Journal of Technical Education*, January-March 2004, Vol. 27, No. 1, pp. 27-32.
13. Green paper of European Union on Innovation and Technology Transfer Enter-prize Unit DG, EUFO, 2296_I 2920 Luxemburg, so also website CORDIS.
14. *Ibid.*
15. *The Human Nature of a University*, Robert E. Goheen, Princeton University Press, 1969.
16. Creating Knowledge—Strengthening Nations, the Changing Role of Education, Edited by Glen A. Jones, Patricia L. McCartney and Michael L. Skolinik University of University Press 2002.

17. *Op. cit.*, Ref. 1.
18. *Ibid.*
19. Government of India, 2009, Technical Education Quality Improvement Program (TEQIP) Phase-II Project Implementation Plan (PIP).
20. The role of Science Parks in the promotion of innovation and transfer of technology, Proceedings of the Science Parks Association, Annual Conference, 6-7 April 1989.

Chapter 17

The Challenge of Globalization for Indian Universities

Setting a tone of discovery, innovation, creativity, patenting, spin-off of new technology-based firms, create technology pioneers, etc. is the urgent need in Indian universities.

Indian universities by world standards are far too behind their counterparts in developed countries. They still operate on old lines as if they are an extension of high school system. Whereas universities in developed countries like USA, Germany, and UK are primarily research universities. Research output, especially need based, is their main contribution and education, is their by-product. Bush Commission report, *Science—The Endless Frontier* (1945) gave this philosophy to universities of USA and which is also adopted in other developed countries. National Science Foundation of US has reprinted this report in 1990, and re-circulated it.

The report prescribed that universities main output should be research, patents, new technologies, intellectual property rights. Higher education should be their by-product. Students learn best by researching, and then it is relevant and up-to-date. It is because of this philosophy that the education in universities of US is observed to be innovative and creative in nature. Without research, it is believed that education remains stale and outdated. Normally, two-thirds budget of a university goes to research.

CHARACTERISTICS OF UNIVERSITIES ABROAD

On the campuses of universities like Madison, Cambridge, Edinburgh what we notice is that research companies are flocking round them. Incubators, research parks, innovation centres, patent and intellectual property rights bureaus are distinctly visible. Venture capital companies have opened offices in campuses in search of new technological ideas for commercialization. Universities in developed countries have become like magnets that attract not only scholars but also industry, entrepreneurs and VCF companies from across the world. They are globalizing their operations to meet the world needs both of education and of technology. Students from many countries, so also industries from across the world are coming to their campuses and they feel proud of the same. By virtue of strong research base they are a source of latest knowledge in education and a source of new ideas, enabling companies to win. It is well realized in those countries that new knowledge, that is to say new technology, is an important source to bring about economic change. USA has doubled its industrial output from 1909 to 1949 and that 85 per cent of the credit is attributable to technology change, according to Nobel Laureate Bob Solow.

Universities like Madison are producing patents as many as 100 per year. The university sells patents to companies and earns an income by way of royalty as much as 40 per cent of its budget. They generate wealth through research, which is believed to be the mainstay of high-income economies in the world. According to World Development Report (WDR, 1999), they spend about 4 per cent of GNP on research. Low-income economies like India spend very less, even less than one per cent of GNP on research. The employment generation and income generation is attributed mainly to research in universities.

Young scholars along with the in-service personnel carry-out research, which is disseminated best through teaching in classes. Innovation and research are considered as 'well springs' of economies.

Helping Business to Win

Every university has a patent and technology licensing department engaged in technology sale. The author during the period of his recent three months visit to Germany, UK and USA, sponsored by the UGC, studied in-depth the organization and management practices of universities along with their visions and missions, systems and procedures. Universities in general have huge campuses, with student strength in the range of 20 to 80 thousands and faculty strength from 1000 to 10,000. For example MIT, Boston has around 30,000 students and 3,000 professors, Karlsruhe University in Germany has around 25,000 students and 1,000 professors, all teachers possess PhD and post-doctoral qualification. Faculty represents a wealth of talent and knowledge, which is exploited to benefit both faculty and university financially. In India faculty with PhD qualification are very few less him 10 per cent. Our bright students are thus being taught by lowly qualified and less experienced teachers.

Spin-off of companies from universities is a common phenomenon, so also spin-off technologies. The companies like Yahoo, CISCO, Google were conceived and born in Stanford University. Project ideas were based on their PhD thesis. A foundation is set up in MIT, Boston with the facility of venture capital fund enabling professors and PhD scholars to start new ventures based on technologies, they develop during the period of their research. Every year as many as 15-20 new technology based firms (NTBF) are born in MIT Boston. Three thousand companies owe their origin to MI. The university gives consultancy on retainer basis to them. This is not unique with MIT only. It is true with almost all universities in developed countries. They have created Technology Incubators to enable raw project ideas to be innovated to marketable stages. The entrepreneurs and professors are thrilled when they see their theoretical ideas being converted into practical projects. Thereby they are earning wealth for themselves so also for the university besides credit and satisfaction. Universities have thus become 'Maternity Homes' for safe birth of new enterprises. Such enterprises that are based on brand new technologies help to reduce mortality rate and sickness of other industries.

NEW MODEL FOR UNIVERSITIES

Does Indian economy need such universities? Can we do without them? At what cost? Without such innovative schemes our investments are being made in sunset technologies. Obviously, they cannot be competitive globally. National Council for Applied Economic Research, New Delhi has published the results of a survey which found that of the 657 Indian companies in the study sample that started up recently, 57 per cent were manually operated and 38.7 per cent were semi-automated. In the same period, according to the study, 80 per cent of the start up companies in Japan were fully automated and 20 per cent were semi-automated. It seems then that substantial investment in India is being made in companies which are based on less competitive technologies, and which are therefore handicapped right at birth. Such companies cannot hope to be competitive on global scale. In USA, 36 per cent of capital investment is in new technology-based firms (NTBF) where as in India NTBF are almost non-existent.

However, the shift from old technology to new technology industrial base is not easy to achieve. It presents many technological, social, economic problems, as well as resistance from trade unions. People must unlearn old methods and skills and adopt new technologies and knowledge. Universities must reorient themselves; prepare to offer courses and interest people in learning and becoming more competent. Without this strategy by universities, industries and industrial estates will languish and become sick, which would be looking for foreign collaborators.

Can Indian universities dream of propelling industrial growth?

They must do so forthwith. Otherwise universities may become dysfunctional and economy will run into difficulty. The rate of absorption of new technology in various walks of life depends much on knowledge of people and their scientific and technological capabilities.

NEW VISION FOR NEW WORLD

What Indian universities lack today, is the new vision of new world? They ought to develop connections with best known universities in the world and correct their priorities and strategies. It is no doubt a long journey. Yet, it must begin somewhere. Is it not that thousand miles journey begins with a single step?

Prof. Terman of Stanford University in USA observed in 1950 that,

> Industry so as to remain competitive globally needs access to first class research in universities. So also the first class researches in the universities need access to industry so as to commercialize their research findings.

This is equally applicable to Indian universities at this juncture. They cannot become and remain competitive without the support of each other. Will our universities care to follow today what others did years before?

It is important to know how universities are conceived and started in those countries. The author visited a newly started Harburg University in Germany. This university started 35 years before under collaboration from 15 best universities in US, UK, Japan and Germany. Today this university has 10 thousand students and one thousand professors. It started with a research park, which today contains around 500 research-based companies adding strength to the economy of the region. University is not planned in Germany without an industrial estate and industrial estate is not planned without a university.

The author also visited Harriot Watt University at Edinburgh, which is located on 600 acres of land and has Research Park on 600 acres surrounding the university. The University of Madison (USA) has a strong Alumni Association known as Wisconsin Alumni Research Foundation (WARF), which is managing and maintaining a big research park.

Taiwan has set up a 'Science Town' at Hsinchu with some 13000 researchers in two universities, six national laboratories and around 150 companies specializing in electronics. Tsukuba Science City near Tokyo is another example of university technology park collaboration.

On the other hand, Indian Universities are engaged more in teaching as if they are schools. The vector direction of our universities is wrong. They are largely teaching and examining bodies without research base and hence they are not effective to cope with challenges. Will they learn themselves and adopt what best universities in the world are doing? Will they do correct bench marking?

Universities abroad have opened continuing education departments, more from 1980, for in-service personnel. They are offering short-term refresher courses leading to PhD. The research work done by people in their work places is counted for the award for degree. They have a flexible model "Cafeteria Approach" in which students can choose a wide variety of options. A combination of economics, engineering and music is also possible.

The credit transfer system, from one university to another is common. A student can study for the same degree course in a number of universities. The credits earned in one university are approved in another. European Commission encourages the mobility of students and professors. It has drawn a program known as Leanhardo-da-Vinci to provide financial support to promote such mobility. The students are allowed to get degree from any one university, which they have visited.

LIFELONG EDUCATION

Continuing education has become so common that the in-service part time students studying in universities are three times larger than the full time students. We see three generation students in campus. Learn while you earn lifelong is very common. It is observed in an OECD study that Europe, Japan and USA together represent 80 per cent industrial global outputs. The main contributing factors to this dominance include continuing education policy and practices of universities in developed countries. Continuing education facilities and better management of technology adds significantly to economic success.

Many Indian universities yet do not have continuing education departments, patent and technology licensing departments. Technology Park and incubators are conspicuously absent. They have almost no connection with industry and industries have almost no confidence in universities. The industrial progress in India is propelled by foreign collaborators. Indian Universities have not gone nearer to them, nor have industries established links with universities. Universities have become corporate offices bureaucratic and political in nature. Consequently, what is taught in universities is not wanted and what is wanted is not taught. There is serious mismatch between demand and supply. Rather than motivating and preparing students for the world of work the universities have become organizations which tend to thwart and impede the potential of their students. The National Education Policy (NPE, 1986) recommended autonomy to colleges to enable them to respond to the needs of industry in terms of research, training and technology transfer. However, progress has been slow.

The traditional affiliating system of universities has become a problem rather than a solution. It has stifled the innovation potential of academics and the public is unhappy. Attempts for improvement are being made. The lack of mobility of Indian academic staff and research staff to world-class centres is seen as major problem. Why is India unable to upgrade its universities? Do we realize that the cost of mediocrity is higher than the cost of upgrading? Why do Indian institutes not transfer technology to industry through the use of patents and IPRS?

CONCLUSION

Indian education has lagged behind the world main because of its poor education policies. Globalization of Indian universities in changing time is the pressing need of time. Redefining their scope, missions and visions in the light of worldwide changes ought to be carried out forthwith. Restructuring the organization, methods, systems and procedures, revising the university acts, making colleges autonomous should become the first item on agenda. Research in universities is the most cost efficient and cost effective model for employment and income generation. It should therefore become the focus of university activity.

Universities to a nation are like heart to our body. Outdated universities are more costly than cost of their modernization. They should therefore be revamped urgently. There are no doubts many problems in adoption and implementation of new policies and practices. How to manage the change is certainly a big challenge before Indian universities. They need to take into account the experience of IIT along with experience from abroad. The speed and direction of change in universities in coming years matters most to the well-being of the people. It is hoped that with the given will and skill of leaders in academics, leaders in industries and politics, we will be able to achieve desired goal.

"How fast we integrate with the world will decide the future."

Chapter 18

Universities and Colleges should be Innovative and Enterprising Compatible to Opportunities and Challenges in Globalization

The present is a time of great entrepreneurial ferment where old and staid institutions suddenly have to become very limber, flexible.

ABSTRACT

The paper outlines in brief, the need and importance of building a knowledge-based economy in the context of globalization. This is with a view to enable people to be more competitive to make most of global opportunities. Strong higher education system is, however, a pre-requisite for development, without which India in spite of potential cannot hope to become a strong economy. Urgent steps for strategic changes in creating entrepreneurs, new knowledge, new technology, patents, IPR, establishment of new technology-based firms, etc. are recommended. Conventional wisdom, of institutes as "teaching shops" in present stormy weather of globalization falls too short of purpose, and does not suffice. Teaching without research base and without innovation is found to be ineffective, outdated, irrelevant and obsolete. From experience in the world it is recommended that India should harvest its untapped research, innovation and entrepreneurship potential lying idle in higher education institutes. Brilliant students and faculty are eagerly waiting. The new roles have a potential to convert, brain drain in to brain gain.

INTRODUCTION

Pressures are mounting on higher education institutes like colleges, polytechnics and universities to play a key role in creating knowledge-based economy and bringing about integration of the Indian economy with global. Corporations, governments, and international organizations like UNESCO, World Bank are calling for a more prominent role for education from basic literacy to lifelong professional education. OECD defines,

> Knowledge based that is to say knowledge-driven economy is one in which the production, use and distribution of knowledge and information are critical to the process of economic growth.

Not surprisingly the role of university is central to the emerging knowledge-based economy. World experience tells us that those regions/nations whose institutes can quickly adapt to the rapidly changing economic, political, technological and social climate will have much greater prospect of success. They are identified as major drivers of change to achieve economic growth. A region where more enrolment takes place in institutes, and liberal, broader, quality education is offered, globalization at faster pace takes place. Higher education has considerable potential to reduce adverse effects, and increase impact of globalization in stimulating economic growth. Knowledge inculcated by institutes can enable people to derive maximum benefits from entry in global market. India has the potential to leap frog the educational infrastructures and effectiveness of developed countries. Raw talent of Indians is good and anxiously waiting to be nursed well.

Colleges and universities in India after independence have made a laudable progress, yet they are observed to be poorly equipped and woefully unsuited to the demands of globalization. They are far too behind their counterparts in developed world. Thousands of students every year are going abroad for higher education. Institutes emphasize memorization that is "rote learning," and do not offer innovation, entrepreneurship and leadership skills needed in world market. Institutes, in globalization, have to play a key role in developing knowledge society. They need to be repositioned, and restructured in terms of their relationship with people, government, industry, private sector and the world. Our true wealth resides in educated citizenry. Most profitable investment lies in education. People who are willing to learn, rich as well as poor, need to be educated to fit them in today's complex globalize world. They need to be allowed to grow to the level they are capable for. Otherwise they tend to become a liability and threat to the national as well as world peace. It is being realized that lack of education is closely linked with unemployment and in turn to crime. India should have now to invest with priority in colleges or else it will have to spend more on building prisons for those who do not get education, and wind up in committing crimes. If investment in colleges by choice does not take place government will be forced to invest more on prisons? Should the state therefore not be investing adequately in building institutes? Public Investment in education will have to increase for it is the best use of tax payer's money.

Need and Importance of Building a Knowledge Society

In globalization, intellectual capital has become more important than land, buildings, equipment, etc. Intellectual skills of people in modern job market have achieved more significance than hand skills. Colleges, polytechnics, universities have come to be known as powerhouses producing new ideas. They increase brainpower and enable the nation to win in brain race. They generate and disseminate new knowledge needed to keep the people competitive. Institutes have moved from periphery of development to the centre.

Institutes Produce National Leaders and Captains for Industry

Development to take place fast and remain sustainable requires educated people and visionary leaders. More educated people are observed to choose better leaders. Institutes are now called upon to produce leaders for industry, and leaders for economy, society and every walk of life. They could produce world-class leaders for which essentially institutes would have to be world-class by themselves, which is so essential to win in world economy. We know that today's leaders in politics, industry, economy, etc. were yesterday's students. We must look at today's students as tomorrow's leaders, and institutes as generators of visionary and creative leaders.

Each one is affected by globalization and each one is impacting globalization. We are now the citizens of one world. We have to be competent by world standards. The boundary lines between the nations are becoming thinner. Students and people in globalization would have to develop international perspectives, tolerance and negotiation skills needed in world market. This is essential so as to keep pace with the world development. World over, this is found to be a winning strategy. We should not delay in its adoption. Else, expert leadership, critical skills, professional services, and new knowledge on which its future in globalize world depends would remain subdued.

MORE STUDENTS ENTERING THE PIPELINE

More students entering the education pipeline in India is a welcome sign. This is the critical input for development. As the world due to globalization, is getting more and more interconnected, the higher education which is meant to drive knowledge, creativity, and innovation, in human society is becoming more crucial. Colleges, polytechnics, and universities all over the world have always been the creators of new knowledge and its keepers. They have sought to prepare new generations with the skills, cultural and scientific literacy, flexibility and capacity for critical inquiry and to make their contributions to society. Development of a nation today is said to depend on its capacity to educate people in relevant knowledge and state of the art technology.

No society, region or nation will prosper without good institutes of higher and technical education

They form the core of development and hence need to be reformed with priority. It is the well-educated people, people with capability and competency, who make the investment and efforts in development projects fruitful. It is this interaction between education and development that shapes our collective future as global citizens. World Bank in its report of 2002 has underlined the importance of higher education for creating able leaders for development of nations. A close coupling exists between 'education and competitiveness' of human force which needs to be kept in view, in today's stormy weather of globalization.

In India proportion of students entering the pipe line of higher education of the age 17 to 23 is around only 7 per cent. This proportion in USA is 55 per cent. World average is 23.4 per cent. It is observed that countries with higher levels of education will be least affected due to shift taking place in employment. In globalization people are found to change jobs three to seven times in service career. The proportion of older students for upgrading skills world over is therefore increasing. UK has declared recently skills revolution, and urgent action taken to upgrade people's competitiveness. Most successful nations shall be those who invest in lifelong learning, and create a learning society. Getting educated only once is not enough. Higher education has become critical to win in business. India would have to work and match with its competitors. Are our students and faculty aware of importance of education for economic development? What our institutes are doing to promote lifelong education?

INSTITUTES BUILD KNOWLEDGE SOCIETY

A central theme is emerging in which significant social, economic transformations are taking place on global level. They are challenging the traditional role and traditional position of universities in society. It is argued that these institutions now are a "think-tank". They need to find ways of addressing these important complex challenges facing the nations with imagination. India has many hidden jewel professors. It is necessary to explore, reward and felicitate them professors are expected to be equal to their counterparts in developed world. How are they enabled in India to be so? They should be enabled to establish alliances with world best institutes, political system, social system, and world economic system. They should not be merely teaching but influencing public policies and society. They should be researching themselves and guiding students for research. There is tremendous positive impact on the transfer of science and technology from institutes to private sector and then to economy, thereby creating marvelous number of jobs with high pay off. Institutes now stand for creating a learning society and a learning economy. Institutes in globalization can and should bring about a cultural revolution, and contribute to collective wisdom, so essential for bright future of our children and grandchildren. Questions are being asked, are we educating students to understand global systems? Do the students understand that they have to have tolerance for the culture of others? Knowledge society will give kick start to Cultural Revolution.

Protect Civil and Political Rights for Knowledge Society to Thrive

Protection of civil and political rights is a prerequisite for establishment of knowledge-based economy. There is a close and inseparable relationship between the quality of higher learning on one hand and the quality of effective and democratic governance on the other. Economic development depends on level of education of the people and level of education depends on quality of governance of the nation. Just as it is very hard to imagine sustainable and democratic development without higher education, it is futile to promote higher education in a society where civil and political rights are systematically suppressed and denied. Experience shows that countries that thrive best in global economies are those which are truly open. Openness means open trade, open investment, open borders. It also refers to open societies that invite new ideas, show a high tolerance and open descent and criticism and rethinking, reworking of their own governance. True development occurs when knowledge is owned and operated by communities, and by women and men who form those communities. Higher education is not a luxury for the rich it is a necessity especially for the poor. E-governance is said to provide solutions. Openness and transparency is consciously promoted by State Government through, Right to Information Act. What kind of e-governance? What are the limits? Who will out line the strategies? It is the well educated who can show the way.

Privatization Accelerates Arrival of Knowledge-based Economy

While the importance of higher education world over is increasing, state budget allocated to higher education per student is observed to be decreasing. In countries like USA, UK per capita public investment on education is reported to be falling. Tuition fees are therefore rising. Private and public investment taken together is however observed to be rising. In India the situation is not different.

Increase in tuition fees is resented by students. They are however paying, because higher education is bringing to them benefits like higher salaries, and an opportunity for better jobs which weigh far more. Private investment by philanthropic organizations, industry, and fees paid by students are found to make education responsive to market needs. This is a great advantage. Privatization leads to stimulate competition to get good students, good faculty thus improving relevance and quality of education. Privatization leads to quick response of education to market forces, which the students and economy needs.

The internal rigid structure of government, universities and colleges is a major obstacle to quick changes needed in education. Private institutes have flexible structure. Privatization has an edge over government regulated institutes in this respect. As such there is no substitute for privatization. But privatization may not protect students coming from low income families. Government would have to cover them by scholarships, bursaries, etc. There is no substitute for public funding. Almost 70 per cent of the students in USA are taking education in government-funded institutions. In Germany, all institutions are government funded, and education from KG to PG is free of cost.

Funding alone by government even if it can leads however to mismatch and waste of resources. Therefore both public and private funding must simultaneously go on. Funding by government for poor and deserving is essential. Can we afford to lose students because of high fees? This has to be viewed as an investment in creating leadership from weaker sections of society. All needs of education however cannot be visualized by government. It is the inherent weakness of the government-regulated systems.

Many times advanced education of superior quality by government is neglected, privatization makes up the gap. Public funding alone leads to over centralization, and increase in overheads without commensurate gains. These weaknesses are overcome in privatization. Where lays the golden mean of public and private funding? Who will find? This requires well-educated people.

The model of private and public funding is found to be more rewarding.

Globalization Brought Opportunities

Some view economic globalization as inevitable, and therefore advocate to focus on necessity of institutional reforms to harvest benefits arising out of globalization. Others view economic globalization as unnecessary evil where economic interests have displaced broader social, human and democratic concerns. The later argue in favour of resistance while the former says resistance is futile. Globalization can benefit human civilization as a whole. However, some may benefit more while others less. People in India to benefit more will have to upscale the skills and knowledge of its people. India is a developing country. It remained less developed so far, by world comparison because its economy was localized and less globalized. The region can be richer if the digital divide between the region and developed world is reduced. We must wake up to this reality and act fast with our full strength to accelerate international trade and commerce, which demands more knowledge of the world. Do we share the same planet, same environment? Then we must nurse globalization.

Opportunities are not Risk Free

There is however more uncertainties and more risks involved in global opportunities. So as to harvest them demands new knowledge new skills, and positive human attitude to go round the world. Survival of fittest is the law. There is an impact of new technology on jobs and business. Are our institutes preparing youths to cope with? Are they providing skills required in global market? Globalization means mixing of cultures, shrinking of time and space. Globalization means business at the speed of thought, instant communication, and instant decisions. Globalization means abandoning traditional methods, systems and procedures in favour of modern, which requires education. Keeping the risks to a minimum and harvesting opportunity requires education. Who provides the scientific approach to harvesting opportunities? Higher and technical education will.

Institutes as Drivers of Change

Students and entrepreneurs in search of new knowledge tend to migrate else where because good institutes are inadequate in number. Good institutes are found to function like magnates to attract intellectuals. Institutions in India except IITs are observed to be far too behind their counterparts in US, UK. Thousands of students are seen migrating for admissions elsewhere. After studies many of them do not return. India to that extent looses talent. USA has gained lot of intellectual capital from foreign countries like India, China by creating world-class universities. If India creates world-class institutes, it can reduce brain drain if not eliminate, and attract brains from other developing and developed countries.

Wealth of a region now depends upon knowledge possessed by the people. He who possesses knowledge becomes well to do, hence is its importance. Is it the local people who posses technological knowledge? We must ensure this. Development is said to primarily aim at acquisition of the intellectual capital. It is not merely construction of roads, bridges, factories, etc. Institutes in the state will have to grow to the level of their counterparts in rest of world. Winners are not those who manufacture goods, but those who develop talent.

NEW ROLE OF HIGHER EDUCATION

To produce captains for industry, to commercialize new knowledge, generate new technology, patents and IPR, starting new technology-based firms, research parks? It is high time for institutes to become enterprising and to give kick start

Institutes can and should derive financial advantage of innovation capacity of students. Institutes ought to be autonomous to do that.

Indian higher education institutes are late starters but now after independence, observed to have made lot of progress. The number of universities, colleges has substantially gone up. They are found to be doing a good job. A revolution is noticed in every state and in the whole country. Students are coming to institutes in larger numbers. People are giving high priority to education. Even if they do not have money enough, they are found borrowing from banks, selling land and houses. The job opportunities in globalization are large enough that they get more than they spend on education. Many are taking jobs abroad in countries like USA, UK, and Japan, etc.

Universities abroad are now highly enterprising in creating knowledge-based society. There is a world wide wave in this respect. There is however, a serious deficiency in the institutes in India. They are observed to be too weak in research, innovation, patenting and IPR, and spinning off of new technology-based firms. If we make benchmarking of our institutes with their counterparts in developed countries a big gap is noticed. For example, USA universities are spinning off new technology-based firms very large in number. MIT Boston is obtaining more than 150 patents every year. The royalty earned from patents is 20 per cent of the yearly budget of the institution. It is spinning off around 50 companies every year. A study conducted in the year 1994 found that 4000 companies owe their origin to MIT. They employ 1.1 million people, and generated 232 billion dollars in world trade. In the United States companies employed 7,33,000 people or one out of every 170 jobs in the country. Indian institutes have not taken any financial advantage from creating innovations. Higher education cannot grow where R&D is absent.

The universities in Australia are also quite active in this respect. Each university is spinning of as many as 50 new technology-based companies. Chinese universities are also not behind. Each university in China has set up technology incubator, business incubator and they are pumping new technologies and innovations in industry. Countries like Germany, UK, and France are far too ahead. From 1980 universities in Germany have set up technology transfer and patent centres. The author was given a fellowship by the ministry of education Government of India, in the year 1996 to visit patent and technology transfer centres in universities of Germany. He has personally visited six universities and observed that students acquire innovation, patent skills. They sow the seeds of entrepreneurship while studying.

How many of the universities in India have obtained patent and IPR? How many companies have been born in universities? Do the students learn innovation skills? How much commercial exploitation is done of the PhD thesis? Are they just lying on library cupboard? They are being exploited by foreign companies, for obtaining patents. Many Indian traditional researches like of Haldi, Wheat, Basmati, Ayurvedic medicines, etc. are being exploited by foreigners. It is because our institutes have so far ignored patenting. There is vast untapped potential available for exploitation. Shall we not hurry up in this regard?

Prof. Terman of Stanford University in the year 1950, gave the principle for establishment of research parks, that "University professors need access to industry to make application of the findings of research, so also industry need access to University research to keep industry globally competitive." Based on above Silicon Valley was born, with the backing of Stanford and California University, Research Triangle Park at North Carolina is set up with the lead of Duke University, 128 street in Boston with the initiation of MIT and a large number of university related parks have come up in Japan, Germany, and UK, with a view to induct new knowledge and new technology to make industry globally competitive.

Department of Science and Technology Government of India have started a similar scheme of Science and Technology Entrepreneurs Park (STEP). Twelve such parks are operating in universities in India. University of Pune, Cochin University, IIT Kharagpur, etc. Parks reports are encouraging. IIT Mumbai has started a technology incubator. TIFAC is set up to give fillip to patenting. The schemes need to be driven further with greater strength and vigor.

Transnational Linkages Essential to Build Knowledge Society

Securing the connections between the developing and developed institutes to build capabilities of knowledge generation is essential. We cannot afford to ignore good policies and practices developed else where in the world. IITs were developed in collaboration with foreign. So they are found to shine in world. Rests of higher education institutes were disconnected and although they spent more they lagged behind. Now we cannot afford to ignore the global scene in education. Why our institutes do not stand in the world list? Why thousands of students are going abroad? Strategic international partnerships have a great potential to bring new knowledge and relate knowledge to local conditions. Who will give directions in this respect? Who will caution the government of fatal consequences of not adequately interacting with world? It is the educated galvanized people who can.

EXAMINE HOLD UPS

Higher education institutes world over are declared as primary engines of economic and social development. Our industry has under nourished the relationship with applied research, innovation, in engineering colleges and universities. Synergies in their relationship like in foreign are yet to be achieved. Inventors, discoverers, creators in colleges and polytechnics must have to be respected, honored and rewarded if these activities are to flourish. We must examine why such activities are not being conducted satisfactorily? Not many professors do research. What are the factors holding up? Policies and practices, visions and missions need reconsideration. Who will do it? There are thousands of eligible students who desire to take admission in higher education institutes, but due to various reasons they cannot. The factors need to be identified and solutions evolved, to make accessibility easy.

What can We Conclude?

Demand for higher education in decades ahead will grow exponentially. Advanced education will become even more pressing both for individuals and society. Education will change in profound ways; much of the change will be driven by market forces. We have to develop capacity in institutions to change. This is a big challenge before the nation. Universities must remove constraints. We cannot afford to waste talent.

"Think globally, Act locally", is the first and foremost new role and responsibility of higher education institutes in the present stormy weather of global changes. They should not think routine way like bygone days. Globalization offers new opportunities and is a strong driver of change. Institutes have to perform differently. What is the new role institutes have to play? They have to look beyond instruction in class rooms become enterprising to generate new knowledge, new technology, patents and IPR so as to make knowledge society effective. Institutes should have to volunteer to show leadership in this noble cause.

Another new role is to "Dream Big", "Jump start technology clusters" attached to institutes using youthful talent for research and innovation. They are found to act as major contributors to regional development. Incubators, technology parks act as spark plugs for development. Institutes now should have to produce not only graduates but produce entrepreneurs using New Technology.

Thirdly, higher education in global circumstances has to aim at "corporate development." They must produce captains of world-class industry. Building synergy between the education and business for national growth is essential. New technology is driving business to greater heights, requiring more skilled and flexible graduates. Universities and corporate presidents should establish a new forum of partnership to achieve synergy.

Fourth role is to take a special drive for advanced education. It is becoming ever more pressing both for individuals and society. Much of the change in higher education is being driven by research in technology and market forces. Institutes must take a new look at it, and on mass scale start MTech and doctoral courses.

Fifthly, Indian industry can no longer do all the research, it needs to survive by itself. Engineering colleges/polytechnics, universities in partnership with industry may have to conduct research more vigorously. Leaders in education and leaders in industry must have to walk hand in hand together for national cause.

Last but not least, traditional regulations by universities and government in today's stormy weather of globalization do not suffice. Higher and technical education must remove constraints, and introduce flexibility, and autonomy. Virtual and for profit universities from across the world are on the horizon, and posing a serious threat.

If higher and technical education is not revitalized in the light of above, opportunities will slip out of our hands and economic stagnation may result.

> If you solve the education problem, then you don't have to do any thing else. If you don't solve education problem and do every thing else, nothing is going to matter as much.

REFERENCES

Beach, Charles M., Robio W. Broadway and R. Marvin Melnnis (eds.), *Higher Education in Canada*, Queens University Press.

Bersucan, David, Robert Bothwell, J.L. Ganatsein, *The Crisis in Canadian Universities Petrified Campus*, Random House of Canada.

Betts, Julian R. and Carolyn W.B. Lee, *Universities as Drivers of Regional and National Innovation*, San Diago's Program for Hi-tech Entrepreneurship, Queens University Press.

Bloom, David E. *Globalization and the Need for Higher Education Reform.*

Bowden, Rob, *Globalization: The Impact on Our Lives*, Rain Tree Chicago Publication.

Jones, Glen A., Patricia L. McCarney, and Michael L. Skolinik, *Creating Knowledge Strengthening Nations*, "The Challenging Role of Education", University of Toronto Press, 2002.

Oblinger, Diana G. and Anne-Lee Verville, *What Business wants from higher education*, American Council of Education.

Rhodes, Frank H.T. *The Creation of the Future*, Cornell University Press.

Tornatzky, Lous G. *Innovation U-New Practices Enabling Cultures.*

Tudiver, Niel. *Universities for Sale*, A Canadian Association of University Teachers Publication.

Chapter 19

Making Universities World-Class: Why and How?

WHY INDIA NEEDS WORLD-CLASS UNIVERSITIES?

Universities in knowledge economy, world over, are achieving high significance. Nations are strong where universities are world-class, not otherwise even if the nations are endowed with abundant natural resources. The strength of a nation is measured now not in terms of the size of army or arsenals but the number of world-class universities. They are mandated to produce new knowledge, new technology, and new theories besides graduates. Vector direction of universities is turned to industrial development, and human well-being.

World experience tells us that it is world-class universities which propel the industrial development. India today is technology follower and not leader. India aspires to be a technology power in near future. India has started schemes like Make in India, Start Ups in New Technology Based Companies, Research Parks, skill India, etc. It wants to give boost to hi tech, high income employment for young generation. Industrial development of India previously was propelled by foreign countries. Now it desires to have import substitution driven naturally. The schemes can be implemented more meaningfully only when India has world-class universities.

Indian universities do not yet make a mark in world list. Government of India is quite serious to boost education to world standard, and has started also National Institutional Ranking

Framework (NIRF) from 2015. Small countries like Singapore, Canada, and Australia in spite of smaller population have world-class universities where brilliant students from a big country like India every year go for higher education, by paying huge sums of money, by one estimate Indian students going abroad in sum total pay money enough to build 20 IITs. Many Indian universities have good infrastructure but they lack world-class professors and academic culture which is necessary for a university to be world-class. In the absence of world-class universities in India, thousands of students are going abroad. And foreign universities are coming in. Brain drain is taking place on big scale. World-class universities are needed to arrest brain drain.

India urgently needs to have world-class universities, so as to achieve its dream to become a developed nation by the year 2020. Presence of world-class universities in a nation now is considered to be a distinguishing feature, and differentiating factor between a developed and developing country. World-class universities produce professional leaders, globally competent, for various professions, like engineering, industry, commerce and trade besides politics and administration to ably run country's affairs at local, national and international levels. It is believed that seeds of leadership are sown within the four walls of classrooms. Leader's matters most to speed up the process of development of a nation. Leaders produced by world-class universities are found to be competent to make best possible use of physical and financial resources of the country and bring about meaningful and purposeful development for human welfare.

Mediocare universities produce mediocare leaders and world-class universities produce globally competent leaders. World experience tells us that nations and regions are prosperous where universities are world-class. Others even if they are endowed with ample natural resources like minerals, land, water, etc. are less prosperous. This is because; with the presence of good universities people do get latest knowledge, latest technology which is born from the womb of world-class universities. It is the world-class universities, who produce competent human capital, who interm produce financial capital and other resources. This is essential to remove poverty and increase the standard of living of vast masses. It is on account of this that world ranking of universities, world over, has assumed great significance.

India so far remained a low income economy, in spite of good amount of natural resources. It is mainly because India is a lowly-educated country, having low standard universities. India is economically far too behind the world, because its universities are behind. Now so as to build India a developed country, India with priority will have to build universities offering education of world-class standard, good quality comparable to their counterparts in developed countries. Government should do the following to make universities world-class.

PROFESSORS MATTER MOST

There are many universities in India who have ample land, five star buildings, brilliant students, brilliant faculty, and good amount of money yet the universities do not stand high in the world list. These universities have all the resources at hand but not world ranking professors. The professors have necessary intellectual potential. But due to poor service conditions and world-class growth opportunities they indulge in polities instead of academics. For example, professors do not have facility of sabbatical leave which is essential for a professor to excel. They do not have adequate research budget. Professors are provided far too less opportunity to go abroad, and work with industry nationally and internationally. The universities lack scientific approach in their planning and governance, comparable to world best. How do you create good academic culture? India Government ought to re-engineer policies and practices, systems and procedures, visions and missions, and adopt new strategies for governing the universities. India ought to learn from the experience elsewhere in the world. Indian universities ought to harness the global winds of change. Our universities need to be research based, and not teaching oriented. Professor is a kingpin in making a university world-class. His service conditions need to be redesigned in the light of what prevails in world best institutions. How do you enable a university to be world-class? The enterprising culture, autonomy, and growth and innovation opportunities necessary for a professor to be world-class need to be urgently provided. Research should be their main job; teaching has to be incidental, supporting like in world best universities elsewhere. Present-day universities unfortunately are bureaucratic, working like a government, working like a government office riddled with red tape. The apex bodies like UGC and AICTE are unfortunately managed and maintained by babus, clerks instead of creative and innovative personnel.

Build University—Industry Synergy Urgently, Starting from Top at Ministry Levels

University Industry Interaction in India is conspicuously absent. Ministry of Industry and Ministry of HRD do not have much interaction. They are supposed to be interdependent and not independent. There ought to be lot of interface between the two. But this interface is neglected by both. There is no synergy between the two. There is no shared vision and collective ambition for growth and prosperity at national and state levels. Industrial estate are planned and implemented by industry department with huge sums of money without any financial inputs in universities and colleges for research and innovation. As a result industries do not get solutions to their problems and have to be importing technology from abroad, at heavy cost. As a result they remain technology followers and do not become leaders, remain less competitive and in the course of time even become sick. For example, Delhi-Mumbai industrial project is spending millions of Rupees on land, buildings, roads, water supply, and electricity but not spending a single rupee on strengthening research and innovation in university and colleges in Aurangabad, Nasik, etc. Skill set demanded by industry is not provided by university. What is provided is not useful to industry. There is a huge mismatch, which by interaction can be avoided. It is believed that even if the industry and universities have all the resources at hand but not the synergy between the two, India will lag behind the world. There is no feedback obtained from industries as to how the education and research conducted by university are received by industries. Consequently, mismatch results. On one hand, there are many educated people with degree in hand but they are unemployable. On the other hand, industries are not getting the type of people they are looking for. Their growth prospects are hindered. Universities earlier were reflection centres, taught knowledge coming from abroad. Now they are expected to give birth to new knowledge, new technology, and spin off hi-tech start-ups in new technology-based firms. They have to be idea generators. University and industry both without synergy will remain behind the world. Government should start adjunct professors scheme from industry to teach in university. Twenty per cent of the professors should be from this category. This is the world trend to give professional and practical inputs to students. Only classroom teaching by full time professors is not enough. Adjunct professors are badly needed. Can a university without adjunct professors ever become world-class? If we want a change these things must be done. They do not cost money; on the other hand they save. Universities can become world-class only in partnership with industry and not without.

INSTALL INNOVATION CENTRE, INCUBATION CENTRE, RESEARCH PARK IN EACH UNIVERSITY

You do not see a university abroad without these centres on campus but in India you hardly see a university with such centres. As a result our brilliant students lack in creativity and imagination. They become servants, and termed in USA as technology coolies to do low end jobs in multinationals and not drivers, architects or creators. Innovative centres are the only way to educate students in an innovative manner. Unless we have a swimming pool we cannot learn swimming. The students are learning known knowledge and known technology but innovation skills and research skills without these centres cannot be learned. This makes our brilliant students technology followers and not leaders. Indian universities need to produce professional leaders and not followers. India is not short of resources but is short of synergy between the industry and institutes. Developing a world-class university is therefore not a business of only university or government alone essentially joint effort in partnership with industry. India needs these centres to make education and research compatible to employment and growth opportunities.

Create Innovation Forum in each University, Consisting of Innovators from Industry, University and Civil Society

In knowledge economy of today, the strength of a nation is measured not in terms of the size of army and arsenals. It is measured in terms of people's scientific and technological capability for which world-class universities are necessary. Universities now are expected to produce not only graduates but give birth to new scientific inventions and new technologies. World-class universities by virtue of knowledge organization have come to be known as provides of the economic security to a nation, and creating bright future for young generation. Without world-class universities India cannot get globally competent professional leaders. Nothing is more important for Indian economy at this juncture of time than building synergy between university and industry for faster development. Interaction between the two is now not optional but compulsory. Universities have come to be known, world over, as the drivers of development.

Recognising the need and importance of world-class universities in nation building our Prime Minister has announced government's determination to make a beginning with ten universities world-class in public sector and ten in private sector. Also he declared they will be granted extra funds and granted full autonomy and that they would be unique, falling outside the purview of UGC and MHRD. India is aspiring to be a developed nation as early s possible. It has the necessary potential. So as to unfold the potential it requires giving higher priority in national and state budget to education. Some time back Nobel Laureate, Dr. Amartya Sen, was asked a question by the then Finance Minister, Dr. Yeshwant Sinha what priority India should give in national budget to education. The Nobel Laureate replied first priority. Then he asked what should be second priority in national budget, he again replied education. Third priority should be given again to education. India today is grossly a less educated country. Unless the education level goes up it is difficult for India to climb the ladder and become a developed country. University education today in India by world comparison is far too weak. This does not mean that by just providing more budgets to universities they will shine in world list. They need money and many other important things. Government should do them at earliest.

ABANDON BUREAUCRACY AND RED TAPE

Government should make a difference between government working and university working. It ought to abandon bureaucratic working and red tape culture in university working. Intellectural component in university working is much higher than in government. A committee may be appointed to make comparative study of service conditions and growth opportunities being provided in world best universities, and redesign new service conditions to be provided to Indian academics. Professors ought to be extrovert and not remain introvert. They must remain in touch with their fraternity elsewhere in the world. Indian government has launched many schemes to modernize the universities by upgrading infrastructure. But it has not taken up any scheme to upgrade professors to world level. In fact, professors matter more than infrastructure. Any deficiency in infrastructure can be made up by able professors, but deficiency in professors' costs heavily to quality of education.

STREAMLINE THE UNIVERSITY MANAGEMENT

Organization and management of universities should be innovative and creative. Time has changed, but Indian universities have not. They do not have capacity and ability to change with respect to time. They work in a routine old manner and not in innovative manner. Indian universities by and large open at 10 am and close at 5.30 pm like a government office. The systems of working are designed based on government systems. Whereas world-class universities open at 8 am and work up to 11 pm late in the evening. Libraries remain opening 24/7, so also the laboratories. Professors work with trust and confidence. Professors to India are too dependent on head of the institution and his office clerks. They do not have financial power needed to buy necessary things. More importance is given to registrar and his administrative machinery in university act than to professors. Government should have to charge these things forthwith.

Universities should have to dream big thinks great and show commitment to implement. They should have high ambition. Indian universities do not have high ambition to be world-class, although they have capability. They are almost insulated from their counterparts elsewhere in the world. They have huge assets like land buildings, faculty and staff. The students are brilliant. But these physical and intellectural assets are lying idle, not utilized fully. Full economic returns from these assets are not attempted. Because the universities lack enterprising culture. UGC and AICTE are run by bureaucrates and not by professors, or thinkers or reformers. This is a major weakness, which needs to be corrected urgently. National Knowledge Commission 2006-07 gave recommendations in this regard. But those recommendations are yet to see the light of the day.

Autonomy like in foreign universities should be given to Indian universities and colleges. Autonomy comparable to world best universities should be accorded forthwith. Autonomy does not require additional money, instead it saves. Government has granted autonomy to universities and many colleges on paper. But government has kept the strings in its own hands. The boards of governors are formulated, but they do not enjoy the necessary powers. Intervention by government in the governance is too much. The type of autonomy enjoyed by world-class universities elsewhere in the world should be granted to Indian universities and colleges. Then only they will come up to expectations. Our institutions are too much oriented to memorization for examination and not creativity or learning. The students have no autonomy to choose to subjects of their liking for study. Cafeteria approach is absent. Professors have no autonomy to conduct the research, and teaching. They are too much controlled by authorities. If Indian gives autonomy to universities and colleges, then they will take care of all other things. On the other hand, if we do not give autonomy then nothing will work, situation will perpetuate.

CONCLUSION

(i) Service conditions of professors should be re-engineered and made comparable to world best universities.

(ii) Innovation centres, incubation centres, research parks should be installed forthwith in each university.

(iii) Industry-institute synergy should be built starting from top ministry level. Mismatch in education is a result of lack of synergy. Education is not matching with growth opportunities, in globalization.

(iv) Unless we have world-class universities India will continue to get mediocre graduates and mediocre leaders. India will remain behind the world, brain drain will continue.

(v) Apex bodies like UGC and AICTE need revamping.

(vi) India Government must harness the global winds of change.

(vii) University education and research is of paramount importance for well-being of people.

(viii) Mediocre universities are far more costly than the cost involved in making universities world-class.

REFERENCES

Duderstandt, James, *A University of 21st Century*. The University of Michigen Press.

European Union, *Green Paper of European Union on Innovation and Technological Transfer,* Enterprize Unit DG, EUFO, 2295-2920 Luxumberg.

FICCI, website.

Government of India, National Knowledge Commission (2007), Report, New Delhi, Author.

Jones, G.A. et al., Ed. *Creating Knowledge—Strengthening Nations, the Changing Role of Education*, University of University Press.

Naik, B.M. (2004). Needed Innovation & Entrepreneurship in Higher Education Institutes, *Journal of Technical Education,* Vol. 27, No. 1, pp. 27-32.

Naik, B.M. and Kandlikar, W.S. (2010). *Higher & Technical Education: Book of Knowledge,* Gyan Publications, Delhi.

Naik, B.M. Gap Analysis, Between Indian Institutes and their Counterparts Abroad. *University News.*

Naik, B.M. "Strategies to make universities Globally Competitive, *University News,* Vol. 49, No. 26.

Rhodes, H.T. (2003) *Role of American University: The Creation of the Future,* Council University Press.

US Academy of Sciences (2007). *Rising above the Gathering Storm.*

Zaho, Fang (2004). Academic Entrepreneurship: Case Study of Australian Universities, *International Journal of Entrepreneurship and Innovation,* No. 5, Number 2, pp. 91-97.

Chapter 20

Enhancing Employability, Innovation, Entrepreneurship and Creativity in Changing World

Institutions can do Better. They Need World-Class Visions and Missions. A Spirit to Compete on Innovation.

Education charged with the spirit of innovation, entrepreneurship, discovery and creativity alone can move a nation forward. Future belongs to those who understand this.

STATEMENT OF THE PROBLEM

On one hand, there is so much of unemployment amongst educated youths and on the other hand there is a shortage of entrepreneurs to develop innovative enterprises. There is abundance of natural resources on one hand and shortage of finished goods and services on the other hand. Lucrative opportunities due to lack of entrepreneurs are either dying or being taken away by foreigners. There is an influx of goods from east and west countries in Indian market. Indian industry unfortunately is far too behind the world. Indian ranks as low as 42nd in industrial competitiveness, and 127th in Human Development Index. Government has set a goal to build India a developed nation by the year 2020. So as to accomplish this, young engineers urgently need to depart from their conventional approach and focus their attention on innovation and entrepreneurship. Higher Education Institutions in partnership with industry, in this cause, have a key role to play. They ought to become business oriented, with focus on spin-off of hi-tech start-ups. They ought to capitalize on emerging technology. Can they provide 'Technology Push' matching with 'Market Pull' on sustainable basis? The present frame of universities and colleges without innovation and entrepreneurship centres is not competitive enough to produce leaders of world-class standard. They are producing good soldiers, which is necessary but not enough. They need to produce competent captains to lead in industry and economy. To be able to become so they are going abroad every year, in increasing numbers and many do not return, a great brain drain.

Universities need to be enlarged forthwith to cover centres like, Technology Innovation Relay Centre, Entrepreneurship Development Centre, Technology, Incubator, Business Incubator, Research Park, Venture Capital Foundation, Technology Park, Patent and IPR Centre, Industrial Services Centre, Technology Transfer and Marketing Centre, Corporate Education Centre, which are existing from last more than 50 years in counterpart institutions in developed countries. It is on account of this that those nations have prospered. IITs, IISc have recently started such centres in their campuses. This is good but not enough. Many engineering colleges must take steps to become enterprising.

Institutions should have to initiate a movement for creation of New Technology Based Firms [NTBF] and venture capital foundations, and angel networks. It is a new dimension to be added to our present university and college campuses. They function as profit centres. They are not a liability on university finances, but generate wealth, which subsidizes cost of education and makes education relevant to market needs.

Prof. Terman in 1950 observed,

> Industry so as to remain competitive globally needs access to first class research in universities. So also the first class researchers in universities need access to industry so as to commercialize their research findings.

There is a greater need of University Related Research Parks (URRP), in India. Parks, in isolation from academic institutions being set up are good but cannot substitute University Related Research Parks (URRP). These centrees have to be the key players. They have to be the drivers of technological revolution.

A formal policy of technological innovation in higher education is urgently needed to drive the spirit of innovation and entrepreneurship as a far-reaching change in society, and not just to target potential entrepreneurs.

Need to Produce Leaders in Technology and Leaders in Industry, Captains and Generals Needed and not only Soldiers to Win on Technology Battle Ground

It was presumed in good old days that new technology could be discovered only abroad. Our colleges, universities and companies used to be happy to become best followers. We have been as a result constantly buying the technologies and they are selling. But now Indian talent has become conscious of its capabilities. It has become ambitious to discover new technologies ahead of others. Indians in Silicon Valley have made a mark. It is observed that students, who learn to innovate in college days, are better suited to discover unknown in service career. They are fit to lead in world market. Students who aspire to become leaders in technology and leaders in industry should have necessarily to acquire skills to generate new technologies, new products and new processes and obtain patents. It is realized.

The Key Factor behind Unemployment is Insufficient Technological Innovation and Entrepreneurship

Do the institutes possess visions and missions to generate new knowledge? Have they nurtured culture to produce new technologies? Visions are in short supply and not the capabilities or the resources. We need to acquire them from world-class institutions. Low aim is a crime.

Why do thousands of students go abroad for higher education? They have been going from pre-independence period. How many more years they may have to go? Can all those who desire go? What are the things which foreign universities teach, but we do not? Unless we teach students skills of innovation, skills for generation of new technologies, skills for discovery of new knowledge, patent and IPR, our institutes will remain behind the time and the outflow of talent will continue.

Their institutions are innovative in character, our institutions are conservative. Foreign universities live today as if future has arrived, we exist today as we existed in past. They teach sunrise technologies we teach sunset technologies. They produce leaders we produce followers. They lead a change we follow the change. They are engines of growth we remain bogies. They are not afraid of change we are. They practice creative destruction, meaning thereby weed out old systems to create new.

The challenge now is to create a knowledge based society. It is that society in which new knowledge is not only used but also generated. The mindset of key people in UGC and AICTE needs to be reframed in favour of creating hi-tech entrepreneurship rather than to prepare youths with knowledge for employment in national and Multi National Corporations. Equipping universities in respect of innovation infrastructure is a crying need to achieve the desired goal.

Technological innovation is an essential precondition for growth, maintaining employment and competitiveness. An innovative person never remains unemployed on the contrary he is more in demand. He has a mission in his life, which gives him extra energy and purpose. An innovative person constantly strives to improve. He is always dissatisfied with the prevalent. He wants to create new and again new. The innovation is progressing constantly on the strengths of new ideas of such scholar persons. Can the institutions produce such innovative persons more in number? If they do so institutions will be more in demand like Oxford and Cambridge.

INNOVATORS ARE JOB GENERATORS AND HENCE ARE INDISPENSABLE

Ideas are the real capital. Ideas are needed to succeed. They come from innovation. Idea generated is opportunity generated. Idea killed is opportunity killed.

> Knowledge memorized and stored in brains is important, but more important is the ability to discover new knowledge, new theories and new ideas.

Institutions are the legitimate places, the crucibles of experimentation, for the manufacture of ideas. It is their prime function. They have no reason to exist if they do not do so. Institutions are places to create dreams and to create capacity and imagination in youths to implement dreams.

The importance of innovation to the country's economic future should be realized and infrastructure as stated above provided forthwith in higher education institutions. This will avoid the shortage of suitable persons for innovation and entrepreneurship, which is found to be a major barrier in employment generation.

Most of the students in colleges and polytechnics learn in a passive way. Students learn quietly what is handed over to them. They learn through transmission and are not guided to take active hand in creation of technologies. What did the famous philosopher Socrates teach his students? His taught how to raise pertinent questions. That means institutes have necessarily to ignite the creative minds of students.

The competency of work force today is measured in terms of its ability to innovative. People have to be innovative to see ahead of others the incoming opportunities.

India possesses the largest pool of youthful work force and high quality human capital. This is our competitive advantage. We ought to prepare youths globally competitive, make them enterprising by global standards for global needs.

COMMERCIAL EXPLOITATION OF BRAND NEW TECHNOLOGY

Invention when exploited commercially is known as innovation. Research conducted in universities colleges and polytechnics often result in publication of wonderful papers, but rarely results in commercial exploitation. Thesis written mostly remains on shelf. No conscious effort is made to obtain economic value from them, mainly because vision in this direction is lacking. Students do not get opportunity to learn to convert inventions into usable goods and services. To that extent skill set of students, in spite of potential, remains deficient. This is addition reduces utility of research done and reduces the rate of return on investment.

It is a good sign that higher education in India is growing. But innovation and acquisition of skills for commercial exploitation, which is the demand of time, is lagging.

Multifaceted units in partnership with industry, like research park, innovation centre, patent and technology, transfer centre, entrepreneurship development centre, incubator, venture capital foundation, angel networks, IPR centre etc. which constitute innovation infrastructure, is found to lead to creation on enterprising atmosphere enabling students to acquire innovation skills, More the commercialization of technology more is the wealth generation. In developed countries innovation in academic institutes is a useful practice. This has generated a wave of entrepreneurship facilitating students and the whole community to be creative, tapping the market in the whole world. USA produces leaders who employ followers from countries like India. Unfortunately, this wave of creativity, leadership and outward looking culture is yet to reach the Indian shores.

A NEW VISION OF NEW WORLD

How long students should keep learning knowledge generated by others elsewhere in the world? How long they should join the army of foreign companies, serve in supporting roles and be content with that? If the necessary infrastructure is provided some of the students, if not all, would certainly become "First Mover Entrepreneurs." The institutes and students need to dream high, in tune with global competitiveness. Learning innovation enables students to consolidate their knowledge of basics. Innovation centre is more than a learning place. It gives an inspiration to students besides generating economic surplus. The role of institutions in vision development should not be under estimated.

Innovation in education institutes in India is conspicuously absent. Students do not get global perspectives. This is a serious lacuna. The institutes without innovation are truly incomplete in modern sense. They still follow an old outdated model whose educational and financial efficiency is too less. They live in past, while their counterparts abroad are ahead of time.

Quality of technical education and research can substantially be enhanced and returns on investment increased if innovation policy in universities colleges and polytechnics is introduced. Joblessness and industrial slow down is a result of lack of innovation. When shall we realize this? The situation is to innovate or die. Hence, Government of India has launched the following program.

QUALITY IMPROVEMENT PROGRAM

For reformation of higher and technical education, Government of India has recently launched a massive program, termed as Technical Education Quality Improvement Program (TEQIP). The objectives are, to impart world-class education, to enable students to grow to the level they are capable for, so also reduce dependence on foreign.

From what is reported it is observed that the scheme is good, well formulated in many respects, and well implemented through but in competitive environment it lacks a step towards "Technological Innovation, organizational innovation, and business innovation". Modernization of laboratories, library, classrooms, faculty development as usual are essential but not sufficient it is necessary to think differently, think great going beyond current practice. It is necessary to design new organization structure oriented towards innovation, and enable students to acquire enterprising skills equal to, if not more than their counterparts abroad, which is the need of the hour. This is to say that institutions must provide a portal through which all the students compulsorily should have to pass through, practice of commercial exploitation of the new knowledge that is to say new technology. They should specially target their efforts towards production of marketable technologies, patents, etc. The students should have to do some field surveys to identify level of technology used, productivity, and difficulties in using the latest knowledge. TEQIP has created an impact but greater especially in NTBF is expected.

Can Higher Education Institutes give New Ideas and Leadership to Help Industry to Win?

Jobs will come not from old type of industries and old technologies, but from sun rise industries and sun rise technologies. Surveys conducted elsewhere in the world indicate that NTBF started by young entrepreneurs with origin in academic institutions are far more successful than those started by person with experience in industry. Academic institutions provide a powerful engine to launch the new technology-based enterprises and thereby generate hi-tech, high income employment.

According to a news item published recently, "India slipped to 21st rank from 13th in number of scientific output." The PhDs produced in engineering are far less. According to an estimate given by TEQIP (2009) there is a shortage of 30,000 PhDs. US produces 30 PhDs per million population, Japan produces 28, India produces only 0.5. The number of graduates produced in USA are almost double than in India. Yet all get jobs or become self-employed. Still they have a shortfall. To meet the same they invite engineers from abroad. This is mainly because they produce larger number of PhDs. Who constantly explore new opportunities, everywhere and anywhere in the world.

A critical examination of the schemes of technical education in the light of global winds of change, so as to avoid mistakes is essential. If the infrastructures like entrepreneurs centre, research park, incubator, innovation centre venture capital fund, patent and technology transfer centre, etc. in partnership with industry are not incorporated, it is feared that the whole effort of reformation will remain on traditional lines, preventing change. Massive investment being made will not yield expected results. The education policies and practices should have to come out of old ruts. They are less efficient, unproductive and outdated. You need new ideas to win in new world.

It should be remembered that any investment in present structure, present systems and procedures without introducing autonomy and improving academic culture is like investment to perpetuate and subsidize incompetence, inefficiency leading to failure.

Change is most wanted to replace worn out ideas. The resources should not be frittered away on trodden paths but should be used creatively on the proceed off the beaten paths, essentially importing academic culture and output. Developing countries in general, are hopelessly conservative, inward looking and hostile to change. Innovative societies are essentially outward looking. Individually, Indians are forward looking but society wise not. Unless we change our mind set, brain wash UGC/AICTE and work to accelerate reformation process we cannot progress.

Unless innovative measures like academic autonomy, administrative autonomy, are introduced in higher education the additional investment in infrastructure will not pay dividends. Our own people in college, university and government unknowingly, out of inertia become obstruction to reformation. The authorities who are used to older style of working and for personal benefits do not take initiative to change. Infrastructure created may remain unutilized. However, this should be guarded to avoid failure.

The experience of India—Canada project and World Bank project in the recent past, has taught us many lessons. Financial aid from World Bank to countries like Congo, Zambia indicates that the aid turned out to be counter-productive. The men in charge of governance were accustomed to benefits from the present system. So they did not take any initiative to change. It went towards subsidizing inefficiency, bad policies, corruption, discouraging reformation, etc.

The present case of universities and colleges, which are offering resistance to change, change to use autonomy, reformation as per NKC recommendations is a capability failure. Raising the organization capability, making them competent and amenable to change is the key aspect which must be attended to with utmost care by aid receiving institutions. Without which they may not be able to make most of the aid. Development of an institute cannot be formed from outside. It comes only from within. It is an endogenous growth. Organizational capability need to be developed so as to bring about change. Exposure to developed world needs to be made, time and again, to accelerate arrival of change.

Benchmarking with the Best in the World

What we observe differently in higher education institutes abroad is that research and innovation private companies are flocking round the university in search of the latest knowledge. Students work in these companies in vacations and research entrepreneurs teach in university. Exchange, circulation of innovators is made easily possible. Interaction between industry and institution for research in facilitated. Universities have on their campuses centres like research park, patent and technology transfer centre, entrepreneurship development centre, incubator, entrepreneurship development centre, incubator, innovation relay centre, industrial services centre for outreach, etc. Venture Capital companies have opened offices in the campuses for early commercialization of technologies. Institutes have become sources of new ideas enabling companies to win. An institute functions like a light house for industry. It is these things which have increased productivity and added value to growing economy. Such institutes are functioning like a magnet attracting best of brains from anywhere and everywhere in the world. Benchmarking is considered to be a big driver for improvement.

Systems in World have Changed—Where are We? Can we Afford to be Status Quo?

All these multifaceted centres provide an opportunity to students to learn beyond curriculum, as per their intrinsic motivations. They have been established especially after 1980, in 84 technical universities of Germany, in 125 research universities of USA, and in many universities abroad MIT Boston has a Technology Licensing Office (TLO) in which about 200 people work. The author has personally visited this office. The institute earns about one hundred patents every year and earns as much as 20% of its budget from the sale of technology.

Quality and relevance of education in developed countries is reported to have improved mainly because of the presence of centres in the campus. Enterprising culture is imbibed in students, which leads to spin-off of companies. Around ten companies are born every year in MIT. Institutes have become the maternity homes, where good baby care is taken and companies are consequently born without any congenital defects. This is found to be a good help to budding entrepreneurs. Our institutions are lacking in all such ideas. Can we not adopt these strategies? True that it is a long journey. But it has to begin somewhere. It is not that a thousand miles journey begins with a single step? The vector of learning of our students should have to be made in right direction. Otherwise their efforts, time and money goes astray.

INNOVATION GENERATES JOBS

Cambridge Research Park, Limerick University Research Park, Harburg University Park in Germany, technology-based spin-offs from Sophia Antipolis, university park in France, Oulu Business University Park in Finland, etc. are world famous examples which have benefited most of the students, industry and academia. The author has personally verified by visiting them. China, Taiwan have installed such parks in their institutes and thereby currently have successfully been converting brain drain into brain gain. An OECD study recently reported,

> Those nations which lead in introducing innovation tend to win jobs from those who lag.

Joblessness in India is increasing due mainly to lack of innovation. Insufficient innovative activity in India is due to shortage of people possessing innovation skills because innovation is not taught in colleges. This is cited as a key factor behind under performance of Indian economy and fast growing unemployment.

India must recognize the full scope of the innovation phenomenon without which proportion of sick industries will increase and new born companies will be handicapped at birth itself.

Can Indian academics teach innovation skills by international standards? Can they teach skills of discovery and skills to generate technologies equal to their counterparts abroad? Certainly, Yes! They have the potential. Can India hope to become a developed nation without learning innovation? Should we keep on teaching sun set technologies? Can we hope to reform education without adopting innovative strategies? We cannot generate employment without NTBF. Can students acquire innovation skills without infrastructure for innovation? We essentially need a swimming pool to learn swimming.

CONCLUSION

Education and training in universities, colleges and polytechnics have a major influence on nation's capacity for innovation. The role played by them, however is not satisfactory. Much needs to be done. Scientific methods like in developed countries need to be introduced. Innovation policy needs to be evolved. Can they produce NTBF, and how many is a pertinent question which they should be asked. Do the institutions have innovative character? How can they acquire?

The role of colleges and universities in fiercely competitive world are changing. A new enterprising society in the world is coming into being. Institutions should therefore focus their attention on reorienting students for closer integration with the world. Mobility of academicians at international levels in advocated. This has remained our serious deficiency in the past.

How much knowledge is acquired and stored in brains is important, but how well-innovative skills are learned deserves priority. India in globalization should deviate from traditional methods of learning and take a lead in sharpening the innovation potential of students. They have missed opportunities in the past because necessary infrastructure and direction for self-employment were not available. Now at least they should not miss.

If India does not become a centre for technological/organization/financial innovation then there is no other way to become a developed nation. If we developed systems in colleges to produce new knowledge and new technology, then there is a fair chance to convert brain drain into brain gain.

The knowledge infrastructure proposed in this paper is a profit centre. It generates wealth much in excess of consumption. It is found to subsidize education and research, besides improving the quality and relevance. It should therefore be installed forthwith in each university, college without any delay. Government should play its central role. Systems like autonomy should be perfected forthwith, otherwise infrastructure created may remain idle.

If India desires to become a technological superpower, then higher education institutions must have to throw away the old shackles, and install new innovation and entrepreneurship culture to create NTBF. This is no more an option but compulsion.

Resources are not in short supply, but the visions. Capacity to implement visions matters. Universities must generate leaders and brand new ideas to enable industry to win.

Education charged with a spirit of entrepreneurship, innovation and discovery is not a luxury; it is a basic necessity to make education globally competitive.

REFERENCES

Bowden, Rob (2004). *Globalization, Impact on Our Lives,* Chicago, Rain Tree Publications.

European Union (1996). Green Paper of on Innovation and Technological Transfer Enterprise Unit, EUFO, 2295-2920 Luxumberg.

India, National Knowledge Commission (2007). *Report, 2006-07,* New Delhi, Author.

Jones, Glen A. et al. (2002). *Creating Knowledge—Strengthening Nations, The Challenging Role of Education.* Torronto, University of Torronto Press.

Naik, B.M. (2010). *Higher & Technical Education, Book of Knowledge,* New Delhi, Gyan Publishing House.

National Academy of Sciences (2007). Rising above the gathering storm, report published by National Academy of Sciences, US.

Chapter 21

Indian Higher Education Institutions Need to Harness Global Winds of Change to Nurture Globally Competent Graduates

INTRODUCTION

World experience tells us that in knowledge-driven economy of today, only those nations are developed and found to progress faster which have world-class universities and colleges. Others do not, even when they have ample natural resources. It is mainly because world-class universities produce graduates who are globally competent leaders, highly creative and imaginative to lead in their respective fields of specialization, like law, engineering, medicine, teaching, etc. They lead also in politics in a creative manner, and make most of the national resources to fulfil the rising aspirations of people. They raise the image of country to world level. Governments of various countries with a view to improve the living standard of people have therefore taken to modernization of universities high on agenda. World-class institutes are found to produce world-class graduates, and mediocre institutes produce mediocre graduates. So as to have globally competent leaders' global ranking of universities and colleges world over, is published and has assumed great significance. Government of India is also serious on this point and has started, National Institutional Ranking Framework (NIRF) from 2016.

Health of Indian economy and health of Indian industry depends on health of education of people in general and higher and technical education in particular. Excellent education is found to be the prerequisite for excellent progress. Nations, regions and cities which realise this only will win. Others may work hard and may have all the resources at hand, but without world-class universities and colleges and especially world-class teachers in them, they are destined to lag behind.

India at present is at risk, for want of research based world-class institutes. It is these institutes which produce sunrise technology and market them world over. They enrich human civilization. They are critical in building India an economic power and meet the needs of vast population. Future of India can certainly be better by adopting Make in India, Digital India, Start Up, etc. schemes which are however possible only if at least a few universities and colleges harness the global winds of change and become world-class and not remain mediocre. It is these world-class institutes which produce globally competent leaders, who matter most in effectively using the physical, financial and intellectual resources of the country. Today, Indian universities do not stand high in the world list. They are by and large mediocre producing mediocre graduates, that is to say, mediocre leaders for various professions and also for politic. Prime Minister of India and President are time and again telling the countrymen through public speeches urgent need to improve quality of university education. But universities because of their outdated rules, not matching with the winds of change in world they are not able to succeed.

The strategies adopted presently by Indian Government to improve higher and technical education are not competitive enough by the world standards. They are undoubtedly misplaced. They are something like the well-known saying. "Fire burning at Someshwari and fire brigade going to Rameshwari". India needs to realise that teachers are the architects, sculptors of future generation and accordingly India needs to redesign the service conditions of teachers, authorities and responsibilities and provide them opportunities to grow to world-class level.

By simply pumping more money without revising policies and practices for professors, higher education cannot be improved. The systems and procedures, visions and missions urgently need to be modernised in the light of those in world best universities. Indian universities and colleges ought to think in global context, dream big think great and adopt strategies to build faculty with excellence reaching to global competence.

UGC and AICTE ought urgently to make a comparative study of service conditions of professors in world best universities and adopt the best practices in India. Without this higher education in India and quality of Indian leaders will never be improved. Development of India is critically dependent on professors who teach and research in universities and colleges.

World experience tells us that unless a professor is involved in industry or profession-oriented research he has very little current and relevant knowledge to teach. He tends to teach sunset knowledge incompatible to global opportunities. Classroom teaching gets a force, depth, and sharp edge if professors are engaged in research and innovation. They become imaginative, remain ahead of time, and update their own capacities to be equal to their counterparts abroad, which are needed to capitalize on technology ahead of others. How long India can be run on borrowed knowledge and borrowed technology? How long students should keep going abroad for higher education? Visions and missions of universities and colleges should essentially include corporate development to make industry, economy win in globalized world. This alone will make education relevant and purposeful, and produce able competent leaders, so badly needed to run the nation in a competitive manner. In other words, Indian universities are challenged and required to produce world-class leaders, for which they themselves will have to be world-class. At least a few universities need to produce globally competent leaders for professions and for politics to ably manage its affairs at national and international levels. India will be a developed nation only if its universities and colleges are qualitative and relevant standing high in the world list.

If the government boards of governors and all the professors of college decide and make effort in this direction undoubtedly quality of education can be superb.

STATEMENT OF THE PROBLEM

Why Indian institutes do not stand high in the world list? Why thousands of students every year go abroad? Why foreign universities are coming in India? Is it not because there is a huge unmet demand? Why coaching classes are booming? Why university education is decaying? India is not short of either talent or resources. Poor governance, poor visions and missions, lack of connections with counterparts elsewhere in the world and poor leadership at state, notional and college levels in higher education is the root cause. Indian institutes as well as professors lack ambition and commitment to rank high in the world list. Indian higher education lacks strategies to enable professors to grow to global standards, without which excellence in higher education is impossible.

Higher education is now a global subject. Students are keen on acquiring best of knowledge and for which they are going anywhere in the world, so also international education providers are coming to India. Students demand world-class education. They are ready to pay for this. But not many universities and colleges in India are able to offer. Many students are going to UK, USA, Canada, Australia, and New Zealand.

Countries like Australia, Canada, and New Zealand have too small a population of the order of 3-4 crore but they have developed big world-class universities and colleges, with eminent professors on faculty, and so they are developed. On the other hand, a big country like India with too big a population has established too small universities and colleges with professors having almost no world-class wisdom, and obviously so India is lagging behind. How can India without globally competent professors' produce world-class graduates? How can a big country like India be run successfully by mediocre leaders at national and international levels? Indian economy and politics need world-class graduates so as to make most of its resources. Even if India has talented brains, youthful population all the physical and financial resources at hand but not world-class professors in universities and colleges, it will lag behind the world. India will be prosperous ranking high only if it has world-class professors, not otherwise. This is a writing on the wall. Will the policy makers realise this?

Time has come for India to have not only five star infrastructures but five star professors. Indian institutes need to adopt strategies to enable faculty to grow to excellence. Only increased investment in buildings and physical resources will not make higher education excellent. There are many universities and colleges in India who have abundant resources, five star infrastructures, but yet they do not stand high in world list. They lack systems and procedures. Leadership in higher education at central level, state and college levels in respect of knowledge is far too weak. Do the universities have ambition and strategies to build faculty competent by world standards? Indian Professors in USA and elsewhere have done wonders. Why can they not do in India? Do our systems and procedure prevent them? Why are they mediocre?

There is a story of two armies who were fighting in war with each other. One army had a lion as captain but the soldiers were sheep. Second army had a sheep as captain but the soldiers were lions. Who wins? Guess the army with lion as captain or sheep as captain. Leaders matter. Where are the lenders produced? In knowledge-driven society, leaders are produced within the four walls of class rooms. What kinds of leaders are produced by our universities?

Mediocre universities produce mediocre leaders. World-class universities produce world-class leaders, who are a prerequisite to build a prosperous nation. It is believed in knowledge society that only those nations are prosperous where universities and colleges are world-class. Hence, world over, world ranking of universities has assumed great significance. Globally competent leaders in various professions, engineering, law, medicine, etc. and various walks of life in society and also in politics come from classrooms not of mediocre colleges and universities but essentially of world-class. India needs globally competent professionals, politicians to manage its affairs ably at local, national and international levels. Indian Government is ambitious to make a mark in the world and so is serious about reaching to excellence and hence has from 2016 started national ranking, known as National

Institute for Ranking Framework (NIRF). Higher education in India undoubtedly behind the world.

India has embarked on missions like Make in India, Digital India, smart cities, smart villages, and Start ups movement. Can India ever fully succeed in these missions without excellence in higher education? The third President of USA, Thomas Jefferson realised that the strength of a nation in knowledge-driven world can be measured not in terms of the size of army, or the size of arsenals as much in the number of world-class universities and colleges. Then USA higher education was behind European countries like Germany and England. He told his countrymen that unless and until American universities and colleges perform better than those in European countries, US economy and US industry cannot go ahead of them. He initiated many schemes for improvement, as a long-term measure. As a result today eight out of first ten universities are from USA. 85% of the intellectual property in the world is owned and possessed by USA. It is on account of this that USA is dominating in the world.

It is on the background of above questions and challenges that the governing bodies of higher education and trustees of colleges have to respond and come in action, make introspection and find out what needs to be done. They essentially have to learn how to be effective, from their counterparts elsewhere in the world, essentially by harnessing for the global winds of change. Is it possible to create a culture of self-assessment? What the governing authorities are doing to achieve excellence? Future of children and grand children depends on how well governing bodies perform today. What is the use of governing bodies if they do not ensure educational quality?

TRANSFORMING HIGHER EDUCATION TO WORLD-CLASS STATUS

India after independence has made laudable progress in higher and technical education. From 26 universities and 695 colleges at the time of independence, we have risen to 836 universities and 39,000 colleges today. GER has increased from 0.4% to 23%. However, it is below world average of 30%. Having just higher education institutes is good but not enough. They must be world-class for improving living of people. So as to enable institutes, government has started Technical Education Quality improvement Program (TEQIP), anti Rashtriya Uchchatar Shiksha Abhiyan (RUSA) with a view to improve access, equity and quality in higher education. Twenty-seven new IITs and IIMs, and many more NITs, USERs are started.

India in higher education is larger in size but in quality far too behind the world. President and Prime Minister of India through public speeches time and again have been showing concern to improve rank or India in world list. Yet not much improvement is noticed, whereas Chinese universities have shot up from nil to 35 in first 200. The committee appointed by MHRD under the chairmanship of former UGC chairman Prof. Hari Gautam has given its report recently and said UGC has not been successful in its mandated mission. The committee recommended abolition of UGC and restructuring and naming it as Notional Council of Higher Education and Research. The council is expected to be a think tank and to navigate higher education to world-class level. World experience tells us that universities are successful which give birth to new knowledge, new technology, new theories, patents and hi-tech start ups. Setting a tone of discovery, innovation, creativity, patenting, spin-off or new technology-based firms, create technology pioneers, etc. is the urgent need. Education charged with a spirit of innovation, demand-driven research adding value in business and commerce can alone move India forward. Future belongs to those who understand this.

Future of India depends on knowledge possessed by men and women rather than resources. India is grossly a less educated country. Have we failed as a society to provide adequate opportunities to our youth to be educated in world-class manner? Have we failed in creating a vibrant educational ecosystem that supports cutting edge research? How are their institutes different from Indian? What do they teach which we do not? Where do we go wrong?

Teaching profession in India is a grim affair, whereas it is prestigious in foreign. We have too much of rote learning. They have more of innovation, creativity. All teachers abroad hold doctorate degree, where as in India very few. Why coaching industry in India is booming? Nalanda and Taxshila were the first universities of the world, where scholars used to come from abroad. Now why a shift in culture has taken place and our scholars students going abroad? Is it due to inadequate value attached to discovery of new knowledge, new theories? It is essential at this juncture to make introspection and learn from the world experience especially in science and technology status of India in world, in leadership, income level. The well-being of people depends on its scientific and technological capability. India, to cope with challenges will have to enlarge the scope of institutions to cover high-end research, innovation, creativity, generation of theories, technology creation, patent and IPR, creation of new technology-based firms, etc. What value we attach to above in budgeting? How can we bring back the past glory of Nalanda?

India urgently needs world-class universities and colleges. Cities, regions and nations develop faster only when knowledge institutions like universities and colleges are world-class, not otherwise even if they are endowed with abundant natural resources. The world is now knowledge driven. Realization of dream to make India a technology leader depends on universities and colleges. Knowledge institutions and knowledge professors have achieved significantly high importance. Knowledge has become more important than physical resources like land, minerals and money. Consequently, there are revolutionary changes in institutions of higher education, all over the world, including India. Knowledgeable persons have become a prime asset, even if a nation has a big treasure of natural resources it needs world-class universities and colleges to grow with the world. Nations develop only when world-class institutions exist and not without them. People's education is synonymous to economic development. Status of India in world market depends on status of India in higher and technical education. India is therefore at risk if it does not rank high in the world list of higher education.

If Indian universities keep on producing mediocre graduates, national leadership in professions and politics undoubtedly will be mediocre. I was reading an article written by an American author in the journal, *Fortune*. The American writer was addressing the question, "Can India ever compete with US in software business?" To answer the question he made an analysis of higher education in both countries, and recorded that Indian system is rote learning that is to say mechanical, stereo type based on memorization and not creative thinking. Students are taught known knowledge. Institutions in India do not teach creating new knowledge, new theories. Students are not learning innovation and hence they do not know how to discover unknown. They are reflection centres, technology coolies, teaching that knowledge which comes to them from developed countries. It does not focus on creativity, discovery and innovation. He came to the conclusion that Indian institutions can produce at best followers but not leaders. On the other hand, thrust of US universities is on producing leaders, discoverers, creators, who obtain patents and intellectual property. It is US which are pumping new technology most in the world market. He concluded student's education in universities and colleges is an enabler to competitiveness. A nation creating followers can never compete with a nation creating leaders, unless in future it improves. Universities in India need to incorporate creativity in syllabi and aim to produce leaders.

TRANSFORMATION DEMANDS STRATEGIC CHANGES

Some of the strategic changes requires for transforming the higher and technical education in the country are described below.

Where do the Indian institutes differ from their counterparts abroad: The universities in foreign are innovative in character, Indian institutions are conservative. They teach sunrise technology, we teach sunset. They produce leaders, we produce followers, imitators, copy cats. They are engines of growth, we remain bogies. They are not afraid of change, we are. They embrace change, we resist change. They practice creative destruction, they destroy old outdated systems and procedures, and we cling to past. Their institutions are research based, ours are teaching based, they teach tomorrow's knowledge today, and we teach yesterday's knowledge today. They produce entrepreneurs job generators, we produce employees job seekers. Their universities produce hundreds of patents, new technology-based companies.

Framework of Indian universities by world comparison is far too weak. They create a mind set of students in favour of innovation we create in favours of examination, memorization. Their labs have generated, given birth to new theories, new technologies and are not merely testing what has been discovered long back. In India what is wanted is not taught and what is taught is not wanted. There is a serious mismatch. The institutes abroad are ahead of time, are we behind!

Innovative Professors and Innovative Infrastructure Need of the Hour: Universities abroad have on campus technology relay centres, entrepreneurship centres, technology incubators, business incubators, research park, venture capital foundation, patent and intellectual property centre, corporate education centre, technology transfer offices, knowledge transfer centres for outreach. They are existing from many years we do not have them even today. It is on account of these centres that their nations and people have prospered. These are the new dimensions to be added urgently to our institutions. They are a profit centres and have added to the wealth of universities and the nation. These centres have given a character of innovation to their universities and made education relevant to the needs of the society. They generate new technology in labs and so they are constantly selling and we buying. Our universities and colleges are teaching oriented, teaching that material which comes to them from abroad. They have no original well springs of knowledge.

Universities abroad provide seeds for industrial growth, Can we? Quality and relevance of education in developed countries is reported to have improved because of the presence of such centres of excellence in the campus. Enterprising culture is imbibed in students. This leads to spin-offs of new technology-based companies, spin-offs of brand new technologies, continuous inputs of new technology in industries to make and maintain them globally competitive. Around 40 companies are born every year in MIT, and this figure over a period of years is of the order of 3000. Stanford University has given birth to companies like Yahoo, Google, and CISCO. This is true of almost all research universities, in Canada, Australia, and China, etc. Universities have become the maternity homes, where good baby care is taken and companies are born without any congenital defects. This is found to be a good help building entrepreneurs. Companies born on university research parks are found to be more prospective at national and global levels, than those companies born off the park. Our universities are lacking in all such ideas. Can we not adopt these strategies? Yes, if such approach is adopted then the flow of students and brain drain will be arrested. True that it is a long journey, but somewhere it must begin. Is it not that a thousand miles journey begins with a single step? The vector direction of our students learning should have to be made enterprising, innovative and in right direction considering global experience. Otherwise the efforts, time and money goes astray.

Only classroom teaching or lab working although necessary is not enough to upgrade the quality of education to world-class level. Imagination, creativity of students grows only when they work in research parks, incubators, innovation centres and industry. Creativity, discovery, innovativeness is the character of institutes abroad. Is it so in India?

Industry Institute Interaction Model abroad worth emulation: What we observe differently in higher education institutes abroad is that R&D units of private companies are flocking round and parking on the periphery of universities in search of new knowledge. These R&D units draw on the intellectual capital of the university. They use the expertise of professors, use research infrastructure in university and the innovative talent of young energetic students. The experts in private R&D units with their rich experience are found to deliver lectures to students studying in university. There is an exchange of knowledge and innovative talent continuously between the companies and the university. The interaction between the university and companies enriches both. By doing this, they subsidize each other's cost of education and research. Students learn innovation skills besides known knowledge and technology. This system especially fires the power of imagination of students, and inspires them with creativity. Thus, research is found to subsidize education and education to subsidize research. Do we have such a system in our universities?

This I have personally observed in many universities like McMaster University in Canada, Karlsruhe University in

Germany, Wisconsin University in USA and several others. This is widely prevalent in many universities in foreign from many years. In India we often talk of need and importance of interaction between industry and institute. Do we need to emulate such good policies and practices from abroad?

Indian universities and colleges ought to dream big, think great and show commitment to become world-class, they have the necessary capability, necessary resources, but they lack visions and ambitions.

Professors are the custodians of the brain power of youths in the country. They are architects and sculptors of the future of young generation; some of them are the leaders of tomorrow strolling today in university campuses. Tomorrow's society of India is being created today in university and college campuses.

The central message of the article is that Indian universities and colleges ought to be conscious about their legitimate role to produce graduates as creative leaders, imaginative leaders and not followers or copy cats, which essentially requires world-class professors. Will the policy makers care for?

To be able to do that institutes ought to follow global winds of change, global visions and missions. They would have to be innovative in character. They must benchmark with world best.

How can Indian universities and colleges be innovative? Conventional wisdom in higher education which once served well is no fit for today and tomorrow. The present time demands revolutionary changes. Conventional teaching in classrooms is necessary, but not enough. Higher education institutes without centres on campus for technological innovation, entrepreneurship development, patent and IPR, technology transfer, venture capital, hi-tech start ups, spin-off of technologies are incomplete, irrelevant and non-viable in modern sense. If India dreams to succeed in Make in India mission, the present higher education system needs to be strengthened urgently in respect of above-stated centres. They have to be able to give Technology Push to address Market Pull and turn out graduates as lenders. Universities and colleges would have to think Out of Box to redesign their systems to generate new knowledge, and new technology ahead of others. They would have to install systems as WELL SPRINGS of new knowledge and new technologies. How can the institutions remain ahead of time? Institutions will have to change present frame of institutions in favour to establish above-stated centres afresh in their campuses, essentially in partnership or in association with industry. Restructuring in the context of global changes has to be the main item on national agenda, without which the intellectual resource will continue to be underutilised, wasted and opportunities missed. Colleges and universities should have to do benchmarking with the best in the world, and make gap analysis. This is urgent, because so far we have failed to navigate in proper direction.

The key factor behind unemployment is insufficient entrepreneurship, and insufficient innovation: Shortage of people with enterprising and innovation skills is a major barrier in employment generation. Universities and colleges which have a major influence on nation's capacity for innovation should have to resort to new strategies. They would have to install systems to generate new ideas and new technologies for industry and help them to win. Make in India should have to explore full scope of innovation phenomenon. They should produce leaders and captains competitive by world standards and not only hirelings or followers or technology coolies. Not many are becoming leaders, entrepreneurs at global level, because that is not what we are teaching them to be.

India is not short of resources but is short of globally-proven systems and procedures, policies and practices. The framework of Indian universities is defective. Research and commercial exploitation of research findings is neglected. Budget needs to give priority to research. Today, budget provided to universities and colleges is small and that too is frittered away on no priority activities leaving almost no budget for priority activities of research and innovation.

Universities unfortunately have become examination bodies, research and innovation which is their legitimate job is on back seat. It is a well-known fact that where there is no research education does not grow. Education quality grows where there is research. Research and education are the two sides of the same coin. They subsidise each other. The situation needs urgent correction.

Nations are more prosperous where autonomous institutions exist. IITs were born as autonomous institutes. Right from first day they are autonomous, and so they could shine. MHRD, UGC, AICTE, TEQIP have all recommended autonomy policy. Autonomy does not require more money but it saves. It improves quality of education without any additional expenditure. From 1960 autonomy is being talked, yet very few colleges have become autonomous. There is no dedicated effort made to install autonomy. Affiliating system in India is rampant. This is structurally an inefficient system consuming more funds, and not permitting excellence in education. Colleges have become "Milk cows" and a burden on universities to manage college examination, etc. This system does not exist in any of the developed countries. Our funding for education as a result is going for perpetuation of inefficiency and subsidising incompetency, and not for improving education standards. Economic returns from investment in universities and colleges are far too low than they could be. Economic security of India is threatened due to absence of autonomy. Solutions to improve quality of higher education do not lie in providing more funds but in utilizing available funds more effectively. Our investment is going for the support and protection of inefficient systems, do we realise this? Government, universities and colleges should have to come together to install autonomy. It does not require money on the contrary it saves, yet quality improves. If we do not step up the challenge of creating autonomous institutions, we undermine everything else we are trying to reform higher education.

Alumni are the ambassadors of institutions and a great force to further education. Alumni are important stakeholders, but their strength in India is frittered away and not tapped properly. Alumni elsewhere have contributed immensely. They will contribute in India too. Each top ranking institute in the world has grown to greater heights with the support of alumni. Alma mater is very near and dear to alumni. They are willing to contribute with full might to add value and provide budding graduates with professional information much needed by them. Every institution should draw out a plan to tap the unutilised force of its alumni. Growth of college, university and growth of alumni ought to in fact synergise. This improves the character of college and alumni in society. Efforts made by faculty alone, stuff and students alone, to make institute world-class is not enough. External backing of collective wisdom from alumni is crucial. Colleges should have to share their vision's and missions with alumni. This strength is available to an institution, it is not to be imported and paid for, but it is to be only tapped.

CONCLUSION

The limiting factor for achieving excellence and success in nurturing leaders for future is the availability of world-class universities especially professors with excellence. Service conditions, authorities and responsibilities of professors need to be re-framed in the light of global winds of change in world best universities. Professors need to be nurtured to become world-class with priority.

It is easy to give a slogan, to build India a developed nation with smart society, smart cities and smart villages, but it is difficult to make it happen. It will certainly happen, but only when professors, universities and colleges rank high in world list, and not otherwise. Make in India will happen, only when Indian universities and colleges come in top hundred in world list.

The role of universities today goes beyond education to technology development, innovation, creativity and discovery of new knowledge. They ought to generate new technology for industry and disseminate quickly. Knowledge transfer from university to society is one of the essential conditions to make in India mission succeed.

India for want of research-based innovative world-class institutions and globally competent professors, is at risk of lagging behind in world brain race.

It is mainly the professors who decide the standing of a university/college in world list. Shall we not understand these global winds of change?

The governing bodies of higher education ought to be innovative, creative and reforms oriented, harnessing the global winds of change.

If we enable professors in universities and colleges to be innovative, creative and competitive by world standard, we don't need to do anything else to succeed. It we do not do this, and do everything else, all that is not going to matter much.

REFERENCES

Naik, B.M. (2015). *Education and Leadership—Role of Indian Universities and Colleges in Nurturing Future Leaders*, published by Atlantic Publishers, New Delhi.

US Academy of Sciences (2007). *Rising above the Gathering Storms: Report.*

India, National Knowledge Commission (2006), *Report*, New Delhi, Author.

India, Yashpal Committee Report, 2009. *Report*, New Delhi.

NPIU (2009). Government of India, TEQIP, Phase-II Project Implementation Plan (PIP).

Report from International Institute Education Planning, 7-9 Rue Engne, 75116 Paris.

American Council on Education (2004). *Shifting Ground Autonomy Accountability and Privatization of Public Higher Education.*

Naik, B.M. (2004). Needed Innovation nod Entrepreneurship in Higher Education Institutes, *Journal of Indian Technical Education*, January-March, Vol. 27, No. 1, pp. 27-32.

World Bank (2009). *Working Paper No. 190, Governance of Technical Education in India, Key Issues, principles, and case studies*, Edited by Andreas Boom and Jannette Cheong 2009.

Chapter 22

Envisioning Faculty Growth to Excellence: Need of the Hour

It is believed, world over, that future of a nation in today's knowledge economy depends on knowledge possessed by its men and women rather than resources. Quality of education depends on quality of professors who teach in universities and colleges. If we enable professors in Indian universities and colleges to be innovative, creative and competitive by world standard, then we don't need to do anything else to win in world. If we do not do this and do everything else all that is not going to matter much. Thousands of brainy students in search of state of the art education are going abro add, and many do not return. On one hand, intellectual capital is moving out, and on the other hand we are trying to woo foreign direct investors. It is to be realised that brains are more valuable than money. "Nations are under developed and trailing behind the world not because they are short of resources but because they are short of world-class professors to offer world-class education nurturing good professional and political leaders". Future of India can certainly be far better if universities and colleges have world-class professors, and in any case not without them.

The paper presents in brief, need and importance of faculty growth in Indian universities and colleges to reach to excellence by global standards. Improving competency of professors has become essential so as to create today a brave new India of tomorrow. Globally competent leaders for various professions and for politics tomorrow are produced today in classrooms. Mediocre universities produce mediocre leaders. Hence, world ranking of universities has assumed great significance. Many Indian universities and colleges are therefore making efforts to come up in top 100. Government is supporting them. Many of them have five star infrastructures, far more physical and financial resources. Yet they do not rank high in the world list. It is mainly because they lack professors with excellence. The limiting factor for ranking high in world list is the professors with excellence. It is only such professors who can successfully nurture with global standard professional and political leaders needed to lead India at national and international levels. Only those who realise will win. Others may work hard, may have all the resources at hand, yet for want of professors with excellence they may not emerge winner.

The purpose of this article is to motivate professors for professional growth and deserve to ably discharge the duties and responsibilities by global standard. Professors form a vital component of international fraternity in academic world, and hence they ought to be competitive by world standard.

Another purpose is to acquaint the governing bodies of Indian universities and colleges in public sector and private sector both to provide facilities urgently to enable professors to bloom to world-class standard. They have the first class raw material but their professional growth today is neglected, and hence they remain mediocre lifelong, turning out mediocre graduates by world standard. Mediocre professors are far too costly, than the cost for their growth, brain drain is increasing. Secondly, faculty is often involved in non academic activities, which deviates their attention endangering the future of youths.

The central message of this paper is that Indian institutes ought to be conscious about their legitimate role to produce graduates as creative leaders, imaginative leaders and not just followers or copy cats. Where are the leaders produced? It is said they are produced within the four walls of class rooms. If India dreams to make a mark in the world, mediocre graduates do not suffice. World-class professor is a critical input required for turning out world-class leaders. Do we realise that status of India in world market depends on quality of higher and technical education. India is at risk if its professors do not grow to excellence.

An institute is known by the reputation of its professors. World-class institutes have essentially world-class professors. Mediocre professors even with five star infrastructures do not make an institute world-class. Only those nations win in world that has world-class professors. Success in creating smart society, smart city and smart village which is the dream of India critically hinges on competency of professors. Seeds for which are sown within the four walls of class rooms. Globally competent leaders come not from mediocre universities but from world-class. Hence, world ranking of universities has assumed significance.

Professors in universities and colleges need to be viewed in global context as the architects, artists or sculptors moulding future of younger generation. They mould the creative minds of students. They are termed as a think tank shaping future of a nation. They ought to be involved in high-end research. They are not to be treated as just servants, but much above, and respected. The paper analyses various factors which professors ought to consciously care, to make most of their capacities. World over, professors in knowledge economy are reckoned as the drivers of development.

Indian Universities and Colleges now Need to Expect

Do we realise that "even if a nation has all the resources at hand but not world-class professors in universities and colleges, it will lag behind the world. The nation will be prosperous only if it has world-class professors, to ignite the minds of students in favour of innovation and creativity to become globally competent leaders". Our institutes now expect each professor to grow to his full ability, achieve high pitch, in his respective field of specialization. Each professor ought to become a thought provider of world-class standard to inspire both students and professionals for innovation and creativity. Following questions need to be asked to nurture professors to excellence:

- As a professor are they thinking in global terms?
- Are they globally competent?
- Can they become?
- They need to think great, dream big, and show commitment.
- Are they educating students with global perspectives?
- Are they nurturing students to become globally competent leaders?
- Professors ought to be innovative, creative and imaginative, so as to mould creative minds of students and professionals.
- Can they create globally competitive eco-system?

  Each professor has high potential, but he has to exercise himself, an institute will only facilitate.
- Professors who can transform college in to a world-class occupy high position in the eyes of students.

Professors are a backbone of college. It is they who take the college to greater heights. It is they who ignite the minds of students for innovation, creativity and prosperity.

India has far too few professors who have achieved excellence of global standard. Many institutes in India have abundant resources, five star infrastructures, yet they do not rank high in world list. This is mainly because of the lack excellence in professors.

On account of this, thousands of bright students every year in search of latest knowledge go abroad; nearly half of them do not return, a very valuable intellectual capital "brain drain" takes place slowing down India's clock of progress and on the other hand India to accelerate development is trying to woo foreign direct capital. Do we realise that loosing intellectual capital is a much greater loss than the benefit of getting direct financial capital. This has to be realised. World experience tells us that USA has become world power on the strength of intellectual capital from India, China, etc.

Can an institute produce graduates today to become globally competent leaders to ably address national problems for tomorrow like in start-up, industry, water shortage, unemployment, farmer's problems, make in India, digital India, Smart city, etc.?

Can and should an institute become a "Light House" for industry.

Health of Indian industry & health of Indian economy in knowledge-driven world of today depends on health of knowledge organization; like universities and colleges, and in particular their professors

Technical education in recent past, although grown well in quantity is far too poor in quality. Then President of India Hon'ble Pranab Mukherjee while addressing BRICS nation's conference in November 2015, advised the participating dignitaries', "So as to achieve economic and industrial development equal to developed countries BRICS nations should have to give first priority to build quality education comparable to the one in developed countries".

Unless quality of education is first improved, industrial and economic development he said cannot be equal to them. Brain drain will continue, intellectual capital will move out which any developing country like India cannot afford.

USA went ahead of European countries and became world power, mainly because of its superior education. Eight out of first ten world best universities are from USA. Thomas Jefferson third President of USA then gave the philosophy to excel in education, which USA adopted and mainly on account of that it became world power. Technical education quality improvement program [TEQIP] in its mission gives top priority to faculty development to reach to excellence. Governing Boards of institutes adopts this view. It believes, Institutional development is faculty development to excellence.

Governing boards are installing systems in colleges enabling professors to grow to world-class standard

An institute ought to provide necessary opportunities to professors to grow. India needs globally competent leaders to manage its affairs ably at national and international levels. Our present leaders in professions so also in parliament and leaders in assembly are unfortunately not globally competent. This is so evident from Parliament proceedings we see on TV. India is in the hands of less competent leaders, some of them in the opinion of public are scoundrels. Where are the leaders produced? They are produced within the four walls of classrooms. Students today become leaders tomorrow. Many leaders of tomorrow are strolling today the corridors of universities and colleges. Who prepares them? It is the professors. Mediocre professors produce mediocre leaders. Mediocrity in professors is far too costly. It results in leading a nation by mediocre.

As a result, many people are living below poverty line, and India in the world is categorized as low income economy. What kind of graduate's universities, colleges produce, is of vital importance? An institute envisions nurturing professors to enable them to be globally competitive, to produce competent professional leaders.

No institution is greater than the knowledge possessed by professors. Learning of students and indigenous technological advancement in India is held back due to acute shortage of professors with excellence. Thousands of students not satisfied with present education are going abroad; some of them in those countries are humiliated? They are paying huge fees so much so that on this amount it is said 20 IITs could be run.

Buildings, equipment and rest of the infrastructure are important but faculty is of paramount importance. It is they who are an active resource. All other resources are passive, who do not teach by themselves. Professors ought to be innovative, creative and imaginative, so as to mould creative minds of students. Time demands capacity building of faculty and staff. The college designs schemes and provides means to enable professors to grow to international standards.

Having five star infrastructures is good, but having five star professors is essential. Deficiency in infrastructure can be met by faculty, but deficiency in faculty cannot be met by any other means, and India has to pay heavy price. Firing the imagination of students can be done only by professors.

An institute adopts policies and practices to encourage faculty to become excellent, work in the areas of their choice, add strengths to themselves and to the institution.

An institute affiliated or autonomous has freedom to think and freedom to act but in public interest. Professors are expected to be self-actuating, self-regulated, self-controlled, and self-governed. They should need no supervision but only coordination in their duties and responsibilities.

Professors in knowledge economy have to envision industrial advancement by providing new knowledge, new technology. It has a corporate vision to help industry win.

Success in "Make in India" mission, critically depends on globally competent leaders in engineering, can an institute provide? Employment problem can then be easy.

Why faculty excellency? World is changing, so our universities and colleges must change. They cannot afford to be stationary.

Faculty is the architect/sculptor shaping future of younger generation and create competent technology leaders, which are a prerequisite for successful industrial development. Most of the time faculty is their role model. Professors are supposed to be teachers not only for students but also for practicing engineers. Through research and technological innovation they are expected to elevate the practice of engineering in professions to successively greater heights.

Faculty constitute the main component of governance system. They ought to be responsible and setting a tone to the quality and relevance of education. They are supposed to be self-motivated; self-regulated. There is no place for on the head supervision. A professor has to be truthful having honesty, probity and high integrity. They are a role model for students. Professors ought to have a passion for upbringing the young generation.

Human civilization is enriched by professors. Professors are expected to be an inspiring force, igniting minds as Dr Abdul Kalam used to say. Institutes are known by reputation of faculty.

Professors create brave new India today, fit for tomorrow.

Professors themselves have to exercise to be world-class, and deserve; at best college will help them.

Professors have to dream big, think great and have passion for excellence, tolerance and commitment to implement new ideas and dreams.

Can professors give joy of learning and joy of creativity to students?

How do you make learning joyful? By envisioning seeding and steering technological innovation that is to say problem solving? Professors have to focus on learning by researching and enabling students to acquire research and innovation skills thereby creating innovative college culture. Indian institutions today are not oriented to innovation. India is losing innovation capacity of students, and in tum of India.

RELATE EDUCATION TO INDIAN SITUATION

India today, is not creating job opportunities, as well as learning opportunities for bright brains, and so in increasing numbers many students are going abroad. Intellectual capital is migrating elsewhere in the world, which is not a good sign. Brain drain must forthwith be arrested. Causes and remedies must be found.

Indian engineering colleges presently are working in the direction which does not consider and evolve solutions to Indian problems. Institutions do not show substantial interest in training for improving Indian manufacturing and services. Start-up movement is the need of the hour.

For example, a look at Indian city vis-à-vis city in a developed country reveals that:

1. Street lights in foreign get on with the coming of darkness, and get off when day light is bright. In India we notice at many places lights are on even in day time.
2. Foreign countries don't have early morning sweeping of streets; they have no brooms like in. India, How do they keep streets clean?
3. They do not have water leakage from public pipe lines, like in Indian cities.

4. In India there are many water supply schemes where pipes and taps are laid but water does not flow. People are required to install pumps on pipe line to get water.
5. Buildings' abroad have no leakages at toilet points.
6. In foreign drainage pipes go through foundations.
7. Roads in cities in India arc spoiled due to water stagnating on roads, etc.
8. Electricity failures in India are frequent. Why?

Can our students analyse such problems and evolve solution? Should they not? Should college curriculum not require students to study such problems in depth?

Produce Imaginative Leaders and not Technology Coolies

Youths are made hirelings like that are to say hi-tech coolies rather than imaginative designers and technologies generators. How do you do that? It needs to have a vision for establishment of innovation centre, incubation centre, research park, etc. which can engage the brains of bright graduates in high end research and provide a lead to hi-tech job growth and opportunities of high income in Indian economy. Their education and training ought to retain the talent in India. Will RIT professors give a thought to this?

Creating opportunities for jobs for bright graduates in India, in this knowledge economy should be the top agenda. Our colleges do not generate jobs and revenue for our youths but become profit-making grounds for others, i.e. multinationals. Graduates become hirelings on fat salaries in multinationals and do not opt to become first mover entrepreneurs like Bill Gates and Mark Zukerberg, because that is not what we are teaching them to be. Consequently, our institutions are facilitating only transfer of intellectual capital to developed countries.

Professors have to love students, regardless of their cast creed religion and sex. They should take joy in student learning. They have to be impartial to all learners, especially when assessing their answer books, and conducting their oral examination. They need to benchmark with the world best professors. They need to have an innovative mindset in favour of learning.

Good professors not only do research but apply the findings of research in the professions so as to improve the productivity and current practices. Paper publication, patent and IPR obtaining, creating start-up companies are now important for professors They need to keep a company of scholars, within India and abroad. Then they are likely to reach to excellence. If they achieve excellence, it is an asset lifelong. There is no retirement for excellent professors. They arc lifelong always in demand all over the world.

What an Institute Contributes to Faculty Development?

It contributes all that is needed to enable a professor to be of world-class. It encourages, and gives guidance to learn for MTech, PhD. It deputes them to attend national, international conferences, seminars and industrial experience.

Should a person give priority for earning money or achieving excellence? If earning money is your first priority it is less likely that you will achieve excellence as a professor. Earning money and achieving excellence do not go together; of course if you bead towards excellence one gets money much more than required for living a life. Professors are advised to refrain from acquiring real estate, share business and do anything else which diverts attention from teaching, research and extension. One gets more respect, honour and dignity by developing a taste for excellence.

Many universities have staff training colleges to re-educate the professors. But their impact is far too low. Much more needs to be done. Government would have to pass a law to bind governing boards to provide training say for one month in one year. It should be obligatory and not at mercy of governing board. sabbaticals need to be introduced. A professor is a national asset and he needs to be groomed well to mould the future of youths.

What are the Benefits of Developing a Taste for Excellence?

Students love excellent professors lifelong. Industrial development of city, region could be fast, globally competitive, on sustained basis not otherwise, even if other resources are abundant. This is the public gain. Institute becomes a "Light House". Students love excellent professors, lifelong. They are always honoured, respected and rewarded by society. Of course, they should not be hungry of rewards. The college intends to install on campus centres of excellence like technology incubation, technology innovation, hi-tech start ups entrepreneurship, etc. It intends to boost local economy. Student satisfaction is the reward for professors. They are a category of people who are wanted all over the world. They add value to human society, and human civilization.

Every institute intends to win the hearts and minds of the students, faculty and staff, industry and the people at large.

Quality of education grows where research is present. Quality of education does not grow where research is absent. Education and research are the two ends of a bow; none has a force unless they both are tied by a rope (a professor) to improve education as well as research.

Will faculty of our institutes accept the challenge of achieving excellence and winning trust and confidence of students and industry both?

WHY A STUDENT OPTS FOR A COURSE ABROAD

1. Every student who went abroad opines that Indian system does not promote innovation and creativity and fails on developing student's practical knowledge. There could be more practical learning and research-oriented assignments so as to kindle the inquisitive minds of students.
2. Individuality of the student should be considered by professors and appreciated rather than expecting a monotonous uniform standard outcome from all students. Every student has his own unique strengths. Uniqueness of student should be considered while educating him.

   A bird should not be taught to swim, and a fish should not be taught to fly.
3. Cafeteria approach of subjects should be adopted. Electives should be offered in larger number.
4. Research in Indian system takes a back seat. Research and high-end research should be given importance and

students should be encouraged to carry-out purposeful research. Research labs should be equipped adequately.

5. College ought to install forthwith on campus innovation centre, incubation centre, research park, patent centre, entrepreneurship centre, start up centre, etc. They are an attraction for creative minds, enlarging their imagination power, so essential in globalization. These centres do not require money on the contrary they generate money. Only vision and determination is needed.
6. Students' knowledge and creativity should be valued and not their marks. Their knowledge and research skills should be tested continuously through research-based assignments, individual and group projects, paper presentations and so on.
7. Facilities such as 24×7 library, high speed Wi-Fi, 24×7 lab should be provided so that students can work anytime.
8. Industry institute interaction should be compulsory. Practical training, assignments of innovation need to be introduced.
9. Cross disciplinary courses should be introduced. Subjects like economics, sociology, psychology, management depending upon will and wish of students need be allowed.
10. The focus should be on developing student's autonomy. Students should be made independent and responsible for their own learning.
11. Students should be helped to gain depth in knowledge by providing them with opportunities to work on projects in a team, to present research papers, and to interact with industry. Opportunities to work and meet with people from different places and work with diversity culture.
12. Assessment pattern of students should be changed, from memorization of knowledge to creativity.
13. Colleges should have more students from foreign. Diversity of students promotes competition and understanding of cultures.

14. College should listen to the voice of students. Regular feedbacks from students should be the culture. Feedback needs to be used in changing course of action for future.
15. Learning should be joyful, challenging, and not dull. Students going abroad feel a jerk when they go abroad, because they fall short on many fronts.
16. Learning should be changed from rote learning and exam orientation.
17. Emphasis should be on learning concepts and their application. Quality of education should be in focus.

The numbers of students leaving the shores for abroad are rising from year to year. Intellectual capital is moving out. Can Indian universities not take this challenge? We must raise standard of education to international level, to arrest brain drain. This requires professors with excellence.

- The college expects a professor to work for college, for public good and not only for self.
- He is expected to do much more than minimum duty.
- He is expected to be a thought leader in society, educating students and professionals to be globally competent professional leaders.
- He should add energy, positivity to eco-system of college. There is a great pleasure for professors in giving knowledge to students, and enriching college.
- A professor should be an asset to college and not a liability.

CONCLUSION

India is at risk of being thrown behind in brain race, if the professors in universities and colleges do not grow to international standard. In knowledge economy, knowledge leaders, namely professors need to be globally competent otherwise brain drain will increase. Returns from FDI will be too small. India will be prosperous only if it has world-class professors, not otherwise.

A professor is very important for creating future of young generation. He/she needs to be nursed well and enabled to bloom to its full capacity. Lack of world-class professors is too costly for India than the cost of upgrading them. Universities and colleges need to change their view towards professors as architects of young generation. The present method of faculty growth is far too inadequate.

Indian universities and colleges without world-class professors can never be world-class, and will produce graduates only to become followers, or copy cats. Such institutions will only be agents enabling young intellectual capital to migrate to developed countries profiting them.

Excellent professors produce globally competent professional leaders, some of them to become entrepreneurs on global plane.

Are professors a think tank for a nation? Should an institute not expect each professor to grow to his full capacity, achieve high pitch, in his respective field of specialization? He ought to become knowledge leader, a thought lender of world-class standard autonomous in nature to inspire both students and practicing professionals for innovation and creativity.

Leaders matter: Each professor is a leader. He leads youths to become leaders and followers.

There is a story of two armies which were fighting a war with each other. One army had a lion as its captain, but its soldiers were sheep. The second army bud a sheep as its captain and lions as soldiers. The lion captain employees bold strategies. The other captain, a sheep designs strategies like a coward and loses even though its soldiers are lions, obviously because the soldiers have to follow the strategies drawn by captain. It is the bold strategies which enable the army to win. Situation of India today is something like sheep as captain. India has a strong base of intellectuals, and academicians but strategies which are drawn by leaders in bureaucracy and leaders in politics are far too weak. Academic leadership as a result at national, state, institution levels is crippled. The lion captain grooms his sheep soldiers to become brave like he himself while the sheep captain hammers down his lion soldiers to become cowards like her. It is ultimately the captains that matter. Professors have to lead students boldly like a lion captain to create able lenders of tomorrow.

Chapter 23

University Industry Interaction: What can and should the Best Practices in Corporate Social Responsibility Do?

Universities/colleges, world over, are assuming key role, driver's role, in global economic systems, where new knowledge and highly skilled people are perceived as fuel for economic development.

Industries constantly need new knowledge, new technology to compete in global market, for which they need access to first class university research, so also university needs access to industry to test and commercially exploit the findings of research. Industries can make some research by themselves, but they cannot make all the research they need all alone by themselves. They have to depend on universities and colleges. Industry and university both cannot grow to their potential, without each other's support, even if endowed with abundant natural and financial resources. They, in public interest, should synergise and be interdependent. It is a strategies weakness if they independent.

Small countries like New Zealand, Switzerland, Canada, and Germany have world-class universities, where brilliant students from a big country like India go for higher education. India although big yet does not have world-class universities. This is a great weakness, which now needs to be converted in to strength. It is a challenge to our universities and industry both to synergise and upgrade to the status of world-class universities. We need good university builders, besides good professors.

Nothing is more important to the Indian economy at this juncture of time than to upgrade its universities to world-class level. Do we realise this? No investment from government and especially CSR like in roads, housing, electricity, etc. is more rewarding than investment in research, education in universities and colleges. If India does not do this nothing is going to matter as much. If India does this other necessary things because of resulting improved capability of human force, will automatically take care. Will the policy makers care to provide budget to upgrade universities?

Indian universities ought to dream big, think great to stand high in the world list for which universities ought to interact adequately with industry. Industries in India are importing and foreign countries are selling. Today, India is distinctly a technology follower and not a leader. Import in defence department alone for example, is of the order of 90%. Import substitution is badly needed. Can Indian universities not do that? Yes, universities have to have a big vision and commitment to implement. Industries and university must have to come closer to each other. Organic links between the two is the crying need of time. To facilitate this government has now introduced the scheme of "Corporate Social Responsibility" (CSR). CSR has made it obligatory for every industry to invest two per cent of its profit in social activities, like in education, health, etc.

If a university dreams to become world-class, it will have to benchmark with world's best universities, and make Gap Analysis, more importantly synergist: with industry, for research and innovation. CSR has now come as an aid in this context.

WHAT CSR CAN DO?

India is at risk for want of university-industry partnership. If the university and industry synergies, make shared vision and collective ambition through corporate social responsibility and jointly establish innovative projects like research park/innovation park, corporate education centre, incubation centres, patent and IPR centre, entrepreneurship centre, undoubtedly, universities will rank high in world list, they will then produce globally competent leaders for various professions and also leaders for politics. Leaders mutter. Industry and economy of India will then be globally competitive, and job generation for youths in emerging technology will grow by leaps and bounds.

How can a university become world-class? A university ought to be charged by creative innovative people in both the academics and industry with a spirit of enterprising culture and innovation spirit to move India forward. Will industry wholeheartedly associate the university especially through CSR to do that? University and industry partnership is critical for the growth and prosperity. This partnership alone can give "Technology push", matching with "Market pull". Universities and colleges then become "Light House" for industries. Leaders of today were students yesterday, students today, are going to be leaders tomorrow. They may be in engineering, industry commerce and trade or in politics. They ought to be globally competent. Younger generation will stand to gain best this way.

World-class universities produce globally competent leaders, who in turn lead in their respective professions to be global leaders. Others produce mediocre who follow and not lead. Obviously so, there is a race world over in universities to become world-class. It is the leaders who matter most for growth and prosperity. Where are the leaders born or made? Seeds are sown within the four walls of class rooms of universities and colleges. If university and industry jointly establish research park, corporate education centre possibly with CSR funding it will make industry globally competitive, the university will become world-class, and lead to eradicate poverty. Limiting factor for growth and prosperity in competitive world is not now availability of natural resources like oil, coal, iron ore, etc. but the capability of universities for generation of new knowledge, new technology and competent professors, and other human resources. Hence, world ranking of universities has assumed great significance.

Once I happened to visit international industrial exhibition at Hannover in Germany. In this exhibition there was a pavilion for universities and colleges. This pavilion was most crowded. Visitors came from all over the world. Universities from all over the world came to present their research and innovation output.

They were presenting the patents they obtained, new inventions and new disruptive technologies which are likely to dominate industry in future. Visitors appreciated this very much. Many financial transactions between companies and universities took place. A university in India needs to take this strategic direction. Will industry through CSR associate in this cause?

Health of industry and economy in India depends in health of higher education. If a university produces globally competent Leaders in various subjects like engineering, economics, etc. India will grow fast. How good is present higher education in global context decides economic standing of India in global comparison. Nations/regions are found to be more prosperous where university-industry partnership exists. Education in such nations is innovative, creative, dynamic relevant, and fitting to industrial needs. There is no mismatch in skills demanded and skills provided. New technology-based firms are born and generation of jobs of high income take place. Nations where universities and industry go hand in hand are richer offering better standard of living to its people. They with each other's support create brand new technologies, new products and new processes. Joblessness is then rare. Innovators from industry and innovators from universities frequently meet time and again al innovation parks to show the new way to industries. Incubation centres, research parks, entrepreneurship centres, start ups grow. Majority funding is through venture capital, putting untried, untested virgin technologies in commercial application. "First mover entrepreneurs, Technopreneurs"[1] lead. So far foreign collaborators have propelled the Indian industry. Indian universities, academics, researchers are now called upon to propel industry for which they ought to synergise. University and industry if they set up jointly a "Corporate education centre" in service people will be trained nonstop for lifelong global competencies. Future of younger generation will be secured. Capacity utilization of installed facility will be stepped up. Boston University has a good corporation centre, which I have personally visited. These are the prominent gaps which jointly they should close.

Compatibility between the policy for higher education and policy for industrial development at state and national levels is essential. Will the government adopt this strategy? All world-class universities have Research Parks[2] on campus. New technology-based firms are born in university for example; Yahoo, Google, CISCO and more than 3000 companies are born in Stanford University. Universities in China, Australia, and Europe are not behind. It is they who have generated hi-tech employment with high income. Anil Kakodkar committee[3] has recommended this to Maharashtra Government. China in the recent past has established more than 300 research parks. Their progress is attributed greatly to these research parks.

Which government, which university docs not want Hi-Tech, high income jobs? American industry in association with universities helped to transform America into economic power house. Can Indian industry not do this? The solution lies in jointly establishing research parks, research centres. Now government has launched ambitious projects like, Make in India, Digital India, Smart cities, Smart villages, Delhi Mumbai Industrial Corridor Project, and raising funds through two per cent of profit in corporate social responsibility. What are the roles and responsibilities of universities and its colleges for their successful implementation? What is the role of industry and university to make Indian higher education globally competitive? Their prime role in today's knowledge driven economy is to jointly produce, globally competent leaders, professional and political leaders for industry and for various walks of life. No one else is empowered and can do this. Can the universities ever produce lenders nil alone by themselves without the help of industry? They essentially need partnership with industry. What kind of leaders presently they produce? Mediocrity in universities prevails and mismatch occurs. What is wanted is not taught and what is taught is not wanted. Mackenzie report says only 15% graduates are employable. This is a result of disconnect between university and industry. Industry and university when they come together they stand tall. In isolation, they cannot achieve peak performance. There is a war on talent. Companies are attracting best talent from anywhere and everywhere in the world, by paying attractive salaries and perks. Can our university graduates win in race? How?

Can a university in partnership with industry propel industrial development? Certainly yes it can. Indian professors in USA have done this; they will do so in India also. Universities and industry are interdependent. They cannot be mutually exclusive. They have to be supportive to each other. No industry to be globally competitive howsoever big and strong can do all the research it needs, all alone by itself. It has to depend on public research done in universities. Industry needs access to first class research in universities, so also researchers in universities need access to industry for application of research findings. Growth and prosperity of a region depends now on presence of world-class universities.

Universities are globally competitive only if its professors are globally competent, and not without even if the infrastructure of university is five star. Industries and universities should take a long-range view, come together to attract globally competent professors, and enable its professors to grow to world-class level.

Government ought to emulate foreign universities especially for service conditions, enabling professors to be world-class. Our present job conditions do not grant necessary autonomy and opportunity to grow to global standard. AICTE, UGC will have to examine and make comparative study with world best universities.

Cities and regions grow faster and on sustained basis only when they have world-class universities and not without them even if they have abundant natural resources. Indian industry needs to conduct research and innovation in association with universities, if it is to compete in knowledge-driven economy. Cities, regions are underdeveloped and trailing behind the world not because they are short of resources, but because they lack shared vision with industry to create world-class universities and colleges to nurture globally competent professional leaders. World ranking of universities has therefore assumed, world over, great significance. They have become a determinant factor for region's economy to prosper. The differentiating factor between developed and developing nations is the presence of world best universities.

Industries want to be globally competitive? Then they must emulate industry institute interaction model of "Research Park" from abroad. What we observe differently in higher education institutes abroad is that R&D units of private companies are flocking round and parking on the periphery of universities in search of new knowledge. These R&D units draw on the intellectual capital of the university. They use the expertise of professors, and young innovative students, use research infrastructure, like labs, library, etc. The experts in private R&D units deliver lectures to students in university. There is an exchange of knowledge and innovative ideas continuously between the companies and the university. The interaction between the university and companies enriches both. By doing this, they subsidize each other's cost of education and research. This system especially fires the power of imagination of students, and inspires them with creativity. This I have personally observed in many universities like McMaster University in Canada, Karlsruhe University in Germany, Wisconsin University at Madison in USA and several others. This is widely prevalent in many universities from many years. Industry and university ought to have shared ambition to create enterprising culture.

It is hoped that the leaders in industry, leaders in academia, social and political systems come together, work together, use collective wisdom and give a proper shape to build Marathwada a developed region.

CORPORATE EDUCATION CENTRE

Not only machines become obsolete but men also. Even the one time gold medallists if they do net learn lifelong would soon become obsolete. India's ability to compete in international market depends now on the competence of its work force. Continuing education lifelong, nonstop is the trend elsewhere in the world. This has enabled people in developed countries to keep pace with changing technology, avoid obsolescence and remain competitive lifelong in global market. In Japan, it is believed that employing people without continuing education and training is a mistake on the part of employers. A company is only as good as its people and their lifelong training. In China, training is both a right and obligation. Corporate training institutes are developed to cover 100% work force every year. This has become essential for all serving personnel in India too. A university in partnership with industry ought to create learning society with learning individuals for hundred per cent population of the work force in the region. It should provide an opportunity to upgrade their skills, knowledge and attitude. This will lead to increase in productivity. A university and its college's classrooms, library, labs, etc. could be used in the evening, without adding to any extra cost.

CONCLUSION

Success in globalised world, which is characterised by fierce international competition, depends now on turning intellectual capital into marketable commodities, faster than one's competitors. Future belongs to those who understand this.

Leaders in academics and leaders in industry should have to form a forum; meet frequently for creating enterprising culture.

Without a joint research park, and joint corporate education centre, patent and IPR centre, entrepreneurship centre, howsoever hard in isolation they may work, will remain behind in international competition. Innovation capacity of industry in the region start ups will then increase.

You need a swimming pool to learn swimming. Students need innovation centres on campus to enhance their skill set and power of imagination.

Both industry and university need to change their traditional mind set of remaining in isolation in favour of cooperation with each other especially for research and innovation. They have to become idea generators.

Projects like smart city make in India, digital India, start ups, incubation centres started by government essentially need industry and university coming together. These projects have less meaning without cooperation between university and industry.

World experience tells us that any company unwilling to commit the funds and efforts required by strategic alliances for research and innovation with academicians in university or college will not likely reap benefits of new technology and new knowledge. Those companies in spite of high potential most likely will not be a major force in industry ten years from now.

NOTES

1. USA (2007). Rising above the Gathering Storm, Report.
2. NAU (2011). Driving Regional innovation and growth, the 2012 Survey of North American University research parks, Battelle report, prepared for Association of University Research Parks.
3. Anil Kakodkar (2011). Higher education in Maharashtra. Preparing for future, new ideas and pathways, Report.

Conclusion

Discussions made so far lead to the following conclusions.

Universities/colleges need to be modernised urgently to create leaders of world-class standard, lest India is bound to get mediocre leaders: Universities and colleges should therefore dream big, think great and venture to produce new knowledge, new theories and new technologies. Universities should not remain reflection centres teaching knowledge coming from abroad. They should consciously create well springs of new knowledge. They should produce not bogies but engines that are to say not followers but leaders. Universities should aim to generate intellectual capital. They should produce entrepreneurs like Narayan Murthy who in turn for India create wealth and jobs. Universities in countries all over the world have now taken to up grading universities with priority. We must adopt competitive strategies.

Building a world-class academic culture in an institution deserves high priority. This essentially requires intellectual inputs, systems inputs besides financial. To be able to produce world-class leaders, well-performing institutes of higher education, some if not all, would have first to be helped to jump up to higher orbit, of world-class standard. No nation, region or society, howsoever well endowed with natural resources, can ever prosper without good institutes of higher and technical education. It is they who build a society driven by knowledge. Knowledge society is that in which the production, use and distribution of knowledge drive the process of economic and social growth. They teach people how to capitalise on new knowledge, how to convert new knowledge in to patents and IPR. They give birth to new technology-based firms to operate on national and global planes. They enable society to be enterprising. They have to deserve now to be a "think-tank" and a "light house" for industry.

Universities and colleges are main players to create brave new India: Knowledge is power, but that knowledge which today is relevant and purposeful. Intellectual property is more important than any other property. India cannot progress leaving the institutions behind. In fact, it is they who can best push India on the path of progress. They ought to be the engines of development and no bogies. The role of universities and colleges, in globalization, is not limited to producing simple graduates with paper degrees, but generating new theories and new technologies, besides preserving old. It extends far beyond to the creation of the future of Indian society. Planners while funding for education should bear in mind that tomorrow's brave new India is being created today in universities and colleges. Institutes of higher education are now creating the future of its men and women. Universities and colleges have assumed the new role of "drivers of change". It is they who produce national leaders and captains for industry, to take the nation forward. An institute has come to be known as power house producing new ideas that matter most. It increases the brain power, intellectual capital and enables India to win in global brain race. They generate and disseminate new knowledge needed most to keep people globally competitive, ahead of time.

Indian universities should network with the world best: Restructuring and repositioning of Indian universities and colleges with respect to domestic India and the transnational world is the need of the hour. The conventional wisdom of university system, with outdated visions and missions, systems and procedures, policies and practices in the era of globalization do not suffice. Now, world over, they are being liberated from government clutches. Previously, universities were localised, sheltered and capped by ideas in government. Once upon a time they served well. Then they were under the "grip of government". But after globalization they have to stand on the basis of knowledge they possess and not on government support. Government support does not give them standing any more. Then education was treated as one of the government departments. Now in globalised world, institutes are expected to be a part of international fraternity and stand with head high on their own merit, ideas, scholarship and imagination. The support they were drawing from government is no more effective. It is the other way round that institute has to provide ideas and knowledge to government to manage its public affairs bringing proven knowledge from across the world.

Governments have to provide adequate funds, but yet not interfere in their organization and management so says International Association of University Presidents.

"Government should put trust and confidence in universities and colleges, to carry out their designated public roles without intervention, even if they fail they should be allowed, for failure is the high road to success."

Professors should have exposure and opportunity to visit the world best universities, without which we cannot get professors of international standing. We know that Sachin Tendulkar could become world-class cricketer, mainly because he played international cricket.

It is high time to emphasise research in education. "Education does not grow where research is absent". Indian higher and technical education is suffering most from the deficiency of research. Universities and colleges need to do more research and innovation to jump up to higher orbit and become globally competitive.

Establish research park in each university/college. Universities must have to think in an innovative way, and permit experimentation. Establishment of research park in each university/college is strongly advocated. World experience tells us that success in international competition depends now on turning intellectual capital in to marketable commodities. Both the university and industry so as to remain competitive globally ought in partnership to install research parks. It provides a common platform to both industry and academics for innovation, creativity, technology generation, and product/process development. It is a mechanism to build synergy between the two. This is the only way for university to upgrade quality and relevance of UG, PG, and PhD programs to local and global needs.

The following are some more conclusions.

1. Higher and technical education in today's time of dynamic economy and fast changing technology must be compatible to the opportunities and challenges in globalization. Indian institutes are yet not aligned to world dynamics. They are observed to be poorly equipped and woefully unsuited to the demands of globalization.
2. Education unleashes the hidden God-gifted powers within students. The skill set of the vast population of India is far too low by international standard. We should humbly accept the reality. We should forthwith put up efforts for up gradation for both young and old, people of all ages in rural and urban areas. They should be uplifted in knowledge and skills. They must be enabled to become globally competent. Lack of education leads to unemployment, increase in crime rate, and investment in building prisons. Planners shall have to essentially bear this in mind while budgeting.
3. Each institution should be competitive, not only by national standards but international. The visions and missions of the institutions, policies and practices, systems and procedures should be made responsive to the changing global environment. Just a few years before Indian universities and colleges were ahead of China, now way behind. Do we realize this? Only those who realize will improve.
4. The mechanism of governance at governmental and university levels needs to be made more scientific. It should be flexible, participative, transparent and responsive to the aspirations of youths. Government should devise policies and practices so as to make it inclusive.
5. Government should pass a law empowering professors with the authorities, duties and responsibilities. Professors are the main players, architects of the future of children and grandchildren. The university acts should give details of their powers and authorities. This is to ensure the quality of education. Professors are being robbed off

their powers, having no academic freedom. They have become humble servants of management. This is not desirable for teaching not only known knowledge but imagination to discover unown.

6. The recommendations of National Knowledge Commission (2006-08), and Yashpal Commission (2009) in respect of grant of autonomy to institutions should be urgently discussed, debated and implemented.
7. A proven theory says that the authorities in chair and politicians in power may obstruct even sabotage and slow down the process of transformation. This is usually done out of ignorance or purposefully to keep alive their personal interests. This puts public interest in danger. Therefore, transformation of higher and technical education should not be left totally in the hands of existing authorities. An independent body to plan and monitor reforms in letter and spirit, essentially should be constituted.
8. All good institutions, world over, are essentially autonomous in nature. Professors ought to have freedom to be innovative and creative. They themselves should steer the direction of academic pursuits in public interest. There should be almost no interference in academics from outside. Bureaucracy is least qualified to steer academics. Autonomous status is a prerequisite for transformation. This should be accorded in letter and spirit. If we feel that faculty and staff are not fit to be autonomous they should be trained and retrained, allowed to be mixed with their counterparts elsewhere in the world.
9. The traditional bureaucratic approach in management of academic institutes is no more relevant today, it should be abandoned forthwith. Indoctrination of ideas from government, rigid framework, and inflexibility has no place in academics.
10. Higher and technical education needs to be lifted up from present degraded ruts and taken, to higher orbits. Without which the economic security in global competition will not be ensured.

11. If the reforms are delayed, foreign institutions are likely to establish education hubs in India and exploit the vast education market. Indians will then go subservient to foreign masters. Consequence will be that Indians will be branded inefficient, incompetent and less knowledgeable to govern. They will be dominated by foreigners. Education may go out of hands of Indian education entrepreneurs.
12. Foreign universities once they come in India they will not remain limited to education but interfere in industrial, social and political affairs of the country. Thus, in turn the sovereignty of India is likely to be in danger. India will tend to become like Afghanistan and Pakistan. The dangers must be recognised. This will not happen but is a remote possibility.
13. The professors in the past did not have adequate opportunities to go abroad and integrate with their counterparts. They are not well connected with the world and are not familiar with the global developments. In order that they become equal to world-class professors they need to be granted increased international mobility. Cost of providing international exposure to professors is much less than the hidden cost otherwise.
14. Professors must be viewed as researchers, discoverers, innovators and creators. They should be enabled to grow to the level they are capable for. They should be encouraged and enabled to write books, research papers, obtain patents, etc. How many of us have travelled abroad? How many have written books? How many have published articles in journals? How many have obtained PhD, patents and IPR? Then how shall we inspire younger generation to be innovative, creative? The well-known saying goes, if there is no water in the well from where it will come in bucket? A change in mind set of people in governance is the need of the hour.
15. They must be equipped with necessary freedom to think and freedom to act. This is essential in the interest of people. It is they who design and shape the future of

the younger generation. They create tomorrow's leaders today. This is a very important job. This should be borne in mind by professors, planners and administrators. Institutions must have to be manned by tall people with global visions.

16. Professors should be differentiated from government servants. They are think tanks. They are like racehorses helping India to win in international competition and not like horses pulling carts. They need leisure, vacations to be innovative and creative.
17. Quality of education does not depend only on instructions in classroom and laboratories. It depends also on multi-facetted activities like entrepreneurship, technology incubators, patents and IPR, lifelong education centre for grownups, research parks, enterprise development centres. They should be set up as early as possible. Only classroom teaching, although essential, is not enough to improve quality, and relevance. National Knowledge Commission has recommended establishment of above centres of excellence, as integral components of the institutions.
18. There must be a paradigm shift from teaching to learning, making use of modern technologies like computer, telecommunications, etc. This is found to bring down the cost yet improve effectiveness. Do we permit experimentation? Known knowledge is finite. We must enable students to increase imagination to discover unknown knowledge.
19. Government should increase the budget allocation from present 3 per cent of GDP to 6 per cent, to education and from 0.65 per cent to 2 per cent to higher education. It should be realized that spending on education is far more rewarding. Not spending is a false economy. Not investing in education leads to promoting ignorance and is more costly. Do we realize this?
20. Modernization of education costs but mediocrity costs far more, which India really cannot afford.